THE LIBRARY
ST. MARY'S COLLEGE OF MARYLAND
ST. MARY'S CITY, MARYLAND 20686

75388

13 50/m

REVOLT IN BUSSA

by the same author

WEST AFRICA UNDER COLONIAL RULE

REVOLT IN BUSSA

*A Study of British 'Native Administration'
in Nigerian Borgu, 1902–1935*

by
MICHAEL CROWDER

NORTHWESTERN UNIVERSITY PRESS
Evanston, Illinois

*Printed in Great Britain at
The Pitman Press, Bath
All rights reserved*

ISBN: 0-8101-0416-4

Library of Congress Catalog Card Number: 73-75236

© *Michael Crowder,* 1973

For Lalage Bown

... this supplies an example of one of the most inept pieces of mismanagement of native affairs that I remember to have encountered in Nigeria. The sacrifice of native institutions, desires, tribal sentiments, traditions and customs to the mere administrative convenience of Government and its Officers can hardly ever have been carried out anywhere with more cynical indifference and ineptitude.

H. E. Sir Hugh Clifford, Governor of Nigeria, 1924

I do indeed feel that some reparation should be made to Bussa for the sufferings and sacrifices which have reduced a proud and comparatively populous race to a soured and sporadic handful.

Hon. H. B. Hermon-Hodge, Resident, Ilorin Province, 1926

PREFACE

The idea of writing a book about the 1915 rebellion in Bussa came to me in 1968 after a conversation with His Highness the Emir of Borgu, Alhaji Musa Muhammadu Kigera III. At the time, I had been planning a study of pre-colonial Borgu, but after discussing the colonial period of Borgu history with the Emir I realized that the 1915 rebellion in Bussa might offer a fascinating insight into the problems of British administration in Borgu. Furthermore, I was at the time coming rapidly to the conclusion that a serious study of pre-colonial Borgu would require not only a knowledge of the two principal languages of the area, but longer periods in the field than my administrative duties would permit. When I visited the National Archives in Kaduna, where the early records of Borgu are housed, I found to my delight that there was sufficient material related to the 1915 rebellion to consider writing a book about it. Indeed, the archival sources for Borgu are probably the most complete for any division in Northern Nigeria, particularly those relating to the early period from 1902 to 1914, when the British Protectorate of Northern Nigeria was amalgamated with the British Colony and Protectorate of Southern Nigeria. While the archives were rich in material both on the rebellion itself and on the problems of native administration in Borgu generally, oral data on the rebellion were generally disappointing. For the most part they merely supplemented the records rather than shedding any new light on the rebellion. I was unable to trace any of the participants in the rebellion, who, assuming that they had been at least sixteen at the time, would have had to be over seventy today, a ripe old age for Borgu.

After a number of visits to the archives and to Bussa itself, by 1971 I felt I had gathered enough material to write it up into a book which I hope will give some insight into the problems of colonial administration at the grassroots level.

I am greatly indebted to the Vice-Chancellor of the University of Ife and its Committee on African Studies for a generous grant made to me while I was Director of the University's Institute of African Studies to pursue research on Borgu. I am very grateful to the authorities and staff of the Nigerian National Archives at Kaduna and Ibadan, for all the assistance they have given me. I should also like to express my gratitude to the authorities of the Senegalese National Archives in Dakar. I am

PREFACE

indebted to Mrs. D. Davin, Joyce Cary's literary executor, for giving me permission to use the Cary manuscripts in the Bodleian Library. Some further debts are acknowledged in 'A Note on Sources', pp. 243-7.

I have been greatly helped in both my field work and in particular in my understanding of the rebellion by the Emir of Borgu and his brother, the Ciroma. I should never have been able to handle the complex material on the pre-colonial history of Borgu without the assistance of Mallam Suleiman Haliru Idris, who acted as my research assistant.

A number of people read the manuscript, or parts of it, before it went to press. I should like to thank them for their advice and criticisms, in particular, Mr. A. H. M. Kirk-Greene, Mr. K. Lupton, Mallam Musa Baba Idris, who is himself working in the pre-colonial history of Borgu, Professor R. J. Gavin, Mr. J. E. Lavers and Dr. John Ballard.

I should also like to thank those who have assisted me with preparing the manuscript for press—Mr. Supo Adedokun, Mr. Ishola Oloyede and Mr. Rafiu Ibrahim, who typed the final version of the book.

CONTENTS

Preface		*page* 11
Prologue		17
I	PRE-COLONIAL BORGU	19
II	EARLY FOREIGN ADMINISTRATION IN BRITISH BORGU	44
III	THE END OF BORGU PROVINCE	65
IV	THE DEPOSITION OF KITORO GANI	89
V	SABUKKI'S REBELLION	113
VI	TWO MURDERS IN BUSSA	131
VII	FIRST REFORMS AND A SECOND RISING	142
VIII	THE REIGN OF KIJIBRIM	165
IX	THE RESTORATION OF KITORO GANI	188
X	THE SECOND DEPOSITION OF KITORO GANI	202
Epilogue		224
Appendix I	Administrators of Northern Nigeria, 1900–1935	231
Appendix II	Residents of Borgu and Kontagora Provinces	233
Appendix III	Officers in Charge of Borgu Division, 1917–1935	235
Appendix IV	Kings of Bussa	236
Appendix V	'Yawuri and Boussa: Petition by Peoples of.'	238
A Note on Sources		243
Notes		248
Index		267

ILLUSTRATIONS

Plates

1 Garuba, King of Wawa, 1901 *facing page* 112
2 The King of Bussa, Kisan Dogo, comes to greet Capitaine Lenfant at Malali, 1901   113
3 The King of Bussa, Kisan Dogo, in 'Palaver' with Capitaine Lenfant near the jetty of Malali, 1901   113
4 The Nephew of the King of Bussa and his entourage before the Graphophone, 1901. This is the nephew whom Capitaine Lenfant describes as the heir to Kisan Dogo. It is therefore possibly a photograph of Kitoro Gani   128
5 Repairing the Bussa Residency, 1906   128
6 The Emir Jibrim. Photographed in February/March 1922   129

Maps

1 Pre-Colonial Borgu   *pages* 32–3
2 Northern Nigeria's Provinces, 1906   *page* 51
3 Sketch Map of Kaiama, 1906   68
4 Sketch Map of Bussa, 1906   73
5 The Say-Barruwa Line and Northern Nigeria's Boundaries, 1901 and 1909   77
6 Greater Kontagora Province, 1914   79
7 Greater Yauri Emirate, 1915   109
8 Bussa's Lost Lands, 1915–1927   195

Figures

1 Interior of the Residency at Kaiama (from a letter from Joyce Cary to his wife, 17th October 1917)   166
2 Joyce Cary on trek with the Emir of Bussa (Kijibrim)   167

PROLOGUE

In June 1915, a force of some six hundred warriors, armed with bows and poisoned arrows, occupied Bussa in British-ruled Northern Nigeria. Led by Sabukki, a prince of Bussa, they slaughtered half the members of the Native Administration who had only three months before taken over the government of Bussa from its King, Kitoro Gani, who was Sabukki's half-brother.

This rebellion has so far found no place in the general histories of Nigeria;[1]* and its exact date cannot be ascertained from the archives of the British administration, whose officials only learned of it two or three days after it happened.[2] The rebellion took the British administration by surprise, despite the fact that they had recently undertaken a radical administrative reorganization of Bussa and deposed its ruler, whom they had written off as an inefficient chief as well as an incorrigible drunkard.

Since it had come under effective British rule at the close of the nineteenth century, Bussa and the rest of the British-controlled areas of Borgu, of which Bussa was by tradition the senior kingdom, had been regarded as one of the least troublesome parts of Northern Nigeria, as a backwater with little economic potential. Its sparse population accepted British rule with apparent docility. The records of the first decade of British rule comment with regularity on the peace and order reigning there. Indeed Sir Frederick Lugard, High Commissioner for Northern Nigeria, of which Borgu was then a province, complained that no cases were being tried in the Native Courts of Borgu. 'Why were the Courts instituted if they do nothing?' he asked the Resident of Borgu somewhat petulantly.[3] If there is a general theme in these reports, it is the laziness and apathy which the British ascribed to the people of Borgu, who they believed were not interested in doing anything more than was necessary

---

* Superior numbers in the text refer to the Notes which are listed under their chapters at the end of the book.

to provide them with their bare subsistence. Joyce Cary, the famous novelist, who became District Officer of Borgu shortly after the rebellion, wrote to his wife in England of 'their indolence, their everlasting indifference to the distant future of next month'.[4]

This book is a study of how the alien British administration of Bussa, which at first met with no opposition, following an occupation that had met with little resistance, could provoke a people generally regarded as peaceful into armed rebellion. It will also show how the British, in order to govern these once 'docile' people, were forced to undo the administrative reforms initiated immediately before the rebellion of which they were one of the major causes. It will emphasize that successful 'native administration' depended intimately on the acknowledgement of pre-colonial territorial rights. And, because of the crucial importance of Indirect Rule through the legitimate chiefs of the people the British administered, Kitoro Gani, King of Bussa, will play a central part in the story. Indeed this book can also be considered as a study of the reigns of Kitoro Gani, and his exile from Bussa; because of the role of kingship both in pre-colonial Borgu and in the British system of administration known as Indirect Rule, Kitoro Gani, although he is a shadowy figure in the government reports, and however incompetent he may have been, is the lead actor in the drama. Finally, it is a study of what Sir Hugh Clifford, Governor of Nigeria, described as 'one of the most inept pieces of mismanagement of native affairs that I remember to have encountered in Nigeria'.[5]

I · PRE-COLONIAL BORGU

1. Borgu in Historical Perspective

When the British occupied Bussa in 1898, it was little more than a village surrounding a mean little palace, consisting of some thirty large huts encircled by a mud wall.[1] This was the residence of the King who described himself as Lord of All Borgu. In 1906, Mrs. Larymore, wife of the Resident of Borgu, described it as 'a mere hamlet, or rather, collection of hamlets, straggling along the river bank; a place of no importance whatever, where there is not even the mildest attempt at a market, where trade is nil, and existence about as stagnant as a mind can picture it'.[2] In 1826 Commander Clapperton, who had been impressed by Kaiama and Wawa, the other Borgu towns he had visited, wrote with disappointment of Bussa, to whom the King of Wawa had said that both the King of Kaiama and himself owed allegiance:[3] 'After approaching what appeared to be extensive walls I was much surprised, after entering the gates, to see only clusters of huts here and there, and no regular town, as I had been led to expect.'[4] Eighty years later, shortly after the British occupation, the population of Bussa was estimated at a mere eight hundred and twenty.[5]

The contrast between the historical importance of Bussa, which claimed it was the senior of the Borgu states, and the tiny size of its capital is one of the enigmas of African history. The shock Europeans experienced on discovering it to be little more than a village resulted from the fact that in the nineteenth century it was almost as well known as Benin. For it was on the rapids of the Niger just south-east of Bussa that Mungo Park had met his death. Today these rapids and the site of the capital at the time he died, as well as those which so disappointed Commander Clapperton and Mrs. Larymore, have been flooded by the great dam across the Niger at Kainji.[6]

Bussa in pre-colonial times was situated strategically on important caravan routes from Badagry to Sokoto, the one which Clapperton followed, and from Ashanti and Gonja to Hausaland and Bornu. Commanding the head of the navigable stretch of the Niger from the Bussa rapids to the sea, it was an entrepôt for trade up and down the Niger. Given the geographical importance of Bussa in particular and Borgu in general, it is remarkable that none of its powerful neighbours ever succeeded in conquering it. To the south, Borgu was bounded by the river Moshi, which was the northern limit of the powerful empire of Oyo. To the east, the river Niger provided the frontier with the Nupe state—which likewise until the nineteenth century seems never to have been conquered.[7] To the north-east also, the Niger was the boundary, separating Borgu from the Hausa state of Yauri. To the north-west, Borgu was enclosed by the Atacora mountains inhabited by the Somba, who did not have a centralized state organization, while its south-west frontiers marched with the militaristic state of Dahomey. Despite occasional skirmishes with one or other of these neighbours, none of them was ever able to make permanent inroads into Borgu territory. Even the great Songhai empire met its match in Borgu during its expansion along the course of the Niger. And while the Sokoto Caliphate at the height of its expansion in the nineteenth century extended far south into Yorubaland, making Nupe an emirate and Yauri a vassal, it was only able to make temporary inroads into Illo and Kaoje, north of Bussa.

A great deal of research will have to be done to understand how Borgu, with its strategic geographical position, could have maintained its independence; its organization can at best be described as a loose defensive alliance between states whose rulers had a common tradition of origin and of political system; and its total population during the colonial period was estimated at little more than 350,000, spread over some 70,000 square kilometres.

Captain Mockler-Ferryman, who travelled up the Niger in 1889, wrote that the Borgawa were much feared by their neighbours and were noted for their bravery in the field. Their poisoned arrows enabled them to hold their own with the forces of the King of Dahomey, notwithstanding the latter's muskets.[8] This may be one explanation for the success of the Borgawa* in maintaining their independence. Another

---

* Borgawa = people of Borgu. The names of peoples in Northern Nigeria usually take the Hausa plural form in the records, i.e. people of Yauri = Yaurawa.

may be, that the population of Borgu in the eighteenth and early nineteenth centuries was much greater than at the time of the British occupation. Lander, for instance, on his second visit to Bussa in 1829 attributed its small population to an outbreak of the pestilence shortly after Mungo Park's death.[9] Yet another explanation may be that the dense Borgu bush made movement of invading cavalry and armies very difficult.[10] Whatever the explanation, for our purposes it is essential to realize that this apparently 'docile' people had a fierce tradition of independence which they had defended by virtue of arms and not because their country, like that of some others, was inaccessible.

While Borgu had enjoyed comparative commercial prosperity during pre-colonial times—Clapperton recorded that he saw more articles of European manufacture in Kaiama in two days than in all his time in Yoruba country[11]—during the colonial period it became very much a backwater. This was particularly true of British Borgu, which had very low priority in the eyes of the administration of Northern Nigeria. One and a half times the size of Wales, with a population of barely 40,000, it had no agricultural or mineral resources of interest to government or commerce. The old caravan routes were replaced by the railway which passed through country east of Borgu. Just as it had been an enigma in pre-colonial times, so it remained one in colonial times. On occasions there was not even one administrator stationed in Borgu. The first government school of any kind was not opened until 1924 in Borgu and that was only a rural school in Kaiama. A similar school was opened in Bussa ten years later. It was not until 1939 that the capitals of these two emirates were given primary schools.[12]

The pre-colonial history of Borgu, and in particular Bussa, remains to be studied in depth, but oral tradition, the journals of the European explorers, and the work of Jacques Lombard, the French anthropologist who has made a monumental study of Dahomeyan Borgu,[13] provide us with some background for our understanding of the events that led up to the rebellion of 1915.

Here, however, a word of caution is necessary. So far no anthropologist has conducted field-work on the people of Bussa themselves. While the political organization of Nikki and of Bussa were not dissimilar there were some important differences in their social organization. For instance, the people of Bussa speak Boko, a Mande language, while the people of Nikki and its related chieftaincies speak Bariba, a Voltaic language.[14] Again the Gando, or class of state slaves, are to be found only in Nikki and chieftaincies deriving from Nikki, not in Bussa.[15] Further, there were significant differences in the way in which *Gani*, the state festival, was celebrated in Bussa and Nikki.

Another note of caution must be sounded here with regard to the use of oral tradition. Many of the traditions made use of in the following pages are those recorded at the beginning of the colonial era. While they have the advantage of having been taken down from men who had minimal experience of the Western world, the British administrators made these recordings very much on an *ad hoc* basis, through interpreters, and with little if any contextual knowledge of the history of the area. They had no tape-recorders, and their choice of informants was very often arbitrary. Most important of all, their primary objective in recording these traditions was to ascertain the pre-colonial political structure, and in particular the legitimate political authorities, of Borgu in order to harness these to their policy of governing at the local level through the existing indigenous authorities, a policy which is better known as Indirect Rule. Now, in Africa, oral history had been used to legitimize dynasties, or claims to political power, or ownership of land. We shall see in the course of events that led up to the rebellion and in the attempts to heal the wounds caused by it, the importance of oral tradition as a source of information, and the difficulty of reconciling one tradition with another, especially those of Bussa and Kaiama.

There is, for the contemporary scholar trying to handle oral traditions, the additional problem that such traditions as have been recorded in the past and have been published (for instance those appearing in the provincial *Gazetteers* or in the works of anthropologists) gain a special currency by the very virtue of being in print. The researcher is liable in Borgu to have informants recite almost word for word the synthesis of oral traditions made by Theodore Hoskyns-Abrahall and published in Hermon-Hodge's *The Gazetteer of Ilorin Province* in 1929.[16] Finally there is the problem in Bussa that oral tradition is related to the history of a very small central ruling group, the *Wassangari*, closely interrelated, in which there is a substantial identity of views on history, such divergences as there are arising mainly in matters of recent history, in particular with regard to claims to political position. In the villages, there is little sense of history. Most villages have been on their site for only two or three generations, owing to the pattern of shifting cultivation. Bussa itself has changed its site at least four times since Mungo Park met his death on the Niger Rapids in 1806.[17] With the change of site, the history of the abandoned sites becomes increasingly vague. The fine modern town of Bussa, architect-designed and built in concrete, seems to have little relationship to the mud-and-thatch Bussa over which the waters closed in 1969.

Another obstacle confronting the researcher in contemporary Bussa is the rapid rate at which Islam has spread among the ruling groups during the colonial period. There is an understandable reluctance amongst devout Muslims to discuss the 'pagan' practices of their forefathers. Furthermore, the British imposition on Bussa of a system of local government modelled on that devised for the Muslim emirates of the conquered Sokoto caliphate has tended to obscure memories of the pre-colonial system of government.

With these reservations in mind an attempt will be made in the pages that follow to describe the lands and people of Borgu, and their pre-colonial history. In this, particular emphasis will be placed on the nature of the relationship between the Borgu states; the political organization of the individual states; and the relationship between Bussa and its neighbour across the Niger, Yauri. These are all essential to an understanding of the rebellion of 1915.

2. The Land and People of Borgu

Pre-colonial Borgu comprised five major states. Nikki, by far the largest, and politically the most important, had sovereignty, often of a very loose kind, over all the Borgu territory in Dahomey, though by the nineteenth century its provinces of Kandi, Kouandé, Djougou and Parakou had become effectively independent. Some Nikki dependencies, namely Ilesha, Okuta, Banara and Yashikera, were cut off from it by the demarcation of the Anglo-French boundary between Dahomey and Nigeria. The other four states are to be found in Nigerian Borgu, with only some 40,000 inhabitants as compared with Dahomeyan Borgu's 300,000 or more. Bussa, the first of the Borgu states to be founded, claimed hegemony over the neighbouring states of Illo and Wawa, though as we shall see these latter were to all intents and purposes independent in the nineteenth century. To the south of Bussa and Wawa is Kaiama, which was a Nikki foundation, but which exercised an effective independence of both Nikki and Bussa.

Borgu itself is flat woodland country, with occasional granite outcrops. In Nigerian Borgu one is struck by the apparent absence of any population outside the main settlements. Only along the Niger does the woodland give way in places to areas of intensive cultivation. Today, along the laterite roads that link Kaiama with Wawa and Bussa, one may drive for nearly thirty minutes without seeing a soul.

The chief occupation of the inhabitants of Nigerian Borgu, with which we are concerned in this study, is farming. Fulani, who wander freely across the lands of the farmers with their cows, supply milk, and —when taxes force them to—sell their beloved cattle as meat for consumption by the farmers. The latter value the presence of the Fulani for the manure their cattle provide for the land. The principal crops cultivated by the farmers are yams and sorghum. Generally poor soil, lack of water resources, and a long dry season have prevented the production of agricultural surpluses, which helps to explain the relatively sparse population of the area. Under colonial rule, the only export crop which was developed was shea-butter from the shea tree.

On the Niger a number of villages devoted part of their labour to fishing, one of the main sources of protein for the people. But food was never abundant, even in centres like Wawa which in pre-colonial times enjoyed a relative prosperity from the caravan trade. Clapperton wrote that the slaves of Wawa ate only two meals a day 'which almost invariably consist of paste of the flour of yams, or millet, in the morning about nine o'clock, and a thicker kind approaching pudding, after sunset, and this only in small quantities; flesh, fowl, or fish, they may occasionally get, but only by a very rare chance. Their owners, in fact, fare very little better: perhaps a little smoke-dried fish, or some meat now and then; principally only a little palm-oil, or vegetable butter, in addition to their paste or pudding; but they indulge freely in drinking palm-wine, rum or bouza.'[19] Wine and beer seem to have been a principal source of vitamin for farmers.

In the large towns there was some degree of specialization among the inhabitants, whose main occupation was farming. Joyce Cary, assessing Kaiama for taxation in 1919, recorded that only twenty-two men, exclusive of the old and sick, did not farm, out of a population for the district of 1,092 males, 1,140 females and 1,104 children. Among those with specialized activities were: butchers, weavers, traders, dyers, smiths, barber-surgeons, tailors, carpenters, shea-butter makers, brewers, porridge-makers, spinners, potters, soap-boilers, lamp-makers.[20] The majority of these activities were concentrated in Kaiama town. In precolonial times the concentration of specialized activities in the town, in particular those of traders, would have been greater because of its position on the caravan route. In 1826, when Clapperton visited Kaiama he met a caravan on its way from Gonja and Ashanti to Kano which he estimated as 'upwards of 1,000 men and women and as many beasts'.[21] Clapperton, and later Richard Lander in 1830,[22] both give the impression of Kaiama being vastly larger than it is today. Clapperton hazarded that it had a population of 30,000, which is ten times the population recorded for 1912.[23] The discrepancy between estimates of population made by Clapperton and Lander and those recorded in the British censuses indicates clearly that there was a considerable decline in population during the nineteenth century. Even taking into account the unreliability of visual assessments, the estimates of the number of people and size of Borgu towns visited by these travellers bear little relation to the Borgu occupied by the British. A number of factors may account for this. The trade routes passing through Borgu from Lagos and Badagry to Sokoto and Kano were frequently stopped by the civil wars that intensified in Yorubaland after the fall of old Oyo in c. 1835. This would have meant an exodus of foreign traders and entrepreneurs as well as a good few locals involved in the long-distance trade.[24] In c. 1835, the combined Borgu armies of Nikki, Kaiama, Wawa and Bussa suffered a disastrous defeat at the hands of the Ilorin with the loss of not only the Kings of Nikki, Kaiama and Wawa, but also many of their men. Throughout the century, the adult male population must have suffered considerable attrition as a result not only of defensive battles, but also of the petty, but frequent, internal wars. Furthermore, slave-raiding of the peasant population by the nobles in order to obtain the means to purchase horses to maintain their cavalry further depleted the population. Finally, the French occupation seems to have taken a considerable toll in lives. (See p. 48.)

The present-day inhabitants of Borgu fall into six main groups. The ruling class were the *Wasangari*. The freemen, who could intermarry with the Wasangari, were known as *Batomba*. Beneath them were the *Fulani*, who were technically a servile group, but could demonstrate dissatisfaction with a Wasangari master by leaving their area for the protection of another master. A Wasangari would do anything to avoid this, since achievement of high political office depended on number of followers as well as wealth. The truly servile class were the *Gando*, who were the slaves of the Wasangari. These usually lived in farming settlements, cultivating on behalf of their Wasangari masters. They usually had to intermarry among themselves, and were treated as property by their masters who could sell them. The Gando are a peculiar feature of the Nikki-derived states, and were not to be found in Bussa, Illo and Wawa, though the Wasangari here did possess domestic slaves. The villages of Shagunu, Kagogi and Sangwa consisted of state slaves of Bussa, not dissimilar in role to the Gando of Nikki.

In addition to these four groups who made up Borgu society were two others, who accepted Wasangari authority while not being of servile status. First were the *Dendi*, who were traders of Mande or Sarakolle origin, in whose hands was concentrated the trade that passed through Borgu. Second were immigrant groups of farmers, particularly in Bussa, along the Niger. These groups accepted political authority and paid tribute, but were not in servile relationship to anyone in Borgu. Indeed the Dendi and other groups of immigrant traders were vital to the maintenance of the Wasangari's power, based as it was on cavalry, since the Dendi supplied horses in exchange either for Fulani cattle or for slaves. During the nineteenth century, Hausa traders became almost as important as the Dendi in Borgu, and Hausa was widely spoken.

3. The Origins of Bussa and its Status in Borgu

Bussa, like many other states in Northern Nigeria, claims as its founder the legendary Kisra, a prince from the East.[25] In Bussa, today, it is claimed that Kisra migrated westwards from Arabia after refusing to accept the reforms of the Prophet Mohammed. After a stay in Bornu, he and his followers moved westwards to what is now the Niger. At that time it was a narrow stream, but Kisra performed a miracle and enlarged it to its present size to prevent his enemies from Arabia continuing their pursuit.[26] The sacred role of the Niger as the boundary of Bussa against its enemies was symbolized by the taboo against the King of Bussa's sailing on the Niger. It was only in 1908 that Kitoro Gani broke the taboo when he crossed the Niger supported on each side by a canoe.[27] Kisra died, leaving three sons, Woru, Sabi and Biyo. Woru succeeded his father as leader of the immigrants and his first act was to found Illo, where Biyo, his younger brother, was left in charge. Sabi and Woru split up, with Sabi moving south-west to found Nikki, and Woru moving south-east. After much wandering Woru settled at Bussa which means in the Bussa language, Mabussa—'I am tired and I now need a rest.'[28] On his migration, Kisra had been accompanied by a number of Mallams, or learned men. The head of these was Bamarubere, one of whose descendants, Mallam Toga, founded Wawa. Though he rebelled against the reigning King of Bussa and was killed, his descendants are still rulers of Wawa to this day.

This is the Bussa version of the foundation of the four principal states of Borgu: Illo, Nikki, Wawa and Bussa. In it, Bussa is quite clearly the senior foundation, since it was founded by the eldest son of Kisra. No mention is made of Kaiama which is generally held to have been founded at some time during the eighteenth century. A speculative date for the foundation of Bussa, Illo and Nikki is at least some four hundred and fifty years ago. Clearly some state organization must have been in existence by the end of the fifteenth century in order for Borgu to have successfully repulsed the army of the Songhai empire on two occasions in the sixteenth century.

We must, however, realize that the above version of the Kisra legend is a Bussa version, which clearly makes Bussa the senior Borgu foundation. From Kaiama, immediately after the occupation in 1902, Acting Resident Kemble collected a very different account, which reduces Bussa to a 'servile' status and gives Nikki primacy.

'. . . Kisra crossed over the River Niger which was then quite a small stream and settled at Bussa with his followers, and wives and slaves. At Bussa he lived many years governing the country and here two sons were born to him. These two sons went hunting towards Nikki and were away a long time, and while they were absent their father Kisra died, slaves being sent to inform the sons of his death. When they were found (at Nikki), they sent back to say that all the usual formalities were to be observed at Bussa and that all that was done at Bussa they would also do so at Nikki. Kisra's body was kept a year and a day before anybody was told of his death. The slaves all stopped at Bussa. One of the brothers was then made King of Nikki and whatever he wanted done at Bussa he told the slaves and it was done. The King of Nikki now had two sons and they went out hunting and while they were away, *their* father died. Messengers were sent out to look for them, but they were not found for a long time and therefore a younger brother who had been born during their absence was made King. When the two brothers heard that their father was dead and a younger brother made King, one brother said let us fight for the throne, but the other said no, as our younger brother has been made King of Nikki, we must go to other places and be made King there. The elder then went to Buai, and the younger to Kaiama where they were made kings.'[29]

Here we see that Kaiama, in this version of the Kisra legend told to Kemble by three of its elders, is made a Kisra foundation and the position of Bussa is relegated to that of an ancestral home, where the traditions are maintained by slaves. Traditions collected in Kaiama in July and August 1971 by my research assistant, Suleiman Haliru Idris, grandson of the retired Emir of Kaiama, Haliru, present radically different versions of the foundation of the Borgu states. These traditions, some of which are recorded below, not only show how difficult it is to interpret oral tradition in a historical sense, but also show how traditions have political implications: in this case that Kaiama was not, and therefore ought not to be, subject to Bussa for local government purposes, which it became in 1955.

Mallam Haliru was given accounts of the Kisra legend, containing the following radically discrepant versions of events:

1. That Kisra never reached Bussa.

2. That Bussa was not founded by a member of Kisra's family but by one of his leading subjects/chief servants.

3. That the Kisra immigrants arrived not in northern Borgu, but in the Kaiama area where they asked permission from the ruler to settle. He then referred them to his overlord, the King of Nikki.

4. That after the Kisra immigrants had been given permission to settle, the sons of Kisra went to Nikki, while the eldest of Kisra's followers went to Bussa, where he established himself as ruler. In Nikki, Woru, the eldest son of Kisra, became King, while his brothers became rulers of neighbouring towns. However, Woru and his brothers decided to go to Bussa and pay homage to the eldest of Kisra's followers because, since the death of Kisra, they had considered him as their father.* It is because of this act of homage that Bussa claimed leadership over Borgu. However, from the Kaiama point of view, Bussa cannot claim superiority, since later a prince of the Kisra Nikki dynasty became King of Kaiama, so that while Bussa may claim

---

* This is still practised in Borgu today. The head of the servants of a king or chief is regarded by the children of the latter as their 'father'. [Information: Musa Baba Idris.]

hegemony because of this act of homage, Kaiama's dynasty is of the Kisra blood.[30]

The Yoruba have a parallel situation. Ife is generally acknowledged as the original settlement of the founding ancestor of the Yoruba, Oduduwa. His sons, who vary in number in the various oral traditions, were the ancestors of the present *obas* or crowned rulers of Yorubaland. Oral tradition here is used to legitimize the status of this or that *oba*. While all traditions have a common denominator of about five towns which can claim royal origin, the traditions vary from town to town as to who the others were. Just as with the Kaiama version of the Kisra legend, the Oyo version of the Oduduwa legend has it that his sons dispersed from Ife, leaving a slave in charge of the sacred relics. This is hotly contested at Ife which claims its ruler is the senior of the crowned rulers of Yorubaland.

The important point here is that, whatever the status of the ruling house of Ife, the city itself is revered as the original home of the Yoruba. Similarly, whatever the subsequent declines in the political fortunes of Bussa, whatever status may be ascribed to its ruling house by other Borgu towns, it is accepted as the senior of the Borgu towns, the home of the Kisra relics. At old Bussa, now flooded, the chains and spears of Kisra were buried and guarded by the *Beresondi*, the personal priest of the kings of Bussa.[31] Bussa kept the Gangan Kisra (the Kisra Big Drum) and the Kisra kettle-drums,[32] and in addition had more state trumpets than any of the other Borgu states, fourteen as distinct from Nikki's twelve.[33] Theodore Hoskyns-Abrahall, who wrote the first detailed history of Bussa in 1925, considered that it was the fact that the priestly status of Kisra in Arabia had been handed down to every succeeding Bussa King, which was largely responsible for the ruler of Bussa's 'wide sphere of influence and for the fear which his name has always inspired. Nikki has in time past had territory, following and wealth greater than Bussa but has never denied to the latter first place. Every Sarikin Bussa admits of but one superior, the Shehu of Bornu.'[34] In acknowledging this special relationship with Bornu, the original halting-place of Kisra on his flight from Arabia, it was Bussa which sent presents to the Mai of Bornu, and in return received camels, horses and suits of cloth which were then divided among the rulers of Nikki, Illo and Oyo.[35] This reference to Oyo is interesting, for in Bussa it is believed that the Yoruba were slaves of Bussa, who after many years of service were given their freedom by the King of Bussa. He told them to follow a snake to which he had attached a charm. They were to follow it until it stopped: and there they were to found their capital. Whilst the Yoruba claim that Oyo was founded from Ife, they do not deny that Oyo was settled in Borgu territory nor that there was a close relationship between Oyo and Borgu.

Given the fact that Bussa claimed primacy among the Borgu states, how far was this acknowledged in practice by the other states? Here we come up against lack of evidence before the nineteenth century. However, we do know from the accounts of the nineteenth-century travellers, Clapperton and Lander, that Bussa was considered in some sense suzerain by Wawa and Kaiama. Clapperton himself wrote in 1826: 'I must however go out of my way to visit the Sultan of Bussa, as all this part of the country is nominally under him. The Sultan of Niki is next to him, and equal to him in power.'[36] Clapperton however recognized the separate political identity of Kaiama and Wawa, which he described as petty states, and merely wrote that 'Boussa is considered the head.'[37] Richard Lander, when he visited Kaiama four years later, wrote of 'the King of Boossa, who is acknowledged to be the greatest of all the sovereigns of Borgoo'.[38] Yet, in 1894, the French and British were still not sure where was the senior ruler, or Lord of all Borgu—in Bussa or Nikki. Even at the time of the visits of Clapperton and Lander, the question was a confused one, for though Clapperton insisted that Bussa was the senior kingdom, he recorded that Dahomeyan messengers had told him that '. . . Niki was the capital of Borgoo and not Kiama. . . .'[39] Again, at the end of the nineteenth century, a local Borgu historian, Lamu of Bode, reported: 'Borgu is not divided into independent Kingdoms, but all the divisions, including Boussa, are subject to the King of Nikki.'[40] It was this confusion that precipitated the famous Race to Nikki (to secure a treaty) between the British, represented by Lugard, and the French by Captain Decoeur, since it was argued that Nikki, clearly the most powerful of the Borgu kings, was also the overall king. In Lugard's treaty with Nikki he was described as 'King of Nikki, and of all Borgu Country'.[41]

This confusion as to who was sovereign in Borgu seems to have arisen from a failure to distinguish between the actual political power of the individual Borgu states, which fluctuated during the nineteenth century, and the reverence in which they held Bussa as the original Kisra foundation. Just as Bussa acknowledged Bornu as its 'suzerain' because it was there Kisra first sojourned on his flight from Arabia, so Kaiama, Nikki and Wawa considered Bussa their suzerain because it was the home of the Kisra relics. But just as Bornu exercised no political control over Bussa, so Bussa exercised none over Nikki, Wawa, Illo and Kaiama by virtue of its position of 'seniority' among the Borgu states. Any control it did exercise over them was in terms of actual power, rather than tradition. And in the nineteenth century Bussa had little actual power.

This confusion as to sovereignty arose also from failure to understand the very special political arrangement that linked the states of Borgu. The political system of pre-colonial Borgu was characterized by the centrifugal tendencies of all its component units, so that it is very difficult at any one time to say whether particular states came under the effective control of either Bussa or Nikki. Thus the rulers of the outlying provinces of Nikki were to all intents and purposes independent and owed Nikki obligation only in times of war with outsiders. This was exactly the obligation of Nikki to Bussa.[42] It is in this sense only that Nikki can be said to have been in any way politically dependent on Bussa.

The hegemony of Nikki and Bussa over their dependent states and provinces was equally weak. Kaiama was a Nikki foundation, but by the beginning of the nineteenth century when Clapperton and Lander visited it, it was clearly independent. In 1826 when Clapperton visited Wawa, its ruler was described by him as its governor, not king, and freely acknowledged the suzerainty of Bussa. In 1830 when Lander returned to Borgu, he learnt in Kaiama that the ruler of Wawa had lately received 'a body of Nouffie [Nupe] horse soldiers, consisting of eight hundred men, which has rendered its chief more powerful than either of his neighbours' (i.e. Bussa and Kaiama).[43]

The apparent lack of authority of Nikki and Bussa over their provinces and dependent states is largely explained by the system whereby the throne was filled on the death of a king, a system which could only weaken the new king's authority.

In principle succession went from elder to younger brother. Only when the last brother was dead did a new generation inherit, starting from the eldest living son of the immediately preceding king. In practice the throne was often contested by rival princes. In effect, then, the throne went to the strongest claimant among them. In Bussa, if the choice of the kingmakers was disputed, rival claimants battled for possession of the sacred cob-skin which a new king had to wear for a prescribed period[44]. Unsuccessful princes would move to outlying districts or even live in exile awaiting another chance to take the throne. Sometimes a king would

NOTES by Musa Baba Idris

1. The south-western boundaries of the greater Borgu, i.e. the area south-west of Djougou, extended westwards farther than the map indicates. Borgu imperial expansion had been westwards over the centuries and there is considerable data on this, but not enough to construct a map or base a boundary map upon.
2. The shaded area was the only area absolutely outside the Nikki satellite and controlled by Bussa directly or indirectly as the case applied to Wawa (Gbere).
3. It follows, therefore, that the other provinces were under the influence of Nikki and this depended on innumerable factors which cannot be discussed here. However, it appears that the powers of Bouay, Puissa and Sandilo had waned probably during the eighteenth century; certainly areas of these provinces had been incorporated and came under the direct jurisdiction of the metropolitan province of Nikki.
4. On the other hand, the provinces of Illo, Kandi, Kouande, Djougou, Parakou and Kaiama had acquired immense power vis-à-vis the over-all control of these areas by the *sina-boko* (supreme ruler) of Nikki, the *de facto* ruler of the Bariba empire. On the eve of the colonial occupation, Borgu was virtually heading towards 'city statism' with the boundaries of the states corresponding with the boundaries of the provinces when under the jurisdiction of the metropolis, Nikki, whose metropolitan areas had been taken over by the new province of Perere which had grown immensely powerful towards the

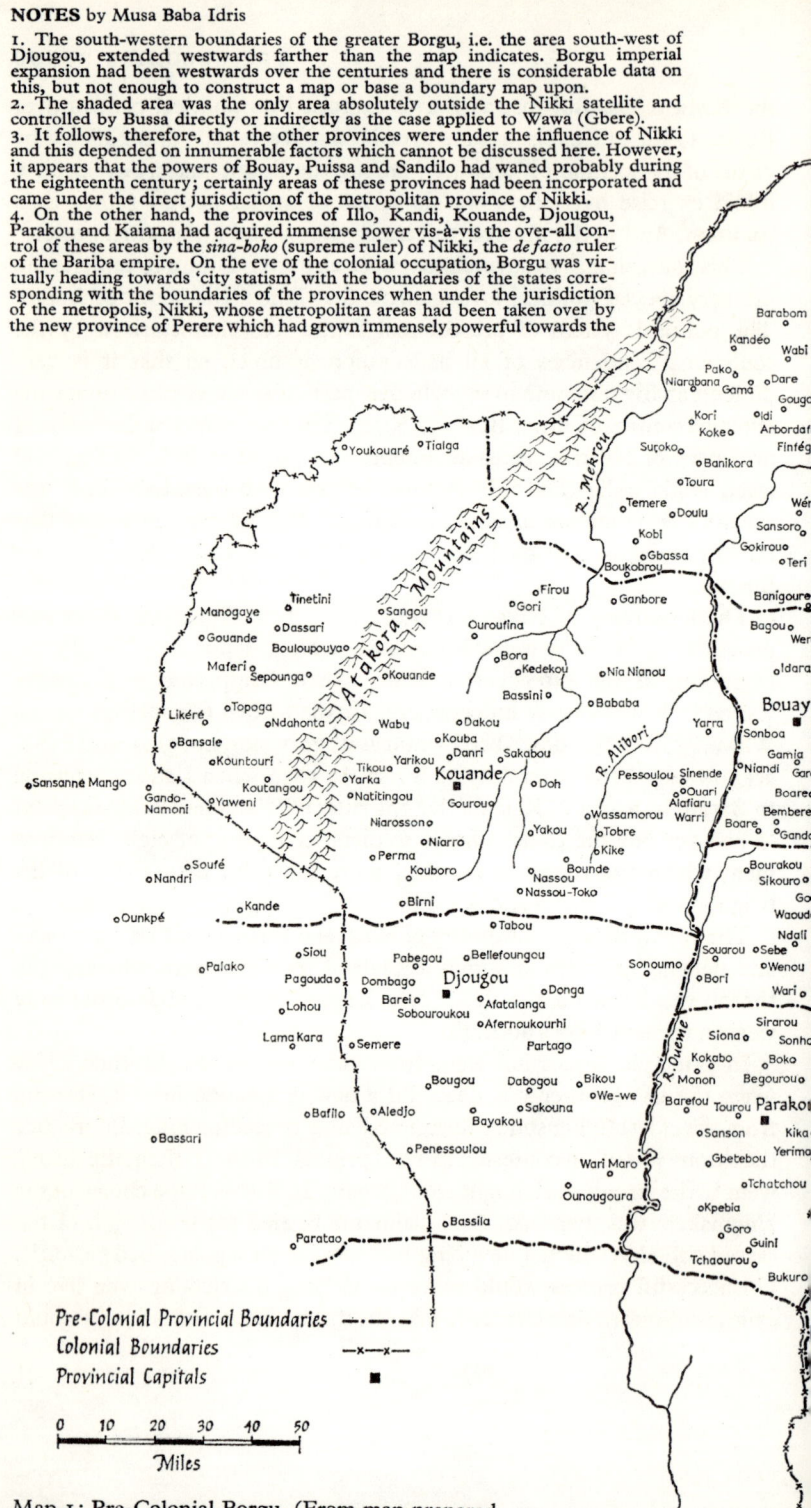

Map 1: Pre-Colonial Borgu. (From map prepared by Mallam Musa Baba Idris)

end of the nineteenth century. This was witnessed by Wolf who visited Borgu in 1891, when the chief of Perere, Koto, was to all intents and purposes the most powerful chief of Borgu.

5. The reasons for this political deterioration lay in the economic situation in Borgu during the century and was escalated by the defeat of the Baribas at the Ilorin war where Sero Kpera, the Bariba leader, was killed after which the succeeding *sina-bokos* were unable to control the provinces.

6. The caravan trade passing through the provincial capitals had made the chiefs extremely powerful so much so that they were in a position to contest the strength of the metropolis, which was in utter chaos at this time owing to dynastic strife.

7. Each province was able to set up its own state administration with similar institutions to those of Nikki and was directly controlled by the chief of the province and did not owe allegiance to Nikki. The same reason goes for the growing strength of the

chief of Perere in whose territory an important trade route passed and whose *wasangari* (princes) were reported by Wolf in April 1891 to have attacked and plundered a caravan of 300 men with 90 donkeys going from Kano to Salaga.

8. Similarly, the area that used to be controlled by Bussa directly as shown on the map was no longer under the jurisdiction of the King of Bussa. Wawa was apparently independent when the Landers were there although there was a nominal respect given to the *Kibe* of Bussa who received the same from the rest of the Borgu provinces.

NOTE by the Author

While Musa Baba Idris considers that Illo had been a province of Nikki, though effectively independent by the end of the nineteenth century, the early British political officers in Borgu considered Illo to be tributary of Bussa. Certainly Bussa when it came under British rule claimed that the southern towns and villages of Illo province, such as Gebbe, Lafugu and Kaoje were within its boundaries.

be attacked by a rival claimant after he had acceded to the throne as in the case of Dan Toro's successor, Kisan Dogo, who was attacked by Nda Galadima, son of Dan Toro. To characterize these succession disputes as civil war which eroded the hegemony of Bussa in Borgu, as Anene did,[45] is to misunderstand the political structure of Borgu, and to ignore the fact that they were just as characteristic of Nikki as of Bussa. The path to the throne was through a combination of the hereditary principle and force. Where a succession in Nikki or Bussa was not disputed, this was because the kingmakers chose the candidate who was clearly the most powerful.

The rulers of Bussa could not be deposed: only die or be killed in battle.[46] There was no concept of permitting the exile of an incumbent monarch. A king faced with exile would rather commit suicide, just as a Borgu commoner would if faced with slavery.

In these circumstances the position of the monarchs of Bussa and Nikki was not a strong one. With little authority over their dependent rulers, and always subject to challenge by rival claimants, their control over their 'states' was in no way comparable to that of the emirs of the Sokoto caliphate. In the case of Bussa, both Wawa and Illo, which paid him tribute, were in practice usually autonomous.

In conclusion, then, while the Kisra legend is important in establishing the primacy of Bussa among the states of Borgu from a spiritual point of view, it does not establish its political primacy. Within Borgu the states were rivals, and did wage wars against each other. Thus in 1830 Kaiama told Lander that it was expecting an attack by Wawa.[47] Clapperton had earlier remarked that when the Borgu states made war on each other Bussa interfered and made both parties pay.[48] However, when the Borgu states faced external threats they were able to unite against them on the basis of their common Kisra origin. It is not clear, though, how these alliances were cemented, whether on the principle of nominal convocation by Bussa as the senior foundation or on that of the leadership of Nikki, as the most powerful state. An interesting parallel might be the way the Greek states organized their armies at the time of Philip II of Macedon in the Delphic League. The best known example of Borgu states allying themselves for defensive purposes was in c. 1834 when Alafin Oluewu of Oyo asked Borgu for support against the Fulani of Ilorin, who were endangering the security of both states. A Borgu army was formed under the leadership of Sero Kpera, King of Nikki, with contingents led by the Kings of Wawa and Kaiama, and by Gajere, nephew of the King of Bussa.⁴⁹ Earlier, they had similarly joined forces, according to Lander, against the Fulani and driven them into the Niger, 'where many of them had perished'.⁵⁰ The acceptance by the other Borgu states of Sero Kpera's leadership indicates, in the view of Musa Baba Idris, the one successful attempt to arrest the centrifugal tendencies among the Borgu states which began in the eighteenth, and continued throughout the nineteenth century. Sero Kpera had sufficient military resources at his disposal to claim leadership of Borgu. His death in the war with Ilorin, however, brought to an end this temporary unity in Borgu and the centrifugal tendencies among the states continued unchecked.

We await the completion of Musa Baba Idris's research on the history of pre-colonial Borgu before the exact nature of the interrelationship of the Borgu states can be determined, particularly with reference to the position of Bussa among them. Perhaps the most we can say now is, as a Bussa guide put it to Lugard when he was about to set out from Kishi for Kaiama: 'the old Bussa king is looked on as a father through all Borgu.'⁵¹ But, as in many families, the sons (Nikki and Kaiama) were richer and more powerful than the father.

4. Kaiama and Yauri

The rebellion of 1915 cannot be fully understood without an appreciation of the nature of the relationship of Bussa with Kaiama, its southern Borgu neighbour, and with Yauri its Hausa neighbour across the Niger. Kaiama appears to have been founded from Nikki some time in the eighteenth century, probably in the latter half. At any rate, by the time Clapperton visited it in 1826, it was a well-established state, certainly independent of Bussa, and largely independent of Nikki. Its southern frontiers marched with those of the Yoruba of Oyo, and all traditions about the founding of Kaiama agree that it was settled only after a successful struggle with them. The founder of Kaiama was Sabi Agba. He was a descendant of Boroboko, a relation of the King of Nikki who had left the capital to found a new town at Bueru.⁵² There it is said Boroboko vanished into the earth and the place of his disappearance is still revered by the people of Kaiama. His successors moved their town on numerous occasions until Sabi Agba finally settled his people at Kaiama after a successful battle with the Yoruba of Oyo. This with reasonable certainty was the war reported by Lionel Abson, Governor of the British fort at Ouidah, which took place in 1783.[53]

There is nothing in Clapperton's account, nor that of the Landers, to suggest that Kaiama was in any way under the political control of either Nikki or Bussa. However, when the King of Kaiama agreed to serve under the King of Nikki in the Borgu army which joined forces with Oyo against Ilorin in c. 1834, it seems that this was as much an acknowledgement of the power of Sero Kpera, King of Nikki, as a recognition of the mutual obligation of the Borgu states to aid each other in time of external threat. Though Sero Kpera's power was transient, Kaiama did acknowledge the precedence of the Nikki kings and it seems clear that when new rulers of Kaiama were selected they had to have the sanction of Nikki or, as a last resort, of Bussa. As a rule Nikki sent a representative to the installation of the kings of Kaiama. Tradition has it that in a succession dispute in Kaiama the matter was referred to Nikki, and if he could not settle it, it was then referred to Bussa.[54] But again this did not mean that Bussa controlled Kaiama. Indeed in the 1880s, in the Gebbe wars against its rebellious Kamberri subjects, Bussa had to call on Kaiama for assistance. Even if, however, Kaiama was as powerful as Bussa, or even more powerful, as witnessed by the effective assistance of the Kaiama army in the Gebbe wars, it could not, in the Borgu conception of the relative status of its rulers, claim equality with Bussa. Mora Tasude, King of Kaiama, put it clearly when he told Lugard in 1894: 'His elder brother was King of Nikki and he was in a sense under Nikki, but paid no tribute to him, in fact was independent. He said Bussa (the eldest of the 3 and looked up to by all), Kaiama and Nikki were all independent Kings, and the only Kings of Borgu.'[55]

Kaiama's frontiers were bounded to the west by Yashikera which was definitely a Nikki foundation and owed no allegiance to Kaiama. Indeed the ruling house of Yashikera could present candidates to the throne of Nikki.[56] Yashikera as a state was founded only in c. 1886 by Ojo (Woru Yaru) son of the Sinolafia, the reigning King of Nikki. It was based on the old town of Kali which Ojo made his capital, changing its name to Yashikera. Prior to that the area seems to have been a collection of villages centred on Kali, and dependent on Nikki,[57] and appears to have been considered as the King of Nikki's farm. Beyond Yashikera were the chieftaincies of Okuta and Ilesha, both tributaries of Nikki, and founded as a result of conquest of Oyo territory. Okuta seems to have been established in the early part of the nineteenth century. Ilesha was founded around the same time, during the tribulations of the Oyo empire which followed the Fulani invasions. In both cases Nikki sanctioned the appointment of new chiefs. However, because Yashikera, Okuta and Ilesha were cut off from Nikki by the Anglo-French boundary agreed in 1898, they were made districts of Kaiama, to which none of the three chiefs in pre-colonial times had owed any allegiance.

A further aspect of pre-colonial Borgu essential to the understanding of the revolt is the relationship of Bussa to its neighbour across the Niger, Yauri. The two states seem to have been on excellent terms in the early nineteenth century. Clapperton records the ruler of Wawa telling him that Yauri owed allegiance to Bussa.[58] The Yaurawa, whilst denying that the kings of Bussa had any territorial rights over them, did admit, according to one British political officer, that the King was their religious 'grandfather'.[59] Madi Adamu, however, in his major study of Yauri history, does not refer to the existence of such a relationship.[60]

In the early nineteenth century, both Bussa and Yauri came under heavy pressure from the Fulani during the early years of the *jihad*.* While Bussa retained its independence, Yauri had to accept protection from Gwandu, to which it paid *jizya*, or that form of tribute paid by a non-Muslim state to a Muslim suzerain if it wished to maintain its own form of government.[61] Bussa (and indeed all Borgu) was sufficiently alarmed by the Fulani threat that no Fulani was allowed to carry a weapon in any of the Borgu states for fear of an internal uprising by the large Fulani community[62] which in the twentieth century was estimated as making up one-fifth of the population of Borgu.[63] Lander records that Bussa was actually taken on one occasion by the Fulani.[64]

Even though Yauri came under Fulani rule, until the accession of Abdullahi Abershi as Sarkin Yauri in 1888 Bussa and Yauri continued to maintain their excellent relations. The friendship of the two states culminated in the 1880s in the joint action of their Kings Gallo of Yauri and Dan Toro of Bussa against the Kamberri of Gebbe. Many Kamberri had migrated across the Niger from Yauri to Bussa because Gallo had been unable to afford them protection from slave-raiding by Ibrahim Nagwamatse, Sarkin Sudan of Kontagora.[65] Gallo was further hampered by civil war. The Kamberri settled on Bussa lands, in particular in the Kunji, Agwarra and Rofia areas. The Kamberri soon asserted their independence, raiding canoes of both Bussa and Yauri. Sarkin Bussa,

---
* *jihad* = a campaign which Muslims should wage against Unbelievers and Unbelief.

Dan Toro, led an expedition against them but had to call in Yauri forces to assist him. These combined forces were at first led by Dangaladima Abershi of Yauri but he had to withdraw on succeeding Gallo as Sarkin Yauri. Dan Toro successfully completed the war and installed his administrator, Barje Bello, to govern the recently subdued districts. Abershi was, however, allowed to appoint the village heads of Kalkami and Kawara to serve under Barje Bello. Then, according to Bussa traditions, Abershi tried to drive out Barje Bello and reassert full Yauri control over its former Kamberri subjects, even though they were settled on Bussa land. Yauri has it, on the other hand, that Dan Toro asked Abershi to rid him of Barje Bello who had overreached himself, but that the latter subsequently made his peace with Dan Toro. As it was, Abershi was ultimately unsuccessful in his attempts to remove Barje Bello, who remained as Bussa's administrator up till his death in 1912. One version has it that the French buttressed Barje Bello's position, another that the Emir of Gwandu called off Abershi and his vassal Kontagora, who had joined forces with Abershi to remove Barje Bello.[66]

Whatever the facts of the matter, as far as Bussa and Yauri were concerned they were now bitter enemies, with Yauri claiming that sovereignty resided in the origin of the people settled in the disputed area, while Bussa insisted that it consisted in ownership of the land. The British administration put an end to open hostility between the two; but if anything, as we shall see, it exacerbated their strained relations through its consistent misunderstanding of the nature of the problem.

5. The Political Organization of Bussa

The monarchy of Bussa can best be described as a decentralized one, for while the king, or *Kibe*, had enormous spiritual importance for his subjects, politically his power was severely circumscribed. In the first place he shared power with representatives of 'the owners of the land', the previous inhabitants of Bussa from whom the Kisra immigrants originally gained permission to settle. Tradition has it that the Kisra party was welcomed by the indigenous inhabitants on condition that they followed the latter's funeral rites and respected their religion. That the Kisra immigrants came to some such peaceful arrangement rather than occupy Bussa by force is borne out by the fact that to this day representatives of the original inhabitants of Bussa, 'the owners of the land', play an important part in the installation and burial of the Kisra kings and in the government of the state. The principal 'chief of the land', the *Bakarabonde*, apart from his position as a kingmaker, acted as regent at the death of a *kibe*. The king's chief minister, the *Badaburude*, was also a representative of 'the owners of the land'. African history is full of examples of such pacts between immigrant groups as 'owners of the people' and indigenous groups as 'owners of the land', whereby the latter accepted the suzerainty of the former on condition that their religious practices and position as owners of the land were respected. The basis of the arrangement was usually the need of the stronger immigrants for land, and the need of the owners of the land for protection.[67] We shall see later that one of the principal functions of the *Kibe* was to offer his subjects protection.

Apart from sharing political power with 'the owners of the land', the kings of Bussa effectively shared it with the rulers of their tributary states of Illo and Wawa. Though these states technically formed an integral part of the Bussa kingdom, in practice they were very largely independent of it. While the King of Illo at the beginning of the colonial period acknowledged that he was a tributary of Bussa[68] and the King of Bussa likewise claimed that such was Illo's status with regard to him, in practice during the nineteenth century Bussa seems to have had little control over Illo. Indeed Lombard states categorically that Illo was not a tributary of Bussa but independent.[69] Neither Clapperton nor Lander refer to Illo as being either subject to Bussa or as being part of Borgu. This may be because at the time it was subject to Gwandu, from which the western sector of the Sokoto caliphate was administered. Gwandu led several expeditions against Illo, including one in c. 1814, and it may be that it was made a tributary of Gwandu for a short while, though this is denied in Illo. It is significant that at this time Bussa did not send Illo any military assistance whilst Nikki did. Certainly by the end of the nineteenth century there was no indication that it was in any way subject to Gwandu; indeed it seemed freely to acknowledge its tributary relationship with Bussa. It claimed the same Kisra tradition as Bussa regarding its foundation: that its first Kisra king was a younger brother of the founder of Bussa. Tradition has it that a quantity of earth was brought from Bussa and placed in the ground near a small gate leading into the palace of the King of Illo. This gate featured prominently in the installation ceremonies of the kings of Illo.[70] In the first five years of British civilian administration in Borgu, however, no problem was experienced in including Illo in the Bussa emirate. (See below pp. 55 and 67.)

Both Clapperton and Lander recorded that Wawa was a tributary of Bussa. Tradition, as we have already noted, has it that the present dynasty of Wawa was founded by a son of the Bamarubere, a descendant of one of the mallams or learned men who accompanied the Kisra 'heretics' to Bussa. To this day Wawa recognizes this origin, and the Bamarubere of Bussa, after gaining the agreement of the King of Bussa, presides over the installation of the kings of Wawa. This fact, however, did not mean much as far as Bussa's political control over Wawa was concerned. Wawa had its own army, which was considerably strengthened by deserting soldiers in the war of succession in Nupe which was taking place at the time of Lander's second visit to Wawa in 1830. Lander recorded that as a result Wawa had become 'more powerful than either of his neighbours', Bussa and Kaiama.[71] Wawa even used its army against Bussa in 1897 when its ruler championed a rival for the King of Bussa's throne. (See p. 48.) Clapperton, when his baggage was detained in Wawa, persuaded the King of Bussa to send armed messengers with his servant, Richard Lander, 'to desire the governor of Wawa to allow my things to go instantly'.[72] Despite this request from his overlord, the King of Wawa procrastinated for several days before releasing Clapperton's baggage. Wawa also appears from the accounts of Clapperton and Lander to have been much larger and richer than Bussa. Indeed Lander described the town of Wawa as 'one of the handsomest, if not the handsomest, in the interior of Africa'.[73]

Over and above the tributary states of Illo and Wawa, a number of Bussa towns and villages, in which princes with ambitions for the throne resided, maintained armies. Since accession to the throne was gained not only on grounds of genealogy, but also by force, eligible princes had to maintain armies against the day the throne became vacant. An ambitious prince, with a sufficiently large army, might even attempt to drive the incumbent monarch off the throne. So the kings of Bussa had to watch carefully the activities of their brother princes.

Within Bussa itself, the King had to contend with a number of individuals and groups who held political power. The office of Kibe was closely associated with that of an official queen, or *Yon Magara*, who was one of his relatives, and was in charge of naming his children. Both Clapperton and Lander found that the reigning Yon Magara exercised considerable influence over the King. She took a major part in their negotiations with him, and Clapperton recorded that she was 'everything with the Sultan'.[74] He recorded that she maintained a completely separate establishment from the King, and also had a great deal of influence over the King of Wawa, whom she described as her brother. The Yon Magara had to be a daughter of a previous king and looked after the affairs of the princesses.

There was also the *Kiwotede*, or heir apparent to the throne, also known as the *Yerima*, who would be the brother or half-brother of the King thought most suitable by the kingmakers to succeed him. This meant that he had to have a powerful following, for in the event of the death of the King he would have to contend, possibly by force, with the claims of rival brothers and half-brothers. He was responsible for the administration of metropolitan Bussa, a sort of apprenticeship for power.

The kingmakers themselves, represented the interests of 'the owners of the land' and 'the owners of the people'. Traditionally there were eight kingmakers.[75] Four represented the inhabitants of Bussa at the time of the Kisra immigration:

The Bakarabonde, who was the chief of the indigenous inhabitants.
The Bamode, who was the 'brother' of the Bakarabonde, and lived at Monai, while the Bakarabonde lived at old Bussa.
The Badaburude, who was responsible for the burial of the deceased king and the investing of the new king in the sacred cob-skin which was the symbol of royal authority.
The Beresuni, who was the priest of the owners of the land and was keeper of the gate of Bussa.
The Kisra immigrants were represented by:
The Batafu or chief minister of the kings of Bussa.
The Beresondi, the chief priest of the kings of Bussa and the Kisra counterpart of the Beresuni.
The Bamarubere, head of the Mallams.
The Madoko, or chief of the King's provincial administrators.
The Zhinkina, the war chief.

Within Bussa there was an important Muslim community. While the rulers of Bussa never accepted Islam prior to colonial rule, they accepted the Muslim community because of the valuable caravan trade they handled. The King appointed a *Liman*, or Imam, to regulate relations between him and the Muslims.

A further element in the political structure of Bussa seems to have been wealth. During colonial times, Kitoro Gani greatly feared his aunt, who, he believed, was not only a witch but was also prepared to use her wealth to put his rival Mai Arki on the throne after poisoning him. Both Clapperton and Lander record the great influence in Wawa of the wealthy widow Zuma, who on several occasions defied the King there.

Finally the King of Bussa governed his subjects through a state council consisting of the Batafu, or chief minister, the Yon Magara, and a number of the princes, including the Kiwotede, or heir apparent. In short the powers of the king were far from 'despotic' as they appeared to Clapperton[76] but were severely limited by the balancing powers wielded by other groups and individuals in the state. In fact emphasis, particularly from the point of view of the colonial experience of Bussa, should be placed on the constraints to the king's authority, rather than its strength.

The principal roles of the king were sacerdotal and protectionist. He was considered divine, and his blessing meant a great deal to his subjects. In the political sphere his main function was that of protector. Clearly the origin of the monarchy lay in the fact that the Kisra immigrants were able to offer the owners of the land protection. And the fact that the kingmakers made their choice not only on the basis of genealogy but also of power, showed its continuing importance in the Bussa concept of monarchy.

The king financed his army through a variety of sources: through tolls on the large caravans passing through Bussa; revenues from his own farms worked by slaves; booty taken in war; annual tribute levied on his subjects. To ensure the collection of this tribute he had royal slave-administrators known as *Wete Futani Gerede*, or as *Kofas* by the British. These slaves came from different tribes. The majority were Nupe, though some were from Bussa itself. These royal slaves took a portion of the tribute collected as their salary, and also grew rich on farming. If a particular village did not produce its tribute, which was due after each harvest, the king sent his royal bodyguard, the *Bere Bere*, identified by the deerskins they wore, to ensure the payment of tribute, which was due from each household rather than from each adult.

These revenues, apart from financing the army and the court, also paid for the main religious feasts, especially the *Gani*. This feast was the principal symbolic demonstration of the unity of an otherwise politically fragmented state. It took place after the harvest and was essentially a feast in honour of the dead kings. To it came all the Wasangari princes to receive the blessing of the living king and that of their ancestors whose spirits were believed to enter the royal drums for the occasion.[77]

The Gani festival was also an occasion for the princes to demonstrate their power. For the occasion they brought in their followings and often any tribute which they had collected from plunder of villages and caravans. Indeed in the month before the Gani in Nikki and Bussa, the caravan trade ceased because of the insecurity of the roads. One of the main features of Borgu was the constant threat to the caravans by highway robbers, often in fact princes collecting booty to strengthen their position in the struggle for the throne. For the princes their prime ambition was the kingship and much of the instability of Borgu at the end of the nineteenth century can be understood in the dictum: that a son of a king had not fulfilled himself if he did not sit on his father's throne.

Thus while at one level the Gani festival symbolized the unity of the extended royal family it also highlighted the rivalries amongst the princes ambitious for the prestige of the throne of Bussa.

Nothing more clearly shows the weakness of the position of monarchs in Borgu than the method by which they acceded to the throne. A by-product of the succession system was the effective parcelling up of the kingdoms of Nikki and Bussa into a series of autonomous principalities, the rulers of which hoped one day to attain the prestige of the kingship. Lombard suggests that but for European intervention this process of fragmentation would have led to the establishment of a multiplicity of small but effectively autonomous political entities in Borgu.[78] This trend certainly helps us to understand how difficult it was for the kings of Bussa in the colonial period to exercise centralized control over the lands of which they were nominal rulers.

II · EARLY FOREIGN ADMINISTRATION IN BRITISH BORGU

1. The Division of Borgu between France and Britain

The scramble for Africa between the major European powers, launched officially by the Berlin Conference of 1884–5, was notable for the rare occasions on which their representatives stumbled across each other's paths in the largely uncharted continent. When paths did cross, diversions were arranged in the chancelleries of Europe and conflict avoided. In Borgu, however, in 1898 British and French garrisons faced each other uneasily a few hundred yards apart in Kaiama, while other Borgu towns were occupied by British or French troops. It is perhaps surprising that Borgu was one of the few areas in West Africa in which there was nearly a conflict between the troops of the two major future shareholders in West African soil, Britain and France.

Largely uninhabited, and with little promise of riches for exploitation, it might seem an unattractive bone over which to risk armed conflict. But by 1898 Borgu had become strategic to the plans for expansion of both powers. In 1885 the Berlin Act had declared that 'The Navigation of the Niger, without excepting any of its branches and outlets, is and shall remain entirely free for the merchant ships of all nations equally.'[1] The Berlin Conference also effectively gave France control of the lands of the upper Niger and Britain control of the lands of the lower Niger.[2] But the dividing line between the two sections was not determined.

By 1890, when Borgu began, quietly at first, to be seen as a potential bone of contention between the two powers, Britain had occupied very little more territory than she possessed in West Africa on the eve of the Berlin Conference. France had been more ambitious in her push across the western Sudan. Even then, she had only just secured her Senegalese base, and it was not until April 1890 that Segu, the capital of the Tukolor caliphate, fell to her forces. For the rest, France maintained coastal footholds in Guinea, the Ivory Coast and Dahomey. Britain had coastal enclaves in Gambia, Sierra Leone, the Gold Coast (Ghana) and in Lagos, just next door to France's Dahomeyan enclave of Porto Novo, and along the Niger coast where the Niger Coast Protectorate and the Royal Niger Company had extended British administration over a large part of south-eastern Nigeria and its hinterland respectively. The Germans were a factor in Togo and Kamerun (Cameroun). Yet as early as 1889 Anderson of the British Foreign Office foresaw than an Anglo-French struggle over Borgu might lie ahead, and warned the Royal Niger Company accordingly.[3]

To understand why Borgu very nearly became the theatre of European hostilities in Africa, one must realize that in 1890, while the European powers possessed little land in West Africa, they laid claim to much. The British through the Royal Niger Company (which had a royal charter from the British Government to govern the African states with which it had made treaties of protection) claimed the vast Sokoto caliphate by virtue of a treaty of 1st June 1885.[4] This had been backed up twelve days later by a treaty with Gwandu, from which the western part of the caliphate was administered. Both these treaties were reaffirmed in 1890. Similarly in 1885 the British had made a treaty with Dan Toro, the ruler of Bussa, assumed to be King of Borgu, which was reaffirmed in 1890. These treaties gave Britain, through the Royal Niger Company, claim to the lower Niger from at least Bussa to the sea, since the Royal Niger Company already controlled the land from the confluence of the Benue and Niger to the coast. Now the rapids at Bussa marked the beginning of the navigable stretch of the Niger to the sea and France was anxious to secure territory below it. Its strategic importance was emphasized by Sir George Goldie, Chairman and founder of the Royal Niger Company, who was to declare in 1896: 'If ever the French get a port on the Niger I will sell up the whole business and clear out.'[5] Bussa became strategic not only because it marked the beginning of the navigable stretch of the Niger, but because it linked the Yoruba hinterland of the Lagos protectorate with the Sokoto caliphate which the Royal Niger Company claimed. For the French, Borgu was essential not only because it would provide a port on the navigable stretch of the Niger but also because it served as the hinterland to its Dahomeyan enclave of Porto Novo. The Germans in Togo too were interested in Borgu on the basis of the doctrine of *hinterland*, by which it was agreed that, given the lack of knowledge of the interior, one European power should not cut off another from its natural back territory. For France in Porto Novo, the question was vital; a large part of Borgu formed a natural hinterland to Porto Novo, and to the kingdom of Dahomey, which France conquered in 1894. As early as 1892, the French explorer Binger had written: '. . . the Nikki-Parakou-Blini (Birni) triangle has the same importance for our colony of Benin (Dahomey) as Kong does for the future of Ivory Coast.'[6] Apart from the doctrine of hinterland, there was the general agreement that boundaries between two powers should take into account local circumstances. Thus while the Anglo-French Convention of 1890 had defined the northernmost limit of the Royal Niger Company's territories as a straight line from Say on the Niger to Barruwa on Lake Chad, 'it was to be drawn in such a manner as to comprise in the sphere of action of the Niger Company all that fairly belongs to the Kingdom of Sokoto. . . .' This ruling, when it came to demarcating the frontier between the French military territory of Niger and Northern Nigeria in 1904, was to have indirect but dire consequences for Nigerian Borgu.[7]

If the principle was to prevail that a power which had a protectorate over a kingdom could claim it, it could work only if it was clear where political authority lay. In the case of Borgu we have seen that the political structure and interrelationship of its constituent states were very complex and not readily discernible by Europeans, virgin in the territory, and equipped with their own notions of sovereignty. A major element in the Anglo-French dispute over Borgu thus became the question as to which had the hegemony over Borgu: Bussa with whom the Royal Niger Company had treaties; or Nikki, which in 1894 had not yet been visited by a European? A further complication was the fact that while the Say-Barruwa line was clear in demarcating the boundary of French and British activities north and south of the line, there was no clear line to demarcate the east-west boundary between the French and British. Lack of agreement over this question, even after both the French and the British had signed treaties with Nikki, meant that the other doctrine which was implemented in the allocation of African soil to European powers, *effective occupation*, came into play. This was to result in the stationing by both France and Britain of troops in Borgu.

The complex series of negotiations which led up to the Anglo-French Convention of 1898, which divided Borgu between the British and French, has been described in detail elsewhere, as has the dramatic race between Lugard, on behalf of the British, and Decoeur, on behalf of the French, to secure a treaty with Nikki.[8] The details need not detain us here. What is of importance for our study is that ultimately effective occupation—not the pre-colonial structure—of Borgu determined how it was divided between British and French. While it seemed that conflict might be triggered off in the Borgu bush in 1898, in fact France and Britain had no intention of this happening.[9] The Borgu dispute, however, formed part of a much larger picture of Anglo-French rivalry overseas, in which a multitude of interests and issues, varying from strictly local considerations to the balance of power on a world scale, were involved. The year before, the Prime Minister, Lord Salisbury, had assured his Ambassador in Paris that neither France nor Britain would risk war 'for the sake of a malarious African desert'.[10] And the Borgu dispute was settled in London and Paris. Nikki was given to the French, but Bussa, and control of the Niger, were given to the British, though France was granted two leases on the Niger, one just below Bussa and one at its mouth, to enable her to exercise her right to free navigation on the river.

2. The Beginnings of Administration in British Borgu

In February 1902 British Borgu came under the civilian administration of Britain's recently established protectorate of Northern Nigeria, of which Lord Lugard was the High Commissioner and Conquistador. Five years earlier, however, French troops under Lieutenant Bretonnet had occupied Bussa, thus securing France a port on the navigable stretch of the Niger, since Bussa's territory extended south of the notorious rapids. The French decision to occupy Borgu was provoked by increasing concern at the activities of the Royal Niger Company in the area, in particular its successful campaigns in early January 1897 against the emirates of Ilorin and Nupe, whose frontiers marched with eastern Borgu.

As early as 1894 a French administrative *cercle* of Djougou-Kouandé in Western Borgu had been created, and an administrative post established at Kouandé. In the first months of 1895 Victor Ballot, the Governor of Dahomey, established small garrisons between the French Residency of Cannotville and Nikki and visited Bussa, technically within the Royal Niger Company's sphere of influence. Shortly afterwards Commandant G. J. Toutée also entered territory claimed by the Royal Niger Company and established a fort at Bajibo on the Niger facing Bussa territory. From Bajibo he went upstream making, amongst others, a treaty with Dan Toro, King of Bussa, who had shown him his treaty of protection with the Royal Niger Company as though it were a certificate of good relations with the 'Merchants of Igga' [Royal Niger Company] in respect of the fifty sacks of cowries which they paid him in lieu of customs duties.[11]

In 1896 the French Resident at Cannotville, in southern Dahomey, had the whole of western Borgu brought under his jurisdiction, including Nikki and Parakou, which was to be his future headquarters. But this was still largely *paper* occupation. The Royal Niger Company's activities to the east of Borgu made *effective* occupation essential.

Three expeditions, including Bretonnet's, occupied the principal towns of Borgu. Thus Borgu's first experience of foreign occupation was French. It was bitterly resented by the rulers and Wasangari who in signing treaties with the Europeans considered that they were treaties in the proper sense, not licences for permanent occupation. In the offers of military protection they saw opportunities to profit in wars against their enemies. As Lombard has put it, when treaties were signed, the advantages were usually emphasized rather than the disadvantages. Certainly the Borgu rulers did not conceive that thereby they would lose their political authority and control of their lands.[12]

The truth of the matter was brought home to them when the French established garrisons in the principal Borgu towns, and constructed forts in them. While the French did not devise a system of administration for their newly occupied territory, they demonstrated that the French garrisons, flying the Tricolor to proclaim 'effective occupation' to the British, had introduced a new and decisive element into Borgu politics. Thus in April Bretonnet gave the recently installed King of Bussa, Kisan Dogo, 1895–1903, support in his attack on his tributary town of Wawa, which was backing a rival candidate to the throne, Kwara, son of Kigwassai, who had himself been the rival of the late Dan Toro for the Bussa throne. The French further helped Kisan Dogo defeat the large army raised in Babana by Kwara, as a result of which he died of his wounds. The French, with Kisan Dogo, apparently crushed Kwara's army ruthlessly, killing the majority of his force estimated at 4,000.[13] Resentment by the Wasangari at French intervention in the political affairs of Borgu led to a general rising against them. By mid 1897, most of Borgu was in revolt or in a disturbed state. In eastern Borgu, which was to be occupied by the British, Wawa and Kaiama had been brought under control soon after the French occupation. Bussa's ruler was indebted to the French. Thus by April 1898, when Lugard, the Commandant of the newly established West African Frontier Force, commenced the British occupation of eastern Borgu, the brunt of opposition to alien occupation had been borne by the French, who did not finally pacify western Borgu until December 1898.

In April 1898, Lugard arranged with Colonel Willcocks, his second-in-command, to establish a base in Borgu at Fort Goldie and then to occupy any towns where the French were not already stationed. Near Kaiama he established a garrison alongside the French one. As far as the local people were concerned, the whole situation must have been mystifying. None of the Borgawa opposed his occupation by force of arms, which must be attributed to the fact that the French had already solved this problem for him. As he himself later admitted, his was a relatively easy assignment. 'As far as the native races were concerned, the French had, of course, a far more difficult task than we had in Borgu. When we arrived it was only to find a submissive population who welcomed us, but it must be remembered they had received a sharp lesson from other white men; they had offered opposition, and had soon learnt that the game was not worth the candle.'[14]

There followed the apparently passive acceptance of the British invasion and the strange spectacle of two sets of Europeans constructing forts, setting up garrisons, signing treaties and raising flags. It is little wonder that the same King of Kaiama, Mora Tasude, who had declared his friendship for Lugard and saved his life by warning him of an ambush on the road to Nikki in 1894, could declare before Willcocks and the French Commander at Kaiama 'I love France.'[15]

On 14th June 1898, the strange confrontation in Borgu was brought to an end when the Anglo-French Convention was signed. Thereafter Kaiama, Bussa, Wawa, Okuta, Ilesha and Yashikera came under British rule, and under West African Frontier Force administration. But there was little time to make administrative plans: the W.A.F.F. were not only thin on the ground, but were to be used in the suppression of the Ashanti uprising and the conquest of the Sokoto caliphate. The first report of the new protectorate of Northern Nigeria, which in 1900 took over administration of the northern territories claimed or occupied by the Royal Niger Company after its Charter was withdrawn, had little to say except 'Borgu was improved greatly during our occupation. The able chief, Kaiama, is making roads in every direction, which he frequently superintends himself.'[16] The second annual report had nothing on Borgu,[17] while the first report on Borgu as a province under civilian rule merely stated: 'Under Mr. Kemble (Acting in charge) the province of Borgu has maintained the character it has always borne since it was administered in 1898 and 1899 by the West African Frontier Force, as an orderly law-abiding district. The excellent chief of Kaiama is as personally keen as ever in constructing roads and helping the Resident in every way.'[18]

Military administration had been slight in touch to say the least. Up till the end of 1901 small detachments of the W.A.F.F. had been kept at Okuta, Yashikera, Illo and Fort Goldie. The Kaiama garrison was removed in 1901, as was that of Ilesha. The garrison at Illo had been established in 1900 only because of Fulani raids. The most accessible British garrison to Bussa was that at Yelwa, 50 miles upstream. When Capitaine Lenfant visited Bussa in 1901 to maintain French navigation rights on the British stretch of the Niger, he found Kisan Dogo, King of Bussa, largely unaffected by the presence of the military. He had consistently refused to go up to Yelwa to give account to the military authorities of his population and resources for taxation purposes. Whenever he was summoned, he invoked the taboo that forbade the King of Bussa to sail on the Niger, since Kisra had enlarged it to protect him from his pursuers. Lenfant believed this taboo to have been a pure invention to avoid obeying the W.A.F.F. summons.[19] We now know that the taboo was a real one. It certainly served to keep Bussa largely independent of the military, who, by the time Borgu had come under civilian rule, were reduced to two token forces at Illo and Fort Goldie, each consisting of an officer and twenty-five men.

3. The First Years of Civilian Administration: 1902–1903

Harry Kemble became first civilian Resident of Borgu Province in an acting capacity. As head of the province he was directly responsible to Lugard as High Commissioner. Lugard, himself, administered a protectorate much of which in 1902 he had not even seen, let alone controlled. He was therefore preoccupied with the more urgent question of bringing the northern part of his protectorate under effective administration, and Kemble and Borgu were left very much to themselves.

In the still extant reports by Harry Kemble for 1902 and 1903, Kisan Dogo, King of Bussa, emerges as a shadowy figure in comparison with

Mora Tasude, King of Kaiama. This is not surprising, since Kemble was stationed at Kaiama, which had been selected as headquarters for the province, and Bussa was some 65 miles away. The only detailed European account of Kisan Dogo I can find is that given by Lenfant who estimated him to be about seventy years old. 'C'est un grand vieillard, très onctueux, sa physionomie ne respire ni franchise, ni bonté. Elle est plutôt empreinte d'une energie farouche et le poids des ans s'est imprimé dans ses traits fatigués.'[20]

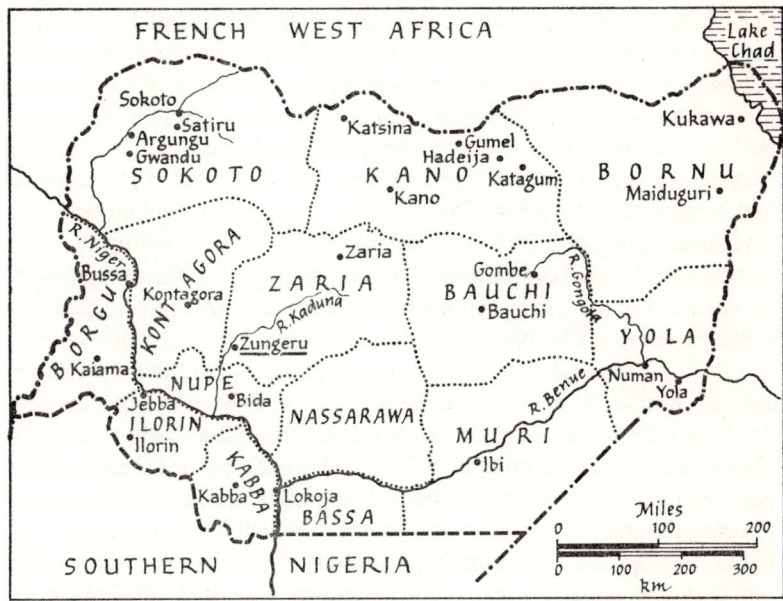

Map 2: Northern Nigeria's Provinces, 1906

The only other European administrator in the province was Mr. Langrishe, stationed at Illo, 100 miles up river from Bussa. From his few encounters with Kisan Dogo, Kemble did not form a good opinion of him. He was 'morose and difficult' though Kemble thought he would improve if he were treated tactfully.[21] Kemble had relatively few dealings with Kisan Dogo, who was clearly left very much to himself. Only two major issues arose that involved Kisan Dogo with the British administration before his death in November 1903 (usually incorrectly given as 1902). The first concerned a charge of murder levelled against the King of Wawa, of whose status vis-à-vis Bussa Kemble was not sure. The second concerned the dispute between Bussa and Yelwa as to ownership of islands in the Niger.

When the W.A.F.F. established their administration in Borgu, the King of Wawa was Kantama, who had been installed by the French shortly after their occupation. He paid tribute to Bussa, on whose behalf the French had fought against his predecessor Kibari who had supported Kwara's candidature to the Bussa throne. However around 1900 Garuba, son of Kibari, Kantama's predecessor, sent complaints against Kantama to Colonel Festing at Yelwa, who thereupon sent one of his officers, Captain Mellis, to investigate. Garuba, ambitious for the throne, told Kantama that the Europeans were coming to seize him, so Kantama and most of the people of Wawa fled to their farms in the bush. Garuba then told the Europeans that he was the rightful King, and Mellis, considering that the fact that Kantama had fled was sufficient proof of the charges laid against him, installed Garuba.[22] In 1901, when Lenfant and his party were at Garafini, he was visited by Kantama. 'This fugitive prince', he wrote, 'is hunted everywhere; he came out from the forest to explain his situation to me. He is a young man, with a proud and energetic face, a Bariba warrior who once fought under our orders and who was enthroned by Vermeersch.'*[23] Early in 1902 charges of murder were made against Garuba, King of Wawa. He was alleged to have beaten a man to death in order to sell his children into slavery. Garuba was brought into Kaiama but was found not guilty. Kemble considered the charge to have been trumped up by Kantama, the ex-King, whose arrest he had ordered. Hearing that the latter was hiding in Bussa, which Kemble was visiting at the time, he sent for Kisan Dogo, and his story of his encounter with him is an interesting example of the directness of methods of administration in those days.

'I sent for the King of Boussa and told him that I had heard that the ex-King of Wawa was in town under the care of his chief headman, and called upon him to produce him. He at first denied all knowledge of the man being there, and I therefore arrested the chief headman and told the King I would take him away as prisoner if the ex-King was not produced. After consulting his elders he said he would send mounted men to go to capture him. I told him I would give him till 6 o'clock that evening to produce the man and rather before that time he was produced and I had him arrested in the presence of some 800

* The French officer in command of the occupation of Wawa.

of the Boussa people. I told the King he had been sensible in giving him up as otherwise he would only have caused trouble to himself and his people for the sake of one man.'[24]

Kemble reported to Lugard that the capture of the ex-King of Wawa 'has, I think, put a stop to the only trouble taking place in this province'.[25] Kantama was brought to trial on May 5th and charged with conspiracy, but the case was dismissed for want of evidence. He was tried again on May 10th, when witnesses had arrived, on three charges of raiding a town, abduction and killing a horse with poisoned arrows. All three charges were dismissed. However, before Bussa had delivered him up, Lieutenant Edward-White, who had himself unsuccessfully tried to capture Kantama, had reported to Kemble that he thought 'it likely that other disturbances will take place unless Kantama is removed from the district'.[26] So, on the grounds that he was a person likely to provoke a breach of the peace, Kisan Dogo and Mora Tasude were called upon to stand security for his behaviour, failing which he would be deported. They signed the bond with Kantama, which is an interesting reflection on the apparently close ties that existed between Kaiama, Bussa and the ex-King of Wawa. Earlier, Kemble had reported that Mora Tasude was on good terms with Kisan Dogo; this is significant in view of the strained relations that developed between Mora Tasude and Kisan Dogo's successor Kitoro Gani.[27]

Trouble however continued in Wawa, and it soon became clear to Kemble that Garuba was the probable cause. Garuba 'is an able man', he wrote, 'with a good firm hold over his people, who obey him without question. At the same time several charges have been brought against him and I fancy there must be some fire with all this smoke.'[28] Nevertheless, though Kantama had recognized Bussa's suzerainty when he was king, Kemble recommended that Garuba's *de facto* independence from Bussa be recognized. He did however note that both Mora Tasude and Kisan Dogo considered him a bad man, but dismissed this on the grounds of the jealousy of which they were accused by the Modibo of Bajibo, 'one of the most trustworthy blackmen I know'. In the King of Bussa's case it was clear that he resented Garuba's independence and would have preferred to have had on the throne Kantama, whom he described as 'his brother', and who would recognize his suzerainty. Anyway Garuba was the son of Kibari who had supported Kwara against him. In the King of Kaiama's case, apparently some of his people had emigrated to Wawa.

By June, Kemble was beginning to have further doubts about the capable Garuba, since new charges of slavery had been brought against him. He started collecting witnesses. By July, after visiting Bussa, he had changed his mind about the independence of Garuba, and recommended that he should be made tributary to Bussa, or else that he be removed and a man chosen by the King of Bussa or the people of Wawa be put in his place.[29] Garuba was accordingly told that he must pay tribute to Bussa but had clearly refused for, in October, Kemble reported that he had again been told to pay tribute. There was, however, dispute as to which of the villages in the Wawa area should pay tribute direct to Bussa and which through Wawa.

Meanwhile, Kemble was asking Lugard to sanction the deposition of Garuba if he continued to refuse to pay tribute, since chiefs could be installed or deposed only with the High Commissioner's approval. The approval apparently did not come through till April 1903, not surprisingly since Lugard was preoccupied with more pressing matters in his conquest of the Sokoto caliphate. In his report for April 1903 Kemble wrote, with obvious exasperation at Garuba's obstinacy: 'Having now received H.E.'s permission to remove Garuba from Wawa should he again misbehave, I have at length determined to do so as he has on two or three occasions done so since the permission was given.'[30] To give himself a clear case for deposition Kemble wrote to Kisan Dogo and Garuba on May 1st to tell them to meet him at Leaba on May 8th to settle the question of tribute. Kisan Dogo turned up, but Garuba travelled only part of the way and then sent a message to say that he was sick. Kemble thereupon sent an escort after him; but Garuba bolted to bush, saying that he refused to pay tribute to Bussa and would fight if the whiteman compelled him to. Kemble then installed Kantama as King of Wawa—an act which he reported 'has been a subject of great rejoicing to all the Wawa people'.[31] Kantama, restored to the throne, agreed to pay tribute to Bussa, and reigned in Wawa until 1945, when at the reported age of 89 he died.

While Wawa was thus restored to Bussa by the British, Kisan Dogo was to lose territory which he claimed to his enemy across the river, the King of Yauri. Indeed, the 1903 Wawa incident was the only occasion recorded in the years before the rebellion in which the British restored to a king of Bussa land which he claimed was rightfully his. The history of early administration in Bussa, as we shall see, was one of continuous whittling away of Bussa's domains. Indeed, the dispute between Yauri and Bussa was to be one of the main factors responsible for the 1915 rebellion. The dispute centred first upon the right of the King of Yauri to collect taxes from those of his people who crossed the river to farm on Bussa lands. Bussa claimed suzerainty over the right bank of the Niger as far as Illo, which it claimed as tributary. Under the military administration, however, permission was given to Yelwa farmers to farm on the right bank. In July 1902, Kemble reported that the King of Bussa was 'very sore' over the fact that Yelwa (Yauri) had been collecting a tax of 1/– a head from villages in his District and also working farms on his land.[32] Unfortunately, Yelwa came under Kontagora Province, so Kemble could do nothing directly about it until he met the Resident of Kontagora. As Kemble complained, it would be difficult for him to get the people to do work on construction of roads in lieu of tax and then have another authority come in and tax them as well. 'All these things combined have, I think, made the King of Bussa surly and unwilling to work for us. From being the second, if not equal with the first King in Borgu (i.e. Nikki) and owner of the second largest amount of territory, he has gradually been coming down and having his towns and villages taken from him till, he says, he will have nothing left.'[33]

This interview with Kisan Dogo was one of the factors in Kemble's decision to make Wawa once more tributary to Bussa. Kemble also protested against the Mounted Infantry from Yelwa collecting taxes from Bussa towns and affirmed Bussa's suzerainty over Illo when he reported that his Assistant Resident, Mr. Langrishe at Illo, found the King there unable to collect his tribute. If it was decided to replace the King of Illo, Kemble reported, Kisan Dogo would certainly want to have a voice in naming his successor.[34] Again, in November, Kemble found a representative of Zuguma, in Kontagora Province, trying to get the chief of Potashi, which Bussa claimed as a tributary, to collect taxes for Kontagora. He therefore gathered together the elders of Potashi who confirmed they were tributary to Bussa, and he told them they would continue to be so. It was at this stage that he recommended that the Niger be the boundary between Borgu Province and Kontagora Province, of which Yauri and Kontagora were constituent emirates.[35]

In March 1903 Kemble was to record yet another incursion into Bussa's territory. The people of Kalikami complained to him that during the military administration the King of Yauri had installed his own headman and their former headman had been forced to flee. Further the King of Yauri had taken prisoner the Magaji (or administrator of the town). Earlier, however, the Military Resident had given Yelwa people permission to farm there. Kemble, protecting Bussa's rights, ordered the Yauri headman out and told the Yelwa farmers they would have to give 10 per cent of their produce to Bussa if they wished to stay.[36]

While Kemble thus stopped these incursions into Bussa territory, he sanctioned the allocation of a number of islands in the Niger to Yelwa. Among these was Rofia Island, whose ownership was to be claimed by Bussa till this day.

Harry Kemble went on leave in May 1903. He was a much more energetic Resident of Borgu than the majority of his successors. By April 1903 he claimed he had visited, with one or two exceptions, every town and village in Borgu, and talked with all the head chiefs. On the strength of this he made the following recommendations. The whole of north Borgu should be placed under Bussa with the exception of the Fulani towns of Kaoje and Lafagu, which should be independent and pay their tax direct to the Government. Southern Borgu should be placed under the King of Kaiama, though he cautioned that it would be unwise to place Woro Yaru, King of Yashikera, under him. The best solution would be to pension him off and remove him altogether from the province.[37] Woro Yaru was a member of the Nikki royal house and a potential claimant to its throne. Yashikera, as we have seen, had never been under Kaiama, and from the beginning Woro Yaru had made it clear he would not accept Kaiama's suzerainty.

In May, P. W. Anderson, a former Army captain, took over charge of Borgu Province from Kemble. He reported in July after a visit to Leaba and Bussa: 'Everybody seemed perfectly happy and peaceful and practically no complaints were brought to me. So far as my experience goes, the Borgu people are very friendly, obliging and hospitable.'[38] The first cases to be tried in the Bussa Native Court were held in July. Lugard minuted on this piece of information 'glad to perceive a start has at last been made'.[39] The only problems he reported concerned Garuba, ex-King of Wawa, and Woro Yaru, King of Yashikera. Garuba was finally caught and tried; though sentenced to imprisonment, he could not under the existing laws be sentenced to deportation after his release from jail. 'If Garuba returns to Borgu', wrote Anderson 'he will, I believe, be a constant source of trouble.'[40] On a visit to Wawa in September, he found that Garuba's supporters there had been spreading rumours that when Garuba was released he would become king again. Anderson therefore spoke to the people explaining that Garuba had been deposed and that if he returned to Borgu he would so do as a small man and never as 'Seriki-n-Wawa'.[41]

Anderson proposed that the best solution for Garuba would be to settle him and his 50–60 'recalcitrant' followers in a village of their own near Fort Goldie. While a European was there they would be under close supervision: if the European were withdrawn it was close enough to the Provincial Headquarters at Kaiama. As far as Woro Yaru was concerned, he had told Anderson all he wanted to do was to live in Nikki. But Anderson doubted that the French would accept him. He proposed that he be pensioned off and sent to Lokoja. In September he reported that the people of Yashikera were prepared to pay Woro Yaru a pension of £18 per annum but that no action could be taken until the question of his successor was settled.

In October Anderson went on leave. During his short tenure as Resident he had apparently had no trouble with Bussa. Indeed he reported on Kisan Dogo: 'I believe that at one time Boussa had the reputation of being a rather troublesome, or at any rate a cantankerous person, but my predecessor told me that he had quite changed now, and all that I saw of him confirmed Mr. Kemble's favourable report.'[42] Anderson handed over to Lieutenant Stevens, having pleaded that a second person be sent to assist this young and inexperienced officer. As it turned out, Stevens in his short term as Resident was to preside over two major events in the history of Borgu: the installation of Kitoro Gani as King of Bussa and the subjugation of Yashikera to Kaiama.

4. The Accession of Kitoro Gani

In November 1903 Lieutenant Stevens, Acting Resident of Borgu, learned that 'the Head-Chief or King of Borgu, Seriki-n-Bussa, Zibiri by name' had died. He also learned that there was likely to be a state of great disorder in Bussa and that some people had already taken to the bush. So he drew up what he called a sort of manifesto calling upon the people of Bussa to be calm and sent letters to the Headmen of the town ordering them to come to Kaiama with their own claimants to the throne. He also said the claimants could come with their followings for this would help to 'feel the pulse of the Mass'. Some 500 men and all the leading chiefs of Bussa together with the three claimants to the throne duly arrived in Kaiama from Bussa to settle the matter. Lugard minuted angrily on the report by Stevens: 'Quite wrong. You should have gone there not called Bussa to Kaiama who is not his suzerain.'[43]

Lieutenant Stevens assembled all the people, the 'Headmen', some of whom were traditional kingmakers of Bussa, and the three claimants. He then convened an *ad hoc* commission of enquiry as to who ought to be king. For the old system of contest was substituted a quasi-legal proceeding in which Lieutenant Stevens recorded in detail the views of each of the headmen as to who should succeed the late Kisan Dogo, who is confusingly described as Zibiri in his report. The result for the modern scholar is one of the few coherent accounts of how African kingmakers, who usually meet in a pontifical conclave, actually came to their decision. Apart from its importance in showing how firm was the claim of Kitoro Gani to the throne, it is an invaluable document on the sort of questions that concern African kingmakers.

There were three claimants to the throne: Gani who was the eldest surviving son of Dan Toro (1862-95), the immediate predecessor of Kisan Dogo (Dan Toro is confusingly described in the evidence as Dogwa); Gera, a very influential person in Bussa, but who did not come of royal stock; and finally Baba, son of Gajere, King of Bussa from 1844-62, described here as Mazza. The eight headmen who came to Bussa were:

Seriki-n-Koenji, described as a senior chief of Bussa (? the Chief of Kunji);

The Liman, (or Imam of Bussa) Abdulai;

The Alkali, or Chief Judge of Bussa, Issa;

The Karabade (Bakarabonde or representative of the owners of the land before the arrival of Kisra, described here as the land-lord of Bussa);

The Ubandawaiki of Bussa, or Prime Minister, Batafo (Batafu);

The Baromiribiri of Bussa, described here as the Marriage Contractor of Bussa. In reality the Bamarubere, or putative descendant of the Chief of the Mallams who came with Kisra;

The Maidoro, or Tax-Collector of Bussa (? the Madoko, or the Chief of the Kofas, or slave administrators of Bussa);

The Dowdu-Bindiga, Mohammedu, or Chamberlain to the King of Bussa. (Not clear who he was.)

Of these, the Bakarabonde, the Batafu, Bamarubere, and the Madoko were traditional kingmakers.

The three claimants were sworn by the Liman to speak the truth, abide by the decision the Resident gave and give loyalty to the successful candidate.

In turn Stevens called on the eight headmen to make their choice. It soon transpired that this had already been done. The second headman called by the Court, the Liman Abdulai, told the Enquiry that after the death of Kisan Dogo, Batafu, the Ubandawaiki of Bussa, called together the people by virtue of his position as regent during the interregnum. In the presence of young and old the general concurrence was that Gani was the rightful successor. In the Enquiry it became clear that Gani's claim to the throne was primarily a genealogical one. It was put most clearly by the Alkali: 'Gani is the right man for the throne. His father was Dogwa (Dan Toro), Chief of Bussa before Zibiri (Kisan Dogo): the late Chief of Bussa has only one brother who ought to succeed him but he is blind, the succession therefore goes back to the dynasty of Dogwa according to Borgu customs; and supposing Gani is elected to be chief the succession will go to his brother Geriayidadi and so on the succession goes to eldest brother, and if no brothers are alive to eldest son or to another branch of the family; the succession does not run from father to son but from brother to brother.' Any lack of clarity in the last sentence of the Alkali regarding whose eldest son the chieftaincy went to if there were no brothers of the last king was cleared up by the Bakarabonde of Bussa, chief representative of the owners of the land. He declared 'Gani is the right and proper successor to the throne of Bussa, because the late chief of Bussa has left only one successor, a blind brother who is unsuitable, and the succession goes back to the reign before to Dogwa's family and Gani is the proper successor in that case.' Four out of the eight headmen cited this genealogical rule in support of Gani. Likewise the claim of Baba who said he was a son of Dan Toro's predecessor was dismissed because it 'is not Borgu custom to skip a family like this, beside which the Alkali himself (recalled by Court) assured the Court that Mazza (Gajere) and Dogwa (Dan Toro) were not father and son, or even brothers, though related through their grandfathers and it would be quite against Borgu custom for anyone but a brother or eldest son to succeed'.

Apart from the genealogical principle, some of the headmen cited Gani's popularity as a reason for accepting his claim. The Chief Tax-Collector told the court that as the official tax-collector he would 'guarantee that the taxes are paid willingly to Gani if he is made chief—but if either of the other claimants *Baba* or *Gera* were made chief he is equally sure the taxes would not be paid'. This was surely a point which must have weighed with Lugard when he read the report, since taxation was at the centre of his administrative ideas. Dowdu Bindiga, described as the keeper of the king's household, concluded the arguments for supporting Gani's claims with the fact that he had plenty of followers and had plenty of money to maintain them. Had he not been sufficiently wealthy, the people of Bussa might possibly not have been so unanimous in their choice.

After the evidence in support of Gani's candidature had been taken, Stevens called for a show of hands, and a large majority favoured Gani. Stevens briefly examined the claims of Gera and Baba, dismissing the former on the grounds that he was not of the royal house, and the latter that he came from the wrong branch of it.

Stevens, in his capacity as Resident, then proclaimed Kitoro Gani King of Bussa. In so doing he exceeded his authority, for though Residents officially installed Chiefs, they had to refer the selected candidate to Lugard for approval beforehand. As Lugard minuted angrily on Stevens's report: 'You have no authority to appoint a chief least of all a 1st Class Chief without reference to H.C. It is these kinds of acts such as your unauthorized actions at Idah with their disastrous consequences —which together with your lack of judicial knowledge and commonsense, make it impossible for me to promote you.'

Stevens, however, followed the full ritual of the British administration for the installation of chiefs, administering the official oath of office to Gani:

'I Gani Seriki-n-Bussa (in succession to the late Seriki-n-Zibiri Bussa) do faithfully promise and swear to be loyal to the Great White King of England, My Father, and to obey all the commands of the High Commissioner of Northern Nigeria his representative and do all that the Resident or Assistant Resident of Borgu Province orders me to do in the High Commissioner's name.

'I swear I will rule my people according to the laws laid down by the High Commissioner of Northern Nigeria and will set my face against slavery and other such bad things and will do my best to be a wise and kind ruler to the people of Bussa. So help me God.'

To this oath, Gani put his mark on 19th December 1903, and after receiving homage from Gera and Baba set off for Bussa where, for the next twelve years, he was to honour his declaration from the British point of view more often in the breach than in the observance.

Gani was already King in the eyes of his people before the Court of Enquiry at Kaiama. He had been through the British administration's rites of installation without the authority of the High Commissioner on December 19th, but the date of his accession from the British point of view was 1904, after Lugard had given it his sanction.[44]

Stevens is unfortunately uninformative about the reaction of Mora Tasude and the people of Kaiama to the spectacle of the next king of Bussa being selected and installed in their midst. There is however a tradition that the bad blood that existed between Kitoro Gani and Mora Tasude was due to the fact that the latter had supported a rival candidate to the throne and had actually pressed his case with Stevens. There is no mention of this in Stevens's otherwise very detailed report. Such an action would indeed help to explain the hatred of Kitoro Gani for Mora Tasude, especially since both his predecessors, Kisan Dogo and Dan Toro, got on very well with him.[45]

Young Lieutenant Stevens seems to have had a chequered career in the Northern Nigerian Service. I have been unable to track down what his disastrous actions at Idah were. But in his short time as Acting Resident at Bussa he managed to lose £112 of government cash, nearly half his annual salary. Because the official safe was rusted, he kept government cash in a large uniform case padlocked to his bedstead. On 27th December 1903 he had dismissed two small boys who were his servants, Awudu and Sule, for continually breaking glass and crockery. Three days later he discovered the loss of money. Apparently his suspicions about the boys were aroused by their lavish spending in the town. He considered it must have been Awudu, aged only 12, who had stolen his keys whilst he was dressing. This loss was referred by Lugard to the Secretary of State for the Colonies, recommending that two-thirds of it be written off and one-third be paid by Lt. Stevens for 'carelessness in leaving his keys in a place in which any of his boys could make use of them'. Awudu and Sule were imprisoned.[46] Lt. Stevens, however, continued on his careless career—losing the key of the safe at Bassa in 1904, for which he had to bear the cost of transporting the safe to Lokoja. Again in 1905 he lost £86 14s 5d at Bassa, for which he had to pay by cheque. Soon after he paid £5 to a political agent without authority.

The cheque for £86 14s 5d bounced. By 1905 Stevens had left the Northern Nigerian service.[47]

Stevens may not have been an efficient officer, and he may have installed Kitoro Gani without authority, but as Harry Kemble was to report on his return to Borgu in January, he did put the right man on the throne;[48] if not, as it turned out, from the point of view of the administration at least from that of the people. This was in fact to become a rare act on the part of the administration in the next twenty years.

The other major act by Lt. Stevens, his attempt at a settlement of the problem of Yashikera, was to remain a sore on the Borgu body politic for the next fifty years. Woru Yaru had been recognized as king of Yashikera by the British in 1900. As we have seen, he refused to serve as a district head under Kaiama, who was made a first-class chief and paramount over southern Borgu. As a member of the royal house of Nikki, he had no intention of abasing himself before Kaiama, whom he considered an upstart. But the British were determined that for administrative purposes southern Borgu should have a paramount. Major Blakeney, Resident of Kontagora in 1911, by which time Borgu had become a division of that province, wrote that had 'Woru Yaru been an able King he would have been made Paramount Chief of South Borgu but he was a useless, helpless individual, and was therefore passed over. . .'[49] To Lt. Stevens fell the task of deposing Woru Yaru and appointing a successor. Rather than go to Yashikera, he sent for Woru Yaru to come to Kaiama. But this was achieved only after a series of exchanges of messages and letters, because of Woru Yaru's hatred of Kaiama. Lugard was to criticize Stevens for forcing Woru Yaru to come to Kaiama: 'It seems quite unnecessary and undesirable,' he minuted. 'He should not in the circumstances have been called into Kaiama by you. He is deposed, he should not have been subjected to this indignity.'[50] Indeed when Woru Yaru was finally persuaded to come into Kaiama, it very nearly caused trouble as Lt. Stevens reported:

> 'Woru-Yaru finally came in and brought with him a large following (for these parts) of some 600 to 700 men who refused to enter the town but camped just outside the Barracks. I gave the Seriki quarters in Barracks and insisted that all weapons carried by his men should be stocked inside the Fort, this was complied with without demur. I next ordered that all his superfluous following should return at day-break next day to Yashikera and that they would have their arms returned

only on this condition that they actually did return, and to ensure this the D.S.P. let me have some of his Police to see them to Yashikera. I did all this as the Seriki of Kaiama was rather alarmed, and because I personally feared a fracas at night in the town, and to obviate the chances of this happening the D.S.P. had a patrol of 16 policemen on duty in the town all night. I had furthermore taken the precaution beforehand in view of such a contingency arising of requesting the O.C. Fort Goldie to augment my escort of 10 men by 12 more, and, also at this juncture some specie arrived from Illo under an escort of 6 men and an N.C.O. so that I had quite a considerable little force to back me up, and I am sure that the orderly termination of the case and the instant obedience to any commands given was due to the presence of these extra troops who to the people seemed to come in just when wanted from North and South Borgu.

'My position was not rendered any the easier either at this point by the news of the sudden death of Seriki-n-Bussa being brought in, and the fact that the town was in a state of disorder owing to the absence of control, and also to the fact that there were three claimants to the vacant throne—I deal elsewhere of this topic in this report however.

'I held a palaver with Woru-Yaru, informed him that he was deposed and in his presence installed the new Seriki a man named Yaru who is I feel sure the right man and sent him to Seriki-n-Kaiama to do homage.

'Woru-Yaru Ex-Seriki and Yaru (Sabon Seriki) the new King, signed in the presence of their respective followers documents and made oaths verbally—the substance of which are embodied in documents relating to this affair which I attach to this report—i.e. "The Yashikera Succession Case" for your Excellency's information.

'*Woru-Yaru* has gone back to Yashikera and with 4 soldiers and my Interpreter John Mill (to act as Political Agent there temporarily) to gather his goods and chattels together preparatory to leaving the Town.'[51]

Woru-Yaru duly left Yashikera for Nikki, taking half the population of Yashikera with him.[52] All that remained in 1907 were 111 males and 119 females of whom 52 were children.

The new King of Yashikera had signed a document prepared by Stevens, which was prerequisite to his accession:

'I further agree to do homage to the Seriki-n-Kaiama the overlord of

South Borgu and pay annual tribute to him as such as laid down by the Resident of Borgu.'[53] Nigerian Borgu was thus divided into two paramountcies or emirates as they came later to be styled: Northern Borgu, where the King of Bussa was Paramount, and Southern Borgu where the King of Kaiama was Paramount. While the King of Bussa could lay a fair claim to suzerainty over the lands placed under him, the King of Kaiama could not. Although only Woru Yaru of Yashikera had protested openly, Okuta and Ilesha equally resented doing homage to Kaiama. Indeed, if they could not be under their overlord Nikki, they would have found it more natural to be under Bussa, as the senior Kisra ruler. To them Kaiama was an upstart. For Bussa, too, the elevation of Kaiama not only to a paramountcy over Southern Borgu, but to equal status as a first-class chief, was in defiance of the traditions of Kisra. Indeed, in the context of Northern Nigeria, the King of Kaiama was put on an equal footing status-wise with the Emir of Sokoto* and the Shehu of Bornu. While this could have been justified for Bussa because of his traditional position, it was quite anomalous for Kaiama. But Mora Tasude, with his sense of administrative efficiency, his claim to personal friendship with Lugard, and his status as first-class chief came almost to eclipse Kitoro Gani in Borgu over the next ten years, much to the latter's chagrin.

* He was not recognized by the British as Sultan until 1915.

III · THE END OF BORGU PROVINCE

1. 1904–1906, Quiet Years

The first three years of Kitoro Gani's reign were quiet. Indeed they showed how light the touch of colonial rule was in the early days of Northern Nigeria. The administration intervened but sporadically. In Borgu there were rarely more than two administrators on the ground at a time, and then one of them was very often ill. The records are full of reports of current illness: Captain Anderson, the Resident, wrote at Kaiama on 21st July 1904: 'Spent most of the day in office work—but have felt so ill that almost every time I write is a painful effort.'[1] Three days later he recorded that Mr. Kemble, now stationed as assistant resident in Illo, had blackwater fever. Earlier, on July 14th when Anderson had tried his interpreter, a Sierra Leonean called John Mill, Mr. Eaglesome, the Deputy Superintendent of Police, had been so weak that he had had to prosecute from a chair. By November Anderson himself was so debilitated by fever and insomnia that he was invalided to the Canary Islands.

Anderson pleaded ill health to excuse an otherwise inexcusable loss of self-control which could have brought about a diplomatic incident.[2] In September 1903, Anderson wrote from Jebba to Lt. Phillips, the officer in charge of the garrison at Fort Goldie, ordering him to detain Captain Fourneau, the French officer commanding the flotilla bringing goods up the Niger to Bajibo for overland transportation to Northern Dahomey. Anderson had felt Fourneau had not given him the correct respect due to his position as Resident. When Anderson dined with Fourneau as his guest there had been some heated words about customs dues. And although Fourneau lunched with Anderson the day he left, he did not pay him a courtesy farewell visit. In what must have been a fit of temper, Anderson ordered his arrest. By a second letter, he hurriedly countermanded the order which Phillips had had the good sense not to carry out.

There the matter might have rested but for a private letter written on 31st January 1904 by Harry Kemble on his return from leave to a friend in Zungeru called Hopkins. 'Anderson', he reported, 'does not seem to have done much outside the office except put people's backs up.' He then retailed details of the Fourneau contretemps. This was then passed on to Lugard's Secretariat and Phillips, Fourneau, Stevens and Kemble were asked whether it was true. Phillips admitted that Anderson did write him a private letter asking him to detain Fourneau but immediately after wrote another private letter countermanding it. Fourneau himself graciously replied that he had dismissed the incident because Anderson's help and 'kindliness to me has made me forget a moment's bad temper excusable in these climates'. Kemble was understandably annoyed by the fact that information from a private letter was used against his superior. Stevens's first reaction was one of irritation that gossip should be the basis of an enquiry against Anderson, who was nevertheless asked to explain himself to the High Commissioner. In a letter dated 6th June 1904 from Kaiama, Anderson admitted that he had had some communication with Phillips giving him 'some instruction regarding the French Flotilla which I found occasion to cancel immediately afterwards, but that it was for the arrest of Captain Fourneau, I feel I may safely deny'. Lugard underlined this passage and minuted on 13.7.1904 that 'it is incredible that a man if in possession of his full abilities at the time of the occurrence should not vividly recollect so very serious a matter as the decision to forcibly detain the officer Commanding the [*illegible*] of a Foreign Power. . . .' Lugard concluded that Anderson must have been drunk at the time. This Anderson denied in a letter of 7th August 1904, saying that he was ill at the time and his memory was greatly impaired by heavy doses of phenacetin and quinine. 'I have found also that when one's head is buzzing with quinine and one is feeling wretched, even important matters sometimes make a less sharp impression than they ought to do and than they would do at other times.' On this denial of insobriety, and the justification of illness causing loss of memory, Lugard let the matter drop.

Recurrent illness and shortage of staff were not the only factors that prevented close supervision of the province. The amount of paper work required of the Residents interfered with frequent touring. When Kemble moved to the new Headquarters of Borgu Province in Bussa on 23rd March 1905, his Political Diary reads almost constantly: 'worked in office all day' and this included Sundays. Right up until August 10th the record continues uninterrupted: 'worked in office all day'. On Sunday April 23rd Kemble noted: 'Took a whole day off for the first time,' by which a later political officer pencilled: 'A sad bitter day.' Even though Headquarters were now in Bussa, the Political Diary, where at least one would expect comments on Kitoro Gani, reveals only 'The Seriki came to salute'. In such circumstances it is hardly surprising that the chiefs of Borgu learnt little of what was required of them by the British and carried on very much as before.

Life in Borgu from 1904 to 1906 was so uneventful that the only really interesting reading provided by the Resident's Political Diary are such items as the discovery of an old woman found tied up and bleeding from her head on the road in Kaiama. Apparently she was suspected of being a witch. Anderson wrote: 'I have had her made as comfortable as possible and have given her a glass of champagne. She clearly required a stimulant and I happen to have nothing else just now.'[3] In February 1904 the death occurred of the Chief of Illo, who was recorded as being a half-brother of the late King of Bussa. He was succeeded by one of his half-brothers who accepted that he was a tributary of Bussa.[4]

The major event of the period was Lugard's visit to Kaiama from 2nd to 4th July 1904. Anderson was fit at the time, but Kemble was down with blackwater fever. The High Commissioner's visit was, however, not altogether a success for Anderson apparently greeted him outside the gates of Kaiama dressed in a brown shirt with its sleeves rolled up. Lugard took offence at this and, after the visit, Anderson was sent a letter of reprimand. He apologized for being improperly dressed, but had thought that brown shirts were in order for civilian Residents, since the late Resident of Zaria used to wear one on official occasions. As to the state of his shirt sleeves:

'I know that they were turned *up* when I passed out of the Kaiama Gate, but my belief was that they were turned *down* long before Y.E. and I met—and I know that on the previous evening I had made a point of seeing that there were buttons on the cuffs for that very purpose.'[5]

Lugard reported that Kaiama was 'a mere village of about 300 persons, and presents a poverty-stricken appearance, typical of Borgu'.[6] During his visit, he decided to move the Provincial Headquarters to Bussa, and selected a new site in Kaiama, outside the town, where the Assistant Resident who was to be stationed there should live. (Up till then the Residency had been inside the town in the old French Fort, built there

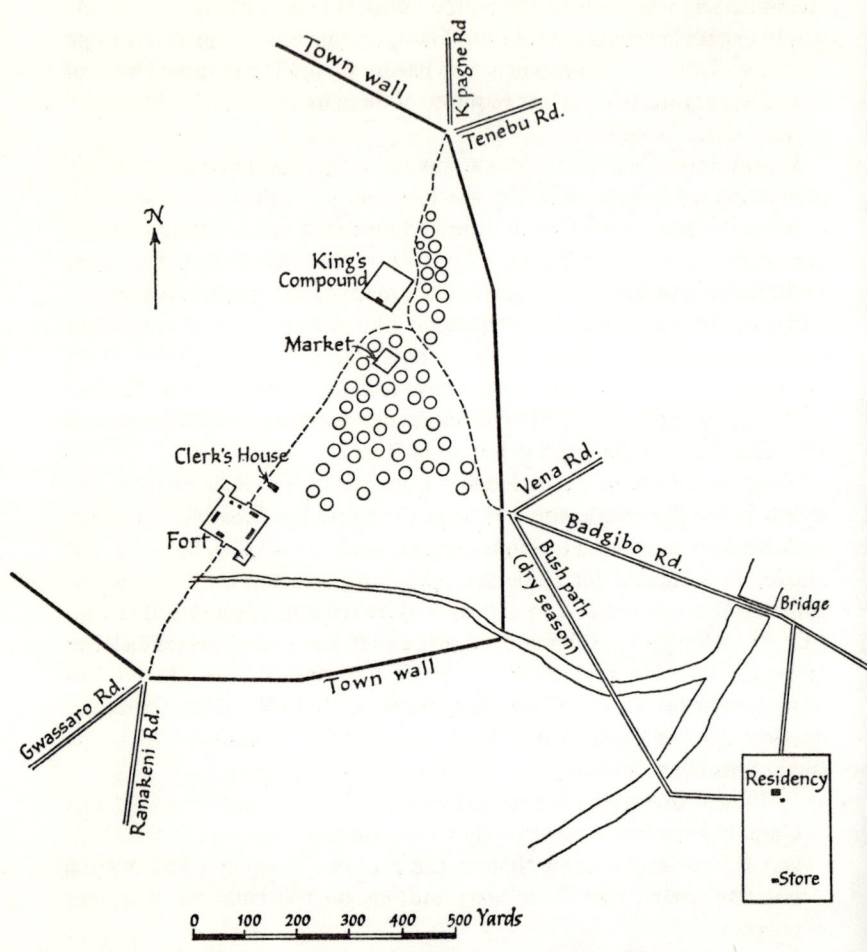

Map 3: Sketch Map of Kaiama, 1906. (From map by Feargus Dwyer)

in 1897.) Lugard chose Bussa because it was more central for administrative purposes, and was on the Niger; its king 'is, moreover, the most important chief in the province'.[7] He was, however, unable to visit Bussa personally and left the Resident to choose a suitable site.

In August Anderson went to Bussa to discuss the plan for the new headquarters with Kitoro Gani, whom he found a fine specimen physically, 'but he is timid and nervous—and apparently in great fear of his life'.[8] The Emir,* as he was now being called, had refused to allow a powerful woman, Babanawara, his aunt, who he thought wished to poison him, to come to Bussa. The Resident had been petitioned to let her come back to her home town, 'but saw no reason, for a case of this sort, for upsetting the new Paramount Chief of North Borgu'.[9] He reported that Kitoro Gani appeared greatly pleased with his decision. Anderson then chose the site for the new headquarters and told Kitoro Gani to clear it. He also told him that he must in future hold his court cases in public.

Fergus Dwyer, Assistant Resident posted to Bussa, did not have the same sensitivity about Kitoro Gani's position. In September, he charged him with being an accessory to an assault on one Woru Kebie. Mai Arki, a rival of Kitoro Gani, and a possible candidate for the throne, sent for the same Babanawara to come to Bussa. She refused unless a white man were there, but sent Mai Arki gifts of kola-nut. Kitoro Gani learnt of this and sent his messenger Makadie to seize the gifts being brought by Woru Kebie, on the grounds that they contained bad medicine meant to kill him. As Kitoro Gani told the Court: 'The woman Babanawara does not like me. I believe she would kill me. She wants to make Mai Arkie King. I sent my messengers to stop Mai Arkie's man. I do not know what medicines they were. No one told me they were bringing medicines. I dreamt it. I am afraid of Babanawara.'[10] Even though Makadie, his messenger, told the Court that he had found medicines with the kola, and two witnesses said they saw the medicines, but did not know what they were for, Kitoro Gani was found guilty as an accessory to the assault, having put in a plea to this effect. Dwyer accordingly ordered him to pay a fine which he paid into court. William Wallace, the Acting High Commissioner, noted sourly:

'I consider this rather tactless proceeding, considering how trivial the case was and that the King believed that the poison was to be

---

* The title Emir was adopted from that used in the Sokoto caliphate for governors of its constituent provinces or emirates. In Northern Nigeria,

administered to him. This sort of thing must tend to lessen his authority over his people which we wish to uphold.'[11]

In November, Kemble, acting as Resident for Anderson, reported that he had to go down to Ilesha and Okuta to quieten the people and 'make them understand that Your Excellency has made Kaiama the Paramount Chief of S. Borgu. . . . I shall be touring for some weeks, no whiteman having done these since the S. Kaiama was installed [1903] with the exception of Mr. Eaglesome's brief visit a month or so ago which I am afraid did no good'.[12] In the same month he received a message from Kitoro Gani that people from N'Gaski, in Kontagora Province, were settling in his villages and refused to go back. Kemble informed him that they could not cross into Borgu without the High Commissioner's permission.

In the New Year Kemble, as Acting Resident, went to Bussa to present Kitoro Gani with his staff of office as a first-class chief. He spent two weeks in Bussa but the only record of discussion with Kitoro Gani concerns some villages in Dahomey which Bussa claimed. He returned to Bussa on 23rd March 1905 to sort out the new Provincial Headquarters there. But, office-bound as he was, there is nothing of interest he reports concerning Kitoro Gani. Actually, the criticisms levelled against Kemble by his predecessor about his preoccupation with office work are not altogether fair. Captain Anderson appears to have gone to pieces. Kemble found him at Bussa very ill, his sight and memory having completely failed him. £7 10s 0d in cash was missing. Papers, principally confidential ones, were also missing. Several of the books were not up to date and the Provincial Record Book had never been opened. 'I am sorry to say everything was in a regular muddle.'[13] Kemble, who had received praise from Lugard for having built 'perhaps the best (roads) we have seen (other than those of the Public Works Department)',[14] was clearly determined to sort out the office. The only problem outside the office that seemed to catch his attention was that of the continued immigration into Bussa territory of farmers from Kontagora Province.

It is perhaps difficult for us to imagine on what a slender budget and with what scarce resources in personnel the early administrators of Borgu were meant to run the huge, sparsely populated province, where roads were largely impassable during the rainy season. Apart from at most two

---

however, it was sometimes used to describe non-Muslim rulers like Kitoro Gani, even though strictly speaking it could not be borne by non-Muslims.

white administrators, the following were the approved African staff for the Political Department of Borgu Province.

*Approved Permanent Native Staff, Political Department, Borgu Province**

Office	Name	Date of 1st Appt.	Rate p.a.
Clerk	R. T. Johnson	—	£99
,,	M. A. Ankrah	—	£72
,,	Vacant	—	£60
Political Agent	Adamu Darazo	10.6.01	£36
Interpreter	J. Mills	11.9.03	£48
,,	Abu Bakare	1.7.02	£24
,,	Vacant	—	£24
Couriers	Adeshina	1.6.02	£18
,,	Suleman	1.11.03	£18
,,	Musa	17.10.04	£12
Arab Writer	Idrissu	17.6.03	£24
			£435

* Incidentally, this was a larger staff than the District Officer in Borgu had in 1958, immediately prior to Nigeria's independence.

This establishment was approved by Lugard on 29th March 1905, which shows the detailed concern the High Commissioner showed in the administration of his vast protectorate.[15]

In August 1905 Kemble was relieved by Dwyer as Acting Resident. On 9th January 1906 Captain Larymore took over the province, arriving there with his wife, one of the first English women to be allowed to accompany the official to whom she was married to Nigeria. She recorded her impressions of Borgu in *A Resident's Wife in Nigeria*, and, as we shall see, took a very jaundiced view of it.[16] Curiously enough the year 1906 is a fruitful one for published memoirs of European life in Borgu; Fremantle who took over from Larymore on December 10th also kept a journal, which was subsequently published.[17]

Larymore noted in his first report that Dwyer had written that the whole district of Kaiama was strongly opposed to Mora Tasude, who was always boasting of his personal friendship with the High Commissioner, 'to whom, he declares, he frequently reports privately as to the state of affairs of the district'. To ensure closer supervision of Mora Tasude, Dwyer had advocated a revolutionary course of action, which strangely enough Larymore had recently put forward, that South Borgu should be placed in Ilorin Province. As additional justification he argued that in Southern Borgu there were many Yorubas, the principal ethnic group of Ilorin Province, and the Borgawa appeared to get on exceptionally well with them.

Echoing his wife's shock at her first inspection of Bussa, Larymore wrote to Lugard:

'I wish Y.E. could have seen Bussa. To me it seems a pity that we should spend a penny on the place or on its Chief, the latter cannot conceive what the role of a man should be in the position in which he has now been placed. He drinks, he is very ignorant, and I fear that the more tribute we share with him, the worse will become his habits. His personal following, who should, in some degree, reflect his own dignity, consist of ragged, unkempt, dirty villagers. I am doing my best to make him realize his own importance in the place, but it is uphill work.

'But regarding the place itself. It is unfortunate that no caravan route passes through it; it is of course, away from the trade route, by road, from North and South, and by water, for most months in the year, the rapids above and below it, make navigation practically impossible, and at any time very risky. When in addition to the above objections, the lesser one of unhealthiness—judging by the experience of others as well as myself—is also present, one is much inclined to advocate another change of headquarters.'[18]

It is from this date that the European administrators begin to put in unsympathetic, later hostile, reports on Kitoro Gani which, accumulated, were to be used in support of his deposition in 1915. Larymore also authorized the return of Babanawara, 'the witch-girl' who had become a wealthy woman, despite the hostility of Kitoro Gani. 'She will be an acquisition indeed in this miserable little place, which, up to now, possesses no market, and whose inhabitants are wholly without interest in anything outside their hut doors.'[19] Babanawara was allowed to return on condition she performed a ceremony warding off calamity from Bussa.

Clearly Larymore's jaundiced view of Bussa was influenced by the presence of his wife, who complained:

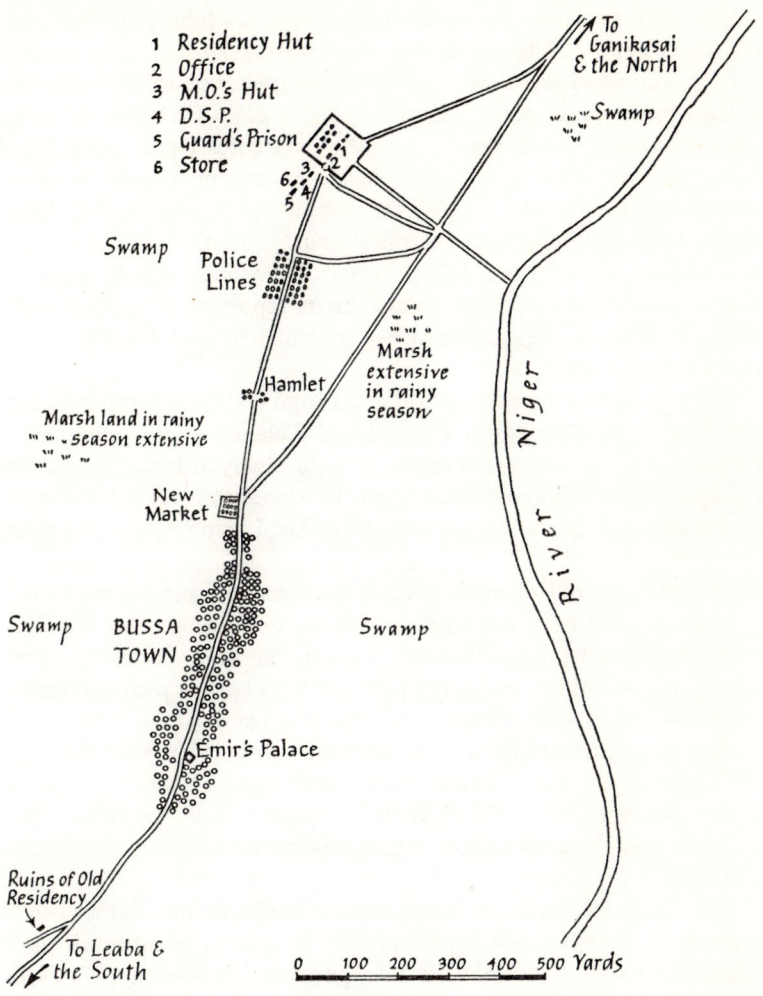

Map 4: Sketch Map of Bussa, 1906. (From map by Captain H. D. Larymore)

'Bussa seemed to me to be much hotter and more unpleasant than any other spot I know. This was partly due to our wretched houses, badly built, ill-thatched mud-dwellings, which afforded little protection from the heat, the inside temperature reaching 103° and 104° every afternoon. The nights were oppressively hot.'[20]

Mrs. Larymore also showed the common prejudice of administrators of her time in favour of the Fulani as a 'higher race'. On a visit to Kaoje, the Fulani enclave in Borgu, she said the Larymores' 'spirits, which had rather dropped at the apparently hopeless poverty and desolation of our new province, revived a little at the sight of brisk, intelligent Fulanis, replacing the apathetic, ignorant dull Borgus'.[21] No doubt she influenced her husband to recommend the transfer of Provincial Headquarters to Kaoje.[22] This was supported by the sanitary report made on March 31st by Dr. Williams on the European quarters, which he said 'most Europeans find extremely depressing'.[23]

The Larymores were at least different from their predecessors in that they toured their province. They visited Kaiama, where Kemble was now Assistant Resident. Larymore thought highly of him. 'Cannot say enough for his willing assistance, and his desire to meet my wishes in every respect.'[24] Mora Tasude impressed Mrs. Larymore, but confirmed Dwyer's earlier report:

'The Sariki of Kaiama is a highly intelligent old gentleman, though he bears a distinctly bad character among all his neighbours for high-handed bullying and dishonesty. . . . He has always been very loyal to the Government, and it is a pity that he is held in such detestation by his own people, though perhaps only natural that, with native cunning, he should have used his boasted friendship with the High Commissioner as an universal threat to all whom he wished to intimidate. He goes in terror of death by witchcraft or "medicine" (i.e. poison) and solemnly assured us that quite lately he had had a wonderful escape. . . .'[25]

Mrs. Larymore's general impressions of Borgu, written shortly before leaving the province, are worth quoting *in extenso*, being much more frank than those given in the official reports, and indicating the attitude that was to predominate among the British administration in Borgu over the next few years.

'The Borgus today, whatever their previous record may be, could not, by any stretch of imagination, be called a war-like race. They are absolute pagans, and appear to be still very low in the order of civilization; their progress has perhaps been hindered by their being somewhat apart from the large Emirates and busier centres of the Protectorate . . . they are the quietest and most law-abiding folks imaginable—indeed, I have heard it said of them that "they have not the intelligence to commit a crime". They do not trade, and appear to have an unlimited capacity for sitting silent and motionless, dirty and unclothed, before their huts, gazing vacantly into space. Their farming is as scanty as their need for foodstuffs will permit. . . . They are more deeply steeped in "ju-ju" and superstition of all kinds than any African natives I have come across. One firm article of faith is the "Tsafi" a "speaking of oracles" the message being received by a priest.'[26]

Larymore himself, a product of Westminster School and an army officer who had served in India, Jamaica and the Gold Coast, clearly found Bussa and its ruler difficult to treat seriously after serving in the Muslim North. As his wife recorded, in 1904 when Larymore met the Emir of Hadejia, an emirate of the Muslim North, it was much as feudal potentates would do.[27] He was equipped with all the arrogant prejudices of the early British Imperialist administration. When some Syrians travelled through Borgu, obtaining free accommodation on the grounds as he put it that they were whitemen, he wrote:

'I recognise that the country must be opened up, but it seems unfortunate that so early in the process of enlightenment the primitive Borgus should have to discriminate in a matter, to them so difficult, as the difference between Syrians and ordinary "whitemen"—a fact these Syrians were, apparently, very quick to take advantage of.'[28]

Kemble, his able assistant, and effective Resident of Borgu till his arrival, showed prejudices of a similar vein. In 1902 he had written:

'I do not believe in any religious education for, at any rate, some years to come. In fact I think the native a better man as he is.

'Neither do I believe in any secular education other than Technical and Industrial. What are wanted in this Protectorate are Mechanist [sic], Masons, Carpenters, Blacksmiths and Labourers not clerks and school masters. The blackman as soon as he learns to read and write thinks he is above field labour, and field labour is what is wanted or will be wanted here. A native always does best when he has something to copy from.'[29]

In December Major J. M. Fremantle arrived to take over the province from Larymore. He reported that he had found the office in excellent condition, and Captain Larymore had apparently evolved order out of chaos. To this a minute was added in headquarters by the Acting High Commissioner. 'Very pleased to learn this as it has been the worst in the Protectorate till now.'[30]

2. Borgu Amalgamated with Kontagora Province

Kitoro Gani and his entourage came out to welcome the arrival by canoe of the new Resident of Borgu, Major John Fremantle, on December 10th. Unfortunately Fremantle was paddled north of the point of reception, so he missed the King. Fremantle was to be the last Resident of Borgu Province, which during the next year was amalgamated with Kontagora Province, and part of it lopped off and given to Sokoto Province.

Fremantle recorded in his diary that the 'Province seems to be in a most peaceable condition; assessment done, very few conundrums and office in excellent order. There is very little doing, and the whole country is stagnant owing to the backward condition of the people—in fact it just *exists*. This I hope will suit my book as far as learning Hausa is concerned, and this I am keenest about.'[31]

Fremantle settled into the Residency, which he considered not up to much, but quite livable in and not worth doing much about since there was already talk of moving the station. He had two Assistant Residents, one at Illo, and one on leave. For once there was a doctor in the province. Jack Fremantle, old Etonian, and 'an example to all of us of what an English gentleman should be' as Lugard wrote after his death,[32] settled down to the easy task of running Borgu Province. He passed the time learning Hausa, which was indispensable to attain the cherished Fulani-Hausa Residencies of the far north, shooting (which he wrote was good) and playing tennis over a fishing-net with home-made bats. He had a private staff of 9—1 cook, 2 houseboys, a 'cookmate', 2 horse-boys, a gardener known as a 'tomato-boy', a government interpreter who had no work to do except on tour 'so helps in the house', and a Police Orderly 'who becomes almost an extra house-boy'. His total expenses for this bevy of servants each month was £9 15s od including their food.[33]

Disappointingly, though the author was stationed at Bussa, the Fremantle journal contains no picture of Kitoro Gani. In his official report he merely considered him to be satisfactory, though he did not despair of him. He found him not only willing but eager to visit his towns with his Resident, something which had never been tried before. But he considered Kitoro Gani's 'idea of being a "big King" seems confined to owning land and adding to his land, not in showing himself worthy of the name.'[34] However when Sarkin Ilesha, 'a wizened-up, gruesome old creature who ought to be in an alms-house', tried to insist on his royal position 'by having the cheek to carry a chair' before Fremantle, he wouldn't let him sit on it, though he 'allowed him a mat'.[35] Fremantle was however impressed by both the rulers of Kaiama and Illo, since both were men out of whom he could get work.

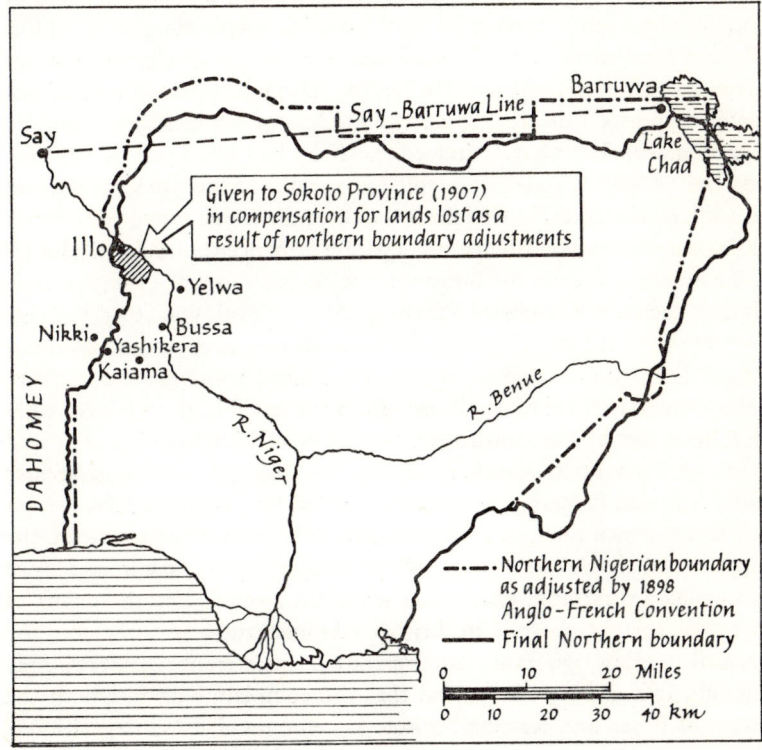

Map 5: The Say-Barruwa Line and Northern Nigeria's Boundaries, 1901 and 190

Fremantle only stayed in Bussa three months and the placid tones of his reports and diaries, showing emotion only where inefficient chiefs were concerned, was to mark the end of an era in Borgu. In 1907 its troubles began. First, the Fulani areas of Northern Borgu, which Kitoro Gani claimed were his territory, and Illo, which he claimed was his acknowledged tributary, were given to Sokoto Province. The reason for this was to compensate Sokoto for territory lost to the French in the adjustment of the Northern Nigeria–Niger boundary. Here it will be seen that the 1890 agreement that the Say–Barruwa line should be adjusted to take into account the actual frontiers of the Sokoto caliphate in practice worked to the disadvantage of Sokoto. (See Map 5.) The Colonial Annual Report for 1904 records that the Emir of Sokoto 'felt deeply the loss of territory ceded to France, which had been assured to him by the government when he accepted British protection. . . .'[36] Thus Illo and the Fulani towns of Kaoje and Gendenne were given as a sop to Sokoto at Bussa's expense. Dwyer, the Acting Resident, found Kitoro Gani 'very much dissatisfied still at the loss of his territory' when he visited him in late 1907.[37] Indeed the King had lost some of his most populous territory, and since people meant revenue this was serious for an already poor emirate. Indeed the revenue for the whole province of Borgu in the last year of its existence as a separate province was under £3,600![38]

The second disaster for Bussa was the decision to make Borgu a division of the new Kontagora Province. At one level, one could say this reduction in administrative status in the British hierarchy might have been a good thing from the chiefs' point of view. Indeed from 1908 to 1912 there was rarely more than one political officer stationed in the whole of what had been one of the constituent provinces of Northern Nigeria, and sometimes no political officer at all. But this did not mean greater independence. It merely meant that for extended periods the chiefs were left to their own devices, their principal obligation being to ensure the taxes were brought in. Then a political officer might come in and try to reorganize everything, only to be withdrawn again. For the chiefs of Borgu a certain rhythm in British administration was replaced by sporadic, often ignorant, administrative interference. Interestingly enough, it is during this period that the complaints against both the rulers of Bussa and Kaiama begin to become regular and deposition is threatened. From the point of view of development, Borgu was now completely out on a limb, with the provincial capital far away in Kontagora, and difficult of access. (See Map 6.)

For a transitional period Borgu and Kontagora had the status of a double province, there being effectively two Residents, though that of Borgu was subordinate to that of Kontagora. Sharpe, the Resident of

THE END OF BORGU PROVINCE

Kontagora, complained as late as April 1908 that Dwyer continued to treat Borgu as a separate province, even though it had formally ceased to have this status.[39]

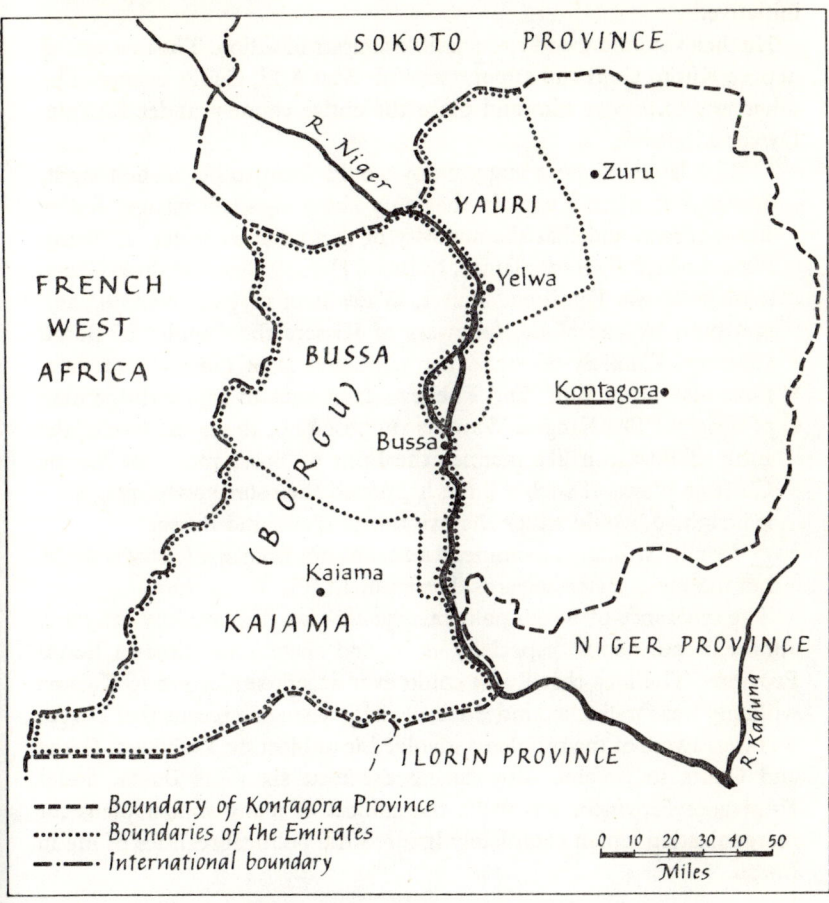

Map 6: Greater Konagora Province, 1914

Dwyer, on his visit to Kitoro Gani in November, had found him not only dejected about his loss of territory, but also 'giving way to his old habit of drink'. Dwyer then proposed the drastic measure that Kitoro Gani be deposed. This is the first time that dissatisfaction with Kitoro Gani's apparent lack of 'modern' administrative ability had led to a recommendation to remove him. This Dwyer expressed with a vengeance, and without the usual *caveat* 'unless he reforms himself'. He reported that he had always been of the opinion that the appointment of Gani as Emir of Bussa was a wrong selection—'he is weak-minded and has no initiative.'

He then recommended two possible courses of action. The first was to depose Kitoro Gani and appoint as emir Mai Arki, Gani's enemy. The other was to depose him and place the entire country under Kaiama. Dwyer admitted:

'The latter of these suggestions would seem to be, at first sight, erratic, but when I explain that only about 14 small villages follow Bussa direct, and that the majority of these consist of ten or twelve huts, the matter seems plainer. In Bussa District there are three Chiefs namely Wawa, Kunji and Puissa. Wawa is of very old standing and was built by one of the followers of Kissera the founder of Borgu Country, Kunji is of the Zaber tribe and is of quite recent date, Puissa is "of the Soil" and I believe dates back to before the coming of Kissera. The King of Wawa is supposed not to see the face of the Emir of Bussa, in like manner the Emir of Bussa must not see the Chief of Wawa, if such a thing happened then some awful plague, it is imagined, would attack the two towns Wawa and Bussa.

'I would strongly recommend a change not from any fear of trouble, but merely as a step towards development.'[40]

The ignorance of Borgu political organization displayed by Dwyer is almost breath-taking, especially as he had spent some time in Borgu Province. The idea that Bussa could ever accept subjection to Kaiama willingly was far-fetched indeed, especially when one recalls that Dwyer was well aware of the problems involved in subjecting Yashikera, Ilesha and Okuta to Kaiama. But during the next six years Bussa, under Kontagora Province, was to be the subject of many similar plans for reorganization which completely ignored the political realities of life in Borgu.

3. Bussa and Kontagora 1908–1912

The first four years of the administration of Borgu by Kontagora were quiet. Characteristic of the administrative reports of these years is the one for the fourth quarter of 1909 on Bussa and Kaiama: 'There is little to report under the heading of Political and Administrative.'[41] The feeling of the British administration, despite the inevitable occurrence of an occasional problem, was that, in the words of Assistant Resident de Putron in 1910: 'The general attitude of the whole division remains as before, eminently satisfactory.'[42] Indeed few problems are alluded to in the reports, and none of them is treated with any urgency or foreboding that it could lead to violent upheaval in what was still considered one of the most peaceful parts of the protectorate of Northern Nigeria. Recruitment for forced labour on the Lagos–Northern Nigeria Railway causes a certain concern. The inefficiency of Kitoro Gani is a recurring theme. The problem of migration from Yauri to Bussa is a constant thorn in the flesh of the administration. But all are treated as part of the day to day problems confronting any political officer. One of the reasons for this false sense of security was a simple one: the sheer lack of knowledge of what was really going on in Borgu. With never more than one British administrator in Borgu at a time, and annual changes of personnel, it was difficult for anybody to familiarize himself with the problems of Borgu at anything other than a superficial level. The Political Officers for Borgu Province from 1907 to 1912 were:

? ? Norton-Traill (1907)
? ? Houlgate (1907–08)
N. M. Gepp (1909)
T. C. Newton (1909/1910/1911)
? de Putron (1910)
J. C. O. Clarke (based on Yelwa: 1911/1912)
A. R. Boyd (Bussa: May–December 1912)
P. R. Diggle (Kaiama: May–December 1912)

The increasing paper-work of the administration competed with the extended absences from headquarters in Bussa which effective touring required. Kaiama, Ilesha, Okuta, Yashikera and the outlying towns and villages of Bussa were but infrequently visited by the political officer during this period. The Resident at Kontagora was certainly aware of the problem, writing as he did in his Annual Report for 1911: 'Borgu, which has an area of over 9,000 square miles, is too big a task for one Political Officer to work efficiently, and though much touring and reassessment has been accomplished much more still remains to be done.'[43] Indeed it is surprising that things worked as well as they did, given the shortage of police as well as administrators. In 1911 the Assistant Resident at Bussa wrote petulantly on July 29th to his Resident:

'Did His Excellency know that I had no Police at Bussa from March 7th ? I imagine in no other province are there 2 totally distinct Emirates looked after by one official.'[44]

Though, hitherto, we have treated the history of colonial administration in Borgu largely chronologically, these four years will be dealt with in terms of the main problems of the Division as the political officers saw them. There is lack of information on day-to-day events in this period, accounted for by the fact that Mr. Boyd reported in 1912 when he took over the office: 'At Bussa the whole office was one mass of white ants and I regret to say that a great pile of records, some of them reference files, etc., were in such a state that the only thing possible was done and that was to burn them.'[45]

The principal problem for the political officer in charge of Borgu Division was how to administer it successfully through the agency of Kitoro Gani. In 1907 the Assistant Resident for Borgu had written that, in effect, he had to fall back on direct rule because of the inadequacies of Kitoro Gani: 'The administrative work has been wholly dependent on myself and staff, indeed to such an extent that if the Emirate of Bussa was done away with, I should be better off, as at present issuing orders through the Emir is only to cause delay and I generally take the matter in hand myself.'[46] Assistant Resident Newton, however, was more charitable about him. 'Seems to be doing his duty in a mild sort of way, but does not appear to be at all self-reliant.'[47] De Putron, who took over from Newton in 1910, considered Kitoro Gani 'too much of a figure head, and . . . not likely to command obedience from his subjects. His officials ineffective, probably not through incapability, but from lack of being kept up to the mark by the Emir, a very great contrast I should say, to the Emir of Kaiama'.[48] Two years before, Major Sharpe, Resident of Kontagora, had however formed a low opinion of Kaiama and threatened to depose him if he did not improve.[49] In fact, the reaction to both Kitoro Gani and Mora Tasude tended to vary with individual officers. Those who favoured strong government tended to get on well with Mora Tasude, who had the reputation of getting things done, even if at the expense of considerable unpopularity among his people. Those who were inclined to a laissez-faire approach tolerated, even if they became exasperated with, Kitoro Gani. At least he was always ready to do what he was told, if not very effectively.

The general view of Kitoro Gani was elaborated by Newton in his Confidential Report on him for 1911, which is worth quoting *in extenso* for the insight it gives into administrative attitudes of the time:

'A weak inefficient ruler unable to deal effectively with any new matter which he is called upon to carry out. In fact putting anything in his hands simply means in many cases delay and constant reference to me before its completion. This is due not only to his weak character but also to the inefficiency of his subordinates at HQ and of his sub-district chiefs.

'The only two men who command respect are the Alkali of Boussa —a Nupe—and Sar. Kunji, who is however now getting rather an old man . . . I am afraid the Emir is little respected.

'He has always had the reputation of being a drunkard. No direct proof. His attitude towards Govt. always quite satisfactory. It is typical of his lack of confidence in himself that he has on one or two occasions asked for police to accompany him to enforce such a thing as the collection of LRNE [railway] labour. Needless to say his requests have not been granted.

'He is very foolish in the way he squanders money, not being strong-minded enough to resist the importunities of his chief men.

'Best I can say of him is that he tries to do as he is told, and he has no doubt improved since the early days of his reign when no one had a good word to say to him. He is ignorant and has few ideas.'[50]

The real problem, as Newton himself discovered, was that politically the kings of Bussa did not have the authority of the Fulani emirs of the conquered Sokoto caliphate. Increasingly a system derived from the Fulani emirates was developing in Northern Nigeria, a pattern of administration which relied on the strong central authority of the Emir, the existence of a regular collection of taxes as in pre-colonial times and the use of district chiefs to administer the constituent districts of the emirates. Such central authority, such regular collection of taxes, such firm district administration did not exist in Bussa. Thus it was that as the British tried to systematize administration in Northern Nigeria the limitations of Kitoro Gani became more apparent. He just did not have the authority required. This was not so much to do with his personality as with the position of chiefs in pre-colonial Borgu. As Newton observed: 'The ties between the Emirs of Bussa and their people have always been weak compared to the strong Fulani methods in vogue elsewhere.'[51] It was because of this that the administration had such difficulty in collecting taxes regularly, in recruiting forced labour and indeed in ensuring regular administration of the outlying districts of the Bussa emirate.

Forced labour, particularly in foreign parts, was completely unheard of in Bussa. Such 'forced' labour as was necessary was performed by slaves, who anyway had their own rights. They would labour so many days on their owners' farms, so many days on their own. The idea of taking former slaves—slavery was now in theory abolished—let alone freemen long distances from home to perform unaccustomed labour had no precedent in Borgu. The nearest parallel was soldiering, but this was an honourable profession. The removal of able-bodied men from the farms, and their separation from their families, incurred considerable dislocation in this already sparsely populated land. Resentment of forced labour was natural in the circumstances. The position of the King of Bussa and his fief-holders, who as we have seen exercised limited control over their subjects in pre-colonial times, was as a result very difficult.

In the first quarter of 1909 the first 383 men were sent from Bussa and Kaiama to work on the railway at Jebba some 150 miles away. In the second quarter a further 150 were sent from Bussa. By the end of the year some 600 men were reported by Newton as having 'been officially sent down' to Jebba from Bussa and Kaiama.[52] The four quarterly reports for 1910 refer neither to additional forced labour being sent to work on the railway nor to any trouble arising from that already sent. However, in the first quarter of 1911, Mr. J. C. O. Clarke, who was temporarily put in charge of the Division, though based at Yelwa across the river, wrote:

'. . . I have had the greatest difficulty in getting the Emirs of Boussa and Kaiama (especially the former) to make any contribution of labour. They put forward all sorts of lame and false excuses, such as their people not being able to get their customary diet of yams at Bokane, and also the collection of tribute was then taking place and that smallpox was virulent.

'The Borguese are a very indolent tribe and addicted to drink, but to ascertain the true reason of their aversion to labour one must look to the poverty of their wants and their growing prosperity under Pax Britannica. With ample food supplies, light taxation (the incidence in Borgu is 1/1d per adult) and industrious wives, no wonder these natives are indisposed to render services to the Government. . . .'[53]

When Newton took over again he complained similarly that the

Bussawa hated railway work, especially when it was far from home. Furthermore Government was now asking for twice as many labourers as before, and new batches were being sent off before the previous ones had returned home.[54] In such circumstances, neither Kitoro Gani nor his kofas and other big men were able to deal effectively with recruitment of labour. Kitoro Gani had had to go in person to superintend the collection which with a great deal of trouble took place on occasions. Threats and even force had to be used, and Kitoro Gani had, under pressure from the administration, to punish a good many deserters. His subjects in western Bussa told him they would migrate to French territory if they were pressed. The naive conclusion of Newton in making this report was that this showed how weak was the hold Kitoro Gani had over his people, especially as he had to give into this particular group.[55] While Newton wrote this in his confidential report on Kitoro Gani, he did in fact appeal to the Acting Resident to remit the required additional 94 Bussa and 60 Kaiama labourers. Apart from emigration to French territory, men were fleeing to the bush on the approach of Kitoro Gani, and the Kunji people were threatening to cross to Illo or Lafagu in Sokoto Province where no labour was being recruited. On top of that the smallpox outbreak in Kaiama made Newton wonder whether there was not a danger of infection in sending men from Kaiama to work on the railway. To this request the Acting Resident E. G. M. Dupigny reacted sharply:

'I hope you are not inclined to indulge in soft sentiment over the wickedness of making the poor natives work on the railway.

'It is a great mistake to think that properly directed labour will do any injury to the native; on the contrary, it is his greatest civiliser and will teach him lessons of self-preservation and maintenance which must be of permanent benefit.

'There is no need for any apprehension as to the Borguese emigrating to French territory or to Sokoto. If they go to the former they will find very different treatment to what is meted out to them in British country and they are quite alive to this fact.

'It is well known that emigrants to the French and German territory invariably return to British country. Over the border they are made to work without compensation, besides paying land rents their sheep and other stock are taxed and the native authorities are despots.

'If they go to Sokoto they have to purchase farms and the land rents are heavier than at Kunji.'

Dupigny did, however, agree to remit the demand for labour on the grounds given by Newton, who did not take the reprimand lying down. From his rejoinder it is clear that the early British political officers had no fear of their superiors:

'I am very far from indulging in "soft sentiment" re the natives. I merely wished to emphasize the fact that, all circumstances considered, the weak Bussa administration had no easy task in many districts in obtaining 2nd and 3rd lots of labour.

'The fact remains that every year a fair number of Borgawa do cross over into French country and do not return, and that it is very rare for French subjects to settle in British Borgu.

'At any rate they would much prefer heavier land rents to being called upon to go some fifteen days journey to the railway work. From what I can gather Illo and Kaoje are not much interfered with by Sokoto.'[56]

The second major problem that worried the administration during these years was that of taxation. As we have already noted, regular taxation was not a feature of pre-colonial Borgu. While dependent towns paid tribute to the king of Bussa, his main source of revenue was from his farms worked by slaves. It will be recalled that the Chief Tax-Collector said that one of the reasons for the popularity of Kitoro Gani was that he was a wealthy man and could support his 'followers'. A further source of income was tolls on caravans passing through Bussa. Finally, it seems that the Kamberri and other subject groups had sporadic and arbitrary levies made on them as officials of Bussa passed through. The idea of individual taxation on a regular basis to be in by a certain time was certainly foreign.

The British, however, insisted on such a system as fundamental to their administration. Furthermore a large part of the tax, $62\frac{1}{2}$ per cent, was to be paid to the government in Zungeru. The agent for the collection of these taxes was Kitoro Gani with his fief-holders, or kofas as they are called in the reports which use the Hausa term.

To have an accurate idea of how much a particular village should pay in tax, and at what rate the villagers should be taxed, the political officers made assessment reports in which they tried to assess the number of the adult population and the wealth of an area, so that they could fix what they considered a fair incidence. For the Bussa emirate they fixed an incidence of 1/1d per adult. Their methods of assessment in the early years were pretty haphazard. Dwyer's was reported as 'to beat a drum and summon all the villagers before him, and make them swear on their "Mayirro" (pagan fetish) that they are all present. *He only assesses those he actually sees.* They get to know this and half of them hide.'[57]

Once numbers and incidence had been 'ascertained' it was the task of Kitoro Gani and his chiefs to get in the tax (called tribute in this period) by a fixed time.

A recurrent theme in administrative reports on Borgu is the difficulty in getting the tax in on time. In 1910, de Putron complained that the kofas of Sarkin Bussa seemed to spend all their time in the capital and think it enough to send out messengers to bring in the tribute.[58] While assessment of the number of people was below the actual level, taxation was not too difficult to collect; but the more accurate the population count became, the more difficult collection became.

One problem involved in taxation that was to add to the bitterness between Yauri and Bussa was that Bussa's incidence of tax was only 1/1d while Yauri's was 2/–. This naturally encouraged Yauri farmers to cross to Bussa land to farm where they would pay less tax. There was the further incentive that Bussa had a large amount of unoccupied and very good farming land. What really riled Kitoro Gani was that these farmers refused to pay him his 1/1d tax, while at the same time they did not pay tax to Yauri, though Yauri also tried to collect tax from its subjects who farmed on Bussa land.

Major Sharpe proposed as a solution to this problem that, while Yauri subjects should be allowed to farm on Bussa land, the incidence of taxation in Borgu should be raised to 2/– to bring it in line with that of Yauri. He went on to say of the Borgawa: 'I think this is the only way of stirring them up a bit, and making them work. They are incorrigibly lazy, and leave their women to do most of the work in the Shea-trade.' The Governor approved the increase in incidence with the caution that Sharpe should go slow.[59]

There still remained the problem of farmers from Yauri who lived on Yauri territory but crossed to Bussa land to farm. This meant that technically they were subjects of the Emir of Yauri and had to pay him tax, yet made their money out of Bussa territory. In 1910 it was agreed that they should pay Bussa 10 per cent of their produce in recognition of his position as chief of the land they farmed. This, as far as the administration was concerned, seemed to have settled the problem. Newton reported:

'The relations between Sar. Boussa and Sar. Yelwa, however, will take some time to become all that could be desired. Sar. Yelwa naturally hates losing the emigrants and the Emir of Bussa is apt, unless he is watched, to use questionable methods in his endeavour to please the immigrants, and is prone to suspect Sar. Yelwa of employing equally questionable means of endeavouring to persuade these men to return to his land.

'However, as Sar. Yelwa undoubtedly drove away these people by his high handed practices and as they have for some years been farming on Boussa land without paying to Boussa anything more than a small Gaisuwa, the solution of the question seems fair (gaisua)* and reasonable: immigrating to Borgu = 2/- assessment per adult.'[60]

However, though the administration thought the problem solved, it was to fester for the next four years.

The administration had not helped things by mooting the separation of Kunji from Bussa and placing it under Yauri, since Kunji was one of the main centres of immigration of Yauri farmers. Fortunately 'native opinion' made itself clear in its hostility to such a transfer, and the administration saw that as Bussa had already lost so much land the separation of Kunji from Bussa 'would cause endless trouble and considerable ill-feeling'.[61] Newton also noted in early 1911 the continuing jealousy between Kitoro Gani and Mora Tasude. If they meet, he said, matters become so strained that 'an open fight between their respective followings is always sur le tapis.'[62] But these seemed to the administration minor problems. At the celebrations in Kontagora for the Coronation of King George V, the leading chiefs of the province met, and Bussa and Yauri in particular effected reconciliations. The Acting Resident, Mr. E. G. M. Dupigny, wrote headily: 'I think it is my duty to say here that the ruling classes of this Province have given the clearest evidence of their loyalty to Government and that a large number of the common people are distinctly well disposed to the officers of Govt. and appreciate the benefits of British rule.'[63]

* gaisua = tribute.

IV · THE DEPOSITION OF KITORO GANI

1. Administrative Policy and Amalgamation

In 1912 the British decided to amalgamate their protectorate of Northern Nigeria with its neighbour, the colony and protectorate of Southern Nigeria. Ever since its inception the protectorate of Northern Nigeria had been running at a loss, subsidized by the Government of Southern Nigeria and an imperial grant-in-aid of some £300,000 a year. To the British Colonial Office and Treasury, whose overall policy for the Empire was that all colonies should be self-supporting, such a situation was intolerable in the long term. As there was no immediate prospect of the Government of Northern Nigeria becoming self-sufficient, it was decided to amalgamate it with Southern Nigeria whose surplus would cover its deficit. This approach was not altogether unfair to the Southern Nigerian Government, since a considerable portion of its revenue was, and would increasingly be, derived from customs duties on imports to, and exports from, the land-locked Northern Government. Another important factor in the decision to bring together the northern and southern protectorates was the need to co-ordinate policy with regard to their rapidly developing railway systems.

To effect the amalgamation, Sir Frederick Lugard was appointed simultaneously Governor of the Protectorate of Northern Nigeria and Governor of the Colony and Protectorate of Southern Nigeria. He arrived in Lagos to take up his appointment on 3rd October 1912. By 1st January 1914 he had completed the task and assumed the title of Governor-General of the Colony and Protectorate of Nigeria.

As far as the administration of Northern Nigeria was concerned, the amalgamation made remarkably little difference. The Governor of the Protectorate of Northern Nigeria now became Lieutenant-Governor of the Northern Provinces of Nigeria; but in day-to-day administration his powers hardly diverged from those of his predecessors. It was only in overall policy that he had to refer to Lagos. From Lugard's point of view, the main function of the Governor-General was to co-ordinate overall policy for the two governments, particularly in the economic sphere. His was very much a one-man show in Lagos, relying on the administrations of the northern and southern provinces to get on with the day-to-day business of governing the people. In so far as he did try to unify the system of administration of the two protectorates, this was to the disadvantage of the South, in that he brought in change to the prevailing pattern there. He introduced to the South the Northern Nigerian model of Indirect Rule as developed in the large emirates of the former Sokoto caliphate.

Crucial to the Indirect Rule system was government of the people at the local level by the legitimate heirs of their pre-colonial rulers, who would as far as possible rule over the same area as they would have inherited if the British had not occupied them. Such chiefs were designated Native Authorities, and usually ruled as sole Native Authority, though sometimes a Chief in Council would be so designated. These Native Authorities had specific functions: the collection of taxes, a portion of which was given to the central government, in this case the Government of the Protectorate of Northern Nigeria, and a portion retained for the administration of the Native Authority's budget through the Native Treasury. The Native Authority, supervised by the Political Officer, ran the budget from which salaries, services and development projects were paid. Taxation, the Native Treasury (or *Beit-el-Mal*) and the preparation of an annual budget under which the Chief, his councillors and district heads were all salaried officials, formed the cornerstone of Indirect Rule as it had come to be understood in Northern Nigeria by 1912. A further distinguishing feature of this system was partial control of the administration of justice, including local police functions, and maintenance of the prisons. The judicial competence of a particular Native Authority depended on its sophistication, and could include, as in the case of Kano, the right to impose the death penalty. All appointments to and dismissals from positions in the Native Authority were in principle under its control, though the Central Government had to sanction the appointment of the chief as head of the Native Authority. The Native Authorities were also legislative bodies which could both legislate on 'traditional matters' and promulgate legislation on such matters as forest reserves, sale and manufacture of beer, etc.

The extent to which a political officer supervised a Native Authority depended on its competence. Ideally, under the Northern system of Indirect Rule the Political Officer acted as an adviser; and divisional reports from those areas outside the large Fulani-Hausa emirates frequently refer to the difficulties of running Indirect Rule, meaning that a political officer was having to interfere more than was thought desirable in the administration of a particular Native Authority. Significantly, when the machinery of government of a particular Native Authority broke down, the Political Officer became Acting Native Authority, until it was restored. Thus while in such cases direct rule was established, the notion of a British political officer *acting* as a Native Authority signified that it was only a temporary measure and the goal was to return to the 'ideal state' of Indirect Rule.[1]

In 1912 Indirect Rule as described above was still unknown in Southern Nigeria and it had not been introduced in many parts of Northern Nigeria, including Bussa. Under the amalgamation, what had long been the goal for all divisions of Northern Nigeria now became the goal for the rest of Nigeria as well.

While Southern Nigeria was greatly influenced by Northern practice in the field of local government and law, the Northern provinces might as well have remained a separate protectorate as far as the day-to-day lives of the people were concerned. The frontiers between the Northern provinces and the Southern provinces remained, and had at times almost the force of an international boundary. Officials of the North and South rarely met, and almost never served in both groups of provinces. Up to the time of the appointment of Sir Donald Cameron as Governor of Nigeria in 1931, the administration of the Northern provinces as far as possible maintained a policy of keeping itself to itself.

2. Administrative Reform in Borgu

In 1912, the year of the amalgamation, the British decided that it was time they did something about the patently inefficient administration of Borgu. Kaiama and Bussa were to be separated administratively and a political officer was to be posted to each. Shortage of political staff, however, made this impossible and until May both Kaiama and Bussa were administered from Yelwa, where the Assistant Resident was at that time J. C. O. Clarke. Clarke was unable to visit Kaiama at all because of the heavy preparations involved in the farewell visit of the Governor,

Sir Hesketh Bell, to Yelwa. But he reported that Mora Tasude 'seems as usual, to have been carrying on the Administration of the Division in an efficient manner'.[2] Bussa appears to have given him no trouble at that time for the Provincial Annual Report contains no reference to it.

In May, A. C. Boyd took over from Clarke as Assistant Resident at Yelwa, in charge of Bussa, while Kaiama was formally separated from Bussa with the appointment of P. R. Diggle as Assistant Resident at Kaiama. Boyd gave Bussa top priority and toured it with Kitoro Gani, being struck by the latter's apparent complete indifference as to whether his orders were carried out or not. While he considered Kitoro Gani a loyal chief, he thought he lacked administrative ability and was highly critical of his kofas. He therefore proposed that the kofa system be abolished and that Bussa be divided up into a series of districts with salaried heads.[3] This idea had been put forward to Newton the year before, and more recently to Clarke, by Major Blakeney, the Resident of Kontagora, who wanted the kofas abolished, and proposed that the new district heads should be made to reside in their districts.[4] Boyd now promised Blakeney that once he had toured the Bussa emirate again, re-assessed and mapped it, he would put forward a scheme for its re-organization into districts with salaried heads.[5] Accordingly, accompanied by Kitoro Gani he toured the whole emirate, remarking that Kitoro Gani told him that it was the first time he had ever made such a tour. Boyd seized the occasion to discuss with Kitoro Gani his administrative defects, 'with the result that I think a glimmering of his responsibility has dawned on him and if he can only be kept up to the mark and a suitable councillor or two (Turaki and Daudin Bindiga at present assist him and the former seems a very capable man) always associated with him there is no reason why with patience he should not improve somewhat in time. He is unfortunately over fond of "gia"* and utters foolish statements when under its influence and also very much "tsafi"† ridden'.[6]

Boyd also discussed his ideas for reform of the administration of the emirate. At first Kitoro Gani was most averse to the idea of abolishing his fief-holders. But Boyd reported that, having seen the way in which tax could be collected by systematic touring such as they had undertaken, Kitoro Gani had come round to the idea and even seemed anxious for the reform.

Thus encouraged, Boyd put forward his scheme for administrative

* Local beer.
† Fetish.

reorganization.⁷ The Bussa emirate was to be divided into six districts: Agwarra, Kunji, West Bussa, Wawa, Leaba and Bussa itself. Bussa District would include those towns and villages in the immediate vicinity of Bussa and would be administered by Turaki, who was Chief Adviser to the Emir and had first been appointed in the reign of Dan Toro in 1885. The old fiefs were to be abolished, and resident headmen would be appointed for each district. In the case of Wawa and Kunji their own kings would be the district heads. In the case of Agwarra, West Bussa and Leaba, district heads would be specially appointed. The scheme was approved and put into effect.

An additional major reform in the administration of Bussa was the establishment in August of a Beit-el-Mal for the emirate. The Beit-el-Mal was the name given to the Native Treasuries established in the Fulani-Hausa emirates shortly after Lugard left Northern Nigeria. These treasuries were subsequently established throughout Northern Nigeria, as taxation became more systematic. As Lugard pointed out in his *Political Memoranda* in 1904–05, the total revenue for the protectorate from taxation was only £21,000 and 'insufficient to pay the salaries of the Native Officials of a single important Province'.⁸ The proceeds of the taxation collected by a Native Authority was paid to the Central Treasury, and a proportion of it, in Bussa's case $37\frac{1}{2}$ per cent, was 're-granted' to the Beit-el-Mal. From this the salaries of Native Authority officials and administrative expenditure were paid. The aim of the Beit-el-Mal was to organize expenditure by the Native Authority on regular lines, and in particular give the Political Officers a chance to supervise their financial affairs. The year after the Beit-el-Mal was established in Bussa, the system was slightly changed. Instead of all taxes being paid to the Central Treasury, that proportion due to the Native Authority was paid direct to the Beit-el-Mal.

These reforms seem to have caused no overt reaction in Borgu. Indeed 1912 was a quiet year in Bussa, though Kitoro Gani had some trouble in Agwarra where the Ubandawaki of Agwarra (Batafu, or traditional Chief Minister) had incited the people to drive out their district head. The Ubandawaki was arrested and given two years in prison by Kitoro Gani. The problem of people from Yauri crossing over to Bussa land to farm and then paying their tax to Sarkin Yauri, continued to be a cause for complaint by Kitoro Gani. The year before, Acting Resident Dupigny had ruled that in such circumstances the stranger farmers should pay their taxes to the Sarkin Yauri rather than Bussa. But now Blakeney ruled that they should pay their taxes to Bussa.[9] In December, Kitoro Gani left for Kano for the Governor's Durbar, where hierarchically, as a first-class chief, he ranked with the Emir of Sokoto (as he was then styled by the British) and the Shehu of Bornu, whom he acknowledged as his overlord.

In their reports for the year Blakeney and Boyd seemed quite satisfied with Kitoro Gani, though concern was still shown for his addiction to drink. Boyd even considered that as a result of his close supervision Kitoro Gani had improved, to which Blakeney replied:

'I am glad to hear of this improvement in the S. Bussa which I hope will continue. We cannot hope for much from the present generation of Native Rulers, but I am sure that treating them with patience and tact goes a long way, in trying to imbue them with a due sense of their responsibilities.'[10]

If Kitoro Gani was deemed to have improved, Mora Tasude certainly was not. When Diggle arrived in Kaiama to re-open the office there, he wrote:

'I regret that I am unable to confirm previous favourable reports on Serikin Kaiama. He has been left too long with no one to look after him. His great idea seems to be to centralize all authority and all power in himself. A great number of persons have left the town of Kaiama because of his treatment of them. On several occasions during the last month the chiefs and headmen of various towns have complained to me that they were frightened to bring tribute into Kaiama because of the Emir and by his impolitic action he has driven a whole village across the Anglo-French boundary.'

He then appended a long list of criticisms of the Emir. To these Blakeney replied, with a note of warning to Diggle:

'I am sorry to hear of your opinion of the Emir of Kaiama, he has always been so well spoken of, doubtless he has been left too much to himself, at the same time you should be very careful about listening to any stories, as there are always plenty of mischief-makers about, who are always against those in authority. You must endeavour to keep him straight, remembering that, the policy of the Administration is to rule through the Emirs.'[11]

Diggle also reported that the Sarkin Yashikera was absolutely unfitted for his job, and that 'the whole of his district refuses to obey him and he has no power to enforce his would-be authority. When he goes anywhere he has to carry his own mat and staff of office'.[12]

THE DEPOSITION OF KITORO GANI

Though Blakeney had shown understanding of Mora Tasude's position, he nevertheless reported him to the Governor who sent a reprimand in Arabic:

'From the representative of the King of England His Excellency the Governor to the Emir of Kaiama—salutations—

'I am informed by the Resident that you have not been governing well and that you are following the dictates of your heart, and not consulting the good of your people, in fact your people are leaving your country because of your action towards them. Know that if I continue to hear such reports of people leaving your lands, there will be no course except for me to take away your staff—therefore make every effort to improve your country and not to spoil it.'[13]

In September Diggle reported that Mora Tasude had substantially improved and more charitably attributed his deficiencies to the long time he had been left to himself. Shortly afterwards on October 7th Mora Tasude died and Blakeney wrote: 'from the purely personal point of view of a Resident here his place will be hard to fill.'[14]

1912 saw a major change in administrative personnel in Kaiama. Sarkin Yashikera was deposed and Mashi, an old soldier of Zaberma, not Borgu, origin, was appointed its District Head. Mora Tasude was succeeded by Jimi, son of Kimora the seventh emir. Blakeney expressed the hope that under Jimi it would be possible to decentralize government and make the district heads more than figure-heads.[15] There were good signs for the new emir in the return from French Borgu of some hundred or more who had fled because of the old emir's autocratic ways. But Diggle sounded a note of caution about Jimi, considering that at first he would not have an easy time administering the Division 'as previous to his appointment he was merely a farmer and had no experience in ruling. Now that the fear in which the late Emir was held has been removed some of the people seem to think they need not pay obedience to his successor'.[16] The hopes expressed by Diggle and Blakeney that under the new emir administrative improvements could be made in Kaiama were not to be realized because of shortage of political staff. After less than a year as Assistant Resident of Kaiama, Diggle had to close down the office, and it was not until 1917, with the posting there of Joyce Cary, that Kaiama was directly supervised by a political officer again.

3. J. C. O. Clarke's Second Administration of Bussa

1913 was to prove a disastrous year for Bussa and, to a lesser extent, Kaiama. J. C. O. Clarke, as we have seen, had already had a brief spell in charge of Bussa, but he had interfered very little in its affairs. He made up for this in his 1913 tour with a vengeance. Unfortunately for Borgu, during most of Clarke's time there he was responsible to a happy-go-lucky Resident, Hamilton-Browne, who failed to perceive the disastrous consequences that would follow from many of Clarke's actions and recommendations. Hamilton-Browne, or 'Hammy' as he was known to his political officers, believed he knew the 'natives' and in particular those of Kontagora Province. In 1917 Joyce Cary was to sum up Hamilton-Browne's character when he wrote to his wife that there would be no change in the administration of Kontagora Province until they changed Hamilton-Browne who was 'simply marking time till he gets his pension. He is an awfully good fellow and as straight as you make 'em but damn slack and that's all about it'.[17]

Clarke himself had joined the Colonial Service in 1905 from the Navy. In 1908 his confidential report described him as possessing 'strength of character, great energy, and perhaps the over-zealousness of youth'.[18] After a quarrel in 1908 with a Mr. Corey, the High Commissioner expressed the hope that he would endeavour to show greater tact in his dealings with 'both Europeans and natives'. As a result he was posted from Niger Province to Yola. He started service in Kontagora Province in 1911 and in 1912 he was recommended for promotion, despite criticisms of his 1912 Assessment Report for Borgu. This ran to only two and a half pages of large manuscript. 'Most insufficient' was the comment at Zungeru.[19] Hamilton-Browne, however, quickly formed a good impression of Clarke, and wrote in 1914: 'Most tactful with Europeans and Clerks. Not popular with all the natives, but this is due to his thorough knowledge of their ways. Mr. Clarke is in my opinion an exceedingly clever political officer. He is untiring in his energy.'[20]

Clarke arrived to assume duty in Yauri with charge of Bussa on 30th December 1912. In his first quarter's report to Hamilton-Browne he put forward his views about emigration from Yauri to Bussa; he believed that the peasants should be kept under their own chiefs and they should be discouraged from crossing into other districts. To this Hamilton-Browne replied that it was a simple solution to a rather difficult question.

With regard to the question of Yauri farmers crossing to farm on Bussa land, Hamilton-Browne was inclined to fix an artificial boundary between the two emirates, which might include the Bussa land they farmed in Yauri. The Niger would thus cease to be the natural division between Yauri and Bussa.[21] He wrote to the High Commissioner that for generations Yauri subjects living on the islands in the Niger had crossed to the left bank and Bussa had never made any claim to control over them until the British had announced the river Niger as the boundary. Kitoro Gani, he alleged, was not averse to such a boundary since it gave him more taxpayers. Hamilton-Browne thus showed his ignorance of the real political situation in pre-colonial times, when the Niger did form the boundary between Borgu and Yauri. This ignorance was to cost Bussa dearly.[22] Clarke was instructed by Hamilton-Browne to conduct on-the-spot investigations, after which Hamilton-Browne would submit recommendations to Zungeru for an artificial boundary.

Clarke visited Bussa and Agwarra districts in March and reported to Hamilton-Browne that the Borgawa were even more backward than the Kamberri, whom he considered the most backward of pagans. This backwardness he thought was due to drink or perhaps their diet. He considered the chiefs very ineffective and incapable of ruling. 'Probably when I know the District better', he added, ominously for Kitoro Gani, 'comparatively capable men will be found and employed as was done in the case of Yauri Division.'[23]

Clarke had been Assistant Resident in Yauri in 1911, and had divided the emirate up into six districts, with Yelwa (the capital) as a separate administrative unit. He had in certain cases replaced inefficient fiefholders by men whom he considered to have administrative ability. Thus the chief of N'Gaski was deposed and the able Tukura, Aliu of Jabo, made Sarkin Yamma, in charge of the Gungawa Islands. In this way Clarke had tried to strengthen the administration of the Emir of Yauri, Jibrilu, son of Abdullahi Abershi, who had succeeded in 1904. He had never had an easy reign, having been placed on the throne by the British to the chagrin of the traditional kingmakers, who were not consulted and constantly intrigued against him.[24] But Clarke, reporting on Jibrilu in 1911, felt he was a fairly competent chief: 'when it is considered that the majority of the population are more or less truculent pagans or at any rate passive resisters, I think he does as well as can be expected under the circumstances.'[25] Clarke had already identified Aliu of Jabo, the

Emir's Tukura * as an 'able lieutenant' and, as we shall see, came increasingly to rely on him in his administration of Yauri.

In his June 1913 report Clarke made two drastic recommendations as far as Bussa and Yauri were concerned: first, that Kunji, which had always been a tributary of Bussa, even if a somewhat reluctant one, should come under Yauri. Secondly, the Bussa land farmed by the Yauris should be annexed to Yauri simply because its farmers were using it.

Clarke was preoccupied with affairs in Yauri and wrote in his September report that though he was now in charge of Kaiama which was once again without a political officer, he had been unable to visit it. The new Emir, 'on probation', appeared to him from reports to be 'slack and inefficient'. In spite of his warnings, he was still importing gin, which was illegal in Northern Nigeria, from the Southern Protectorate. Clarke added that he would probably have to take action soon.[26]

In July Isa, the Sarki of Kunji, died. Clarke, still pressing the case for Kunji's being included in Yauri, wrote in his December report: 'The people of Kunji District are quite distinct from Bussa people. They were until recently all Yauri subjects and Fulani and have progressed much more than the Bussa people and their sarakuna† are much more efficient.'[27] In his Annual Report for 1913 he even went so far as to say that Kunji had been handed over to Bussa a few years after the British occupation, to which a later political officer rightly pencilled the comment 'A.D.O. i/c Yauri biased in their favour. Quite untrue.'[28]

Clarke did put forward one progressive idea during his first full year's administration of Bussa. This was that Bussa should retain 50 per cent instead of $37\frac{1}{2}$ per cent of the taxes it collected. The salaries of the Emirs at £240 a year, and those of the District Heads at £36 a year, were quite inadequate. As he pointed out, with only one political officer attached to the three emirates of Yauri, Bussa and Kaiama since 1911 except for the brief period of Diggle's attachment to Kaiama from June 1912 to March 1913, the work of administration, including policing, was being carried on by the chiefs. Furthermore it was becoming extremely difficult for the chiefs to impose *gaisua* or unofficial taxes, with the result that 'they are in a constant state of pecuniary embarrassment.' This proposal was supported by the Resident, now Major Blakeney, who forwarded it to the Lieutenant-Governor on 20th March 1914.[29] He recommended a

---

* Tukura = Royal Messenger, who on official business would be treated with deference since he represented the king, or in this case, the Emir.

† Chiefs.

£60 increase in Bussa's salary, to make it £300. Temple, the Lieutenant-Governor, concurred and the changed rate was brought into effect in the 1915 Estimates. As Blakeney wrote:

'An income of £240 per annum for an Emir of the 1st Class, such as the Emir of Bussa is, can scarcely be considered sufficient for him to maintain his position with, and I think it is hardly realized the many demands made upon their private expenses, that these men have. Again £36 per annum for District Heads, responsible for the collection of the taxation of their districts, cannot be considered in any way adequate, and must in some cases, I am afraid, lead to dishonest practices.'[30]

The real problem was the fact that the Bussa emirate, 7,500 square miles in area, produced only £1,903 in taxation in 1913. And even this was difficult to collect.

In 1913, when the incidence of taxation was raised by 3d per adult from 2/6d to 2/9d, some relations of Kitoro Gani, among them his half-brother Sabukki, incited the people against paying tax to the District Head of Bussa, Turaki.[31] In this action they had the support of the Batafu, the traditional chief minister, who opposed collection of taxes before the harvest was in.[32] Indeed the refusal to pay tax appears, according to Bussa informants, to have been due as much to resentment of the rise in incidence as to hatred of the power of Turaki and the suspicion that Kitoro Gani was pocketing much of the tax.[33]

Sabukki and other ringleaders were arrested and sent by Clarke before the Emir of Bussa's court. Kitoro Gani then had to try his own brother, and sentenced him to one year's imprisonment. Sabukki and his accomplices, however, escaped from jail, and took to the bush where he lived as an outlaw. It was later believed that he escaped with the connivance of the Alkali and possibly even Kitoro Gani himself.[34] The Alkali, Mallam Isa, was actually brought to trial for his part in the escape and sentenced to six months in jail. His sentence was quashed, but he was deprived of his position.

There were further reports of anti-tax agitation in the first quarter of 1914 in Aliyara District (West Bussa) where Boyd had had some trouble in 1912. The situation appeared sufficiently grave to Kitoro Gani and the District Head of Aliyara, who were responsible for getting in the tax, that they requested that Clarke accompany them there with an escort. If not, they feared things would get out of hand. Clarke recommended a W.A.F.F. patrol, to which Dwyer, Acting Resident, and soon to become

Clarke's enemy, wired 'not necessary'. In reply, Clarke commented, 'it is, I am sure very necessary if we are to avoid regrettable incidents in the future'. Clarke therefore proposed in the absence of the W.A.F.F. to take an escort of Northern Nigerian Police with him.[35]

Clarke, however, went on leave before he could take the patrol to Aliyara. Before he left in 1914, despite his reservations about Kunji's traditional relationship to Bussa, he had to sanction the installation of a new District Head of Kunji by Kitoro Gani. He went on leave satisfied that, despite the problem in Bussa and Aliyara Districts, the emirate was 'progressing satisfactorily and the District Heads are doing good work and after I have carried out a tour of Aliyara's district the whole Emirate will be in a very satisfactory state politically'.[36]

4. The Borgu Patrol of February 1915

While Clarke was absent on leave, no administrative work was undertaken in Borgu Division because of lack of staff.[37] The only event of importance recorded in the Resident's report on Borgu for the second quarter of 1914 was the death of Sarkin Ilesha; and there was the usual note that Kitoro Gani's conduct had been unsatisfactory owing to his habits of drunkenness.[38] In the third quarter, however, Fergus Dwyer, who had taken over at Yelwa, visited Bussa and wrote at length of the problems there. Kitoro Gani complained to him that 'the people of the outlying villages paid absolutely no attention to his orders or instructions'. The village of Yangbasso had been giving trouble. Kanu was reported as out of hand. Sarkin Wawa had taken to heavy drinking. Indeed Kitoro Gani and his chiefs were sufficiently worried about the situation in Bussa to come up river to see Dwyer and ask once more for a police patrol. Kitoro Gani also took the opportunity to complain about Yauri farmers on his territory. 'Illo, Kawogo (Kaoje) and Lafagu . . . were taken from me. Now I am losing all the rest.'[39] Dwyer in return took the opportunity to lecture Kitoro Gani on the subject of his conduct and explained to him that while he was giving in to his attacks of drunkenness the *talakawa* (peasants) would only despise him and refuse to obey him.[40]

The problems of supervising Bussa were exacerbated by the outbreak of the First World War in August 1914 which diverted most of the energies of political officers to the recruiting of carriers for the Expeditionary Force for Kamerun and Togo. Though Kontagora Province had been asked to supply 800 carriers the Resident wisely decided not to recruit any in Borgu. He did, however, express the hope that the problems of Bussa District would be remedied by the posting of Clarke in charge of Borgu.[41]

In October Clarke was in fact posted to Bussa as District Officer and an escort of one N.C.O. and six constables of the Northern Nigerian Police was given him because of the unsettled state of the Division. The exigencies of the war meant that no more could be spared. Before he had time to tour the disturbed parts of Borgu he was transferred to Yelwa, though he was still responsible for Bussa and Kaiama.[42] His escort was recalled to Yelwa.

Once again Clarke wrote to the Resident on the need to tour Borgu with an escort. He suggested the Resident accompany him too. An N.C.O. and 10 W.A.F.F. other ranks, or 15 Northern Nigerian Police, would be necessary. The District Head of Aliyara had been driven out of several towns in his attempts to collect tax. The whole problem of tax collection had been worsened by the fact that the incidence on adult males had been raised by Dwyer from 2/6d to 4/-.[43] Clarke found on his arrival that there had been little progress in the collection of taxes and the people indicated they would not pay until after the harvest.[44]

Again the question of Yauri subjects farming on Bussa land was raised, along with that of Bussa's subjects farming in the Kontagora emirate. The Resident suggested that perhaps in settling for the Niger as the boundary 'historical rights were not understood'. The Acting Lieutenant-Governor replied to this: 'I should not worry too much about the historical rights. They are not of sufficient importance in this case to go beyond the natural boundary.'[44]

The Resident also reported to Zungeru that the taxes were not coming in from the Kaiama emirate and that he would have to ask for a patrol to collect them. The emirate was 'in a most unsatisfactory state owing to lack of European supervision'. Lugard, now Governor-General, complained that the political officers should do more touring to rectify this situation.[46] In his Annual Report, Blakeney however emphasized the fact that office work was preventing him from leaving headquarters. This was regrettable, 'as nothing is productive of so much good as moving amongst the people'.[47]

In February 1915 Clarke was at last given the patrol he had requested and marched through parts of Bussa and Kaiama. In the latter, the Resident reported, the patrol did 'a great deal towards re-establishing the authority of the Native Administration which had been steadily declining since the death of the late Emir'.[48]

The patrol was secured only after more than two weeks of telegraphic exchange between Kontagora and Zungeru as to its necessity.[49] Zungeru was reluctant to commit troops because of the war. On the other hand Hamilton-Browne argued that outstanding tribute could not be collected without a patrol. On 15th January 1915 Hamilton-Browne sent a priority telegram to the Acting Lieutenant-Governor, Temple:

'Regret report District Heads of Kaiama and West Bussa have been driven out and so no collection of Revenue has been made. One Town it is reported commenced repairs on Walls. French Authorities also in trouble on their side. Sanction requested for entire detachment Zuru to establish proper order in disaffected area.'

Persuaded now of the urgency of the situation, Temple recommended to Lugard that troops be despatched to Kaiama. On January 16th Lugard finally telegraphed that there were no troops available at Lokoja, the nearest W.A.F.F. garrison, but that a company was being sent from Udi in south-eastern Nigeria to Kaiama. On January 19th, Hamilton-Browne cabled that the trouble being experienced by the French was due to the appointment of a new and unpopular Chief of Nikki: 'Most of West Borgu crossed border to assist in demonstration against him but trouble is not serious. If dealt with at once can effect lasting settlement without bloodshed.'

Though Lagos had agreed to sending a full company of three sections, they did ask why it was necessary to send three sections of soldiers which 'appears excessive in a country like Borgu. H.E. remarks that we do not of course wish to espouse the French causes of difficulty with natives of their territory.' Very soon, French compulsory recruitment for the European Front was to cause widespread agitation and open rebellion in Dahomey and most parts of French West Africa.[50] Temple replied that it was he who was responsible for asking for a full company of three sections. Hamilton-Browne had originally thought only one section necessary. But Temple felt a comparatively strong force was necessary since the disturbance was on the frontier. He had now, after representations by the Commandant of the W.A.F.F., reduced his request to two sections. These were now *en route*.

The troops finally left Onitsha for Kaiama on January 22nd but did not reach their destination until February 5th. The patrol consisted of Captain Waters and Temporary Lieutenant Farquhar together with 65

THE DEPOSITION OF KITORO GANI

rank and file, one Maxim gun and carriers. They were met at Kaiama by Clarke. Waters, in command of the column, stayed in Kaiama on Clarke's advice until the tribute had all been brought in, rather than going out at once to other disaffected areas. They then proposed marching to Ilesha, Okuta, and Yashikera near the Dahomeyan boundary where they would turn northwards passing through the disaffected border towns. 'It is not expected', Waters reported, 'that serious, if any, opposition will be met with, in which case, I propose, with the sanction of the Commandant, to limit my Progress Report to once fortnightly.'

As Waters had predicted, they had no trouble in Ilesha, Okuta or Yashikera. All the tribute was brought in and there was no fighting. Indeed, between the time of their arrival at Kaiama and their entry to Okuta, Clarke had had no occasion to call upon Waters to order troops to take action in any way. The mere presence of troops had been sufficient to enable the Native Administrations to carry out the collection of tribute. The patrol reached Yelwa on March 24th without meeting any active resistance. Outstanding tribute was collected and indeed there was a £400 increase on that of 1913. Clarke meanwhile arrested the chiefs of Banara and Okuta for their alleged part in the resistance to tax collection and put acting district heads in their place. In West Bussa, Aliyara's district, the ringleaders of resistance to tax collection were similarly arrested.

As far as Clarke was concerned he had successfully shown the flag and order was restored to the Kaiama emirate and the disaffected parts of West Bussa. He and Hamilton-Browne now implemented their plans for a major reform of administration in Nigerian Borgu.

5. The Subjection of Bussa to Yauri

When the Acting Lieutenant-Governor for the Northern Provinces read the Kontagora Report for the first quarter of 1915, he complained that the Resident and his Assistant District Officer had spent 63 days together at headquarters instead of touring his province.[51] But in his office Hamilton-Browne, who had taken over from Blakeney, had not been idle. He was drawing up proposals, based on recommendations by Clarke, for the complete administrative reorganization of the Bussa and Kaiama emirates. In short, these recommendations involved not only the subjection of Borgu to Yauri but also the wholesale removal of its traditional rulers. Since these administrative 'reforms' brought Bussa to the edge of revolt, and led to disturbances in Kaiama despite the recent military patrol, we must ask how Hamilton-Browne and Clarke could have got away with such.

In the first place, Hamilton-Browne had never visited Bussa, Kaiama or even Yelwa before he put forward his recommendations, and so was depending largely on Clarke for his advice. In the second place, he personally seems to have been an easy-going administrator, without much intelligence, inclined to rely too much on the man on the spot. Anything for a quiet time, seems to have been his philosophy; and since Clarke assured him that nothing could be done in Bussa and Kaiama with the present generation of rulers, and that the reforms would be acceptable, or at least feasible, he was prepared to go along with them. Clarke thus becomes the crucial figure in the decisions that led to the 1915 rebellion. In Borgu he is one of the very few administrators out of a long line who is still remembered by the people. He is still known as Dan Tankwa ('the Peppery one') because of what they considered his rash and cruel actions while in charge of Borgu. He was clearly impatient of inefficiency and contemptuous of traditional rulers who could not fit in with his ideas of good administration. He had little conception of the nature or the strength of pre-colonial native institutions, and if they did not fit his bill he was prepared to dispense with them.

Clarke would have fitted much better into a French colonial administration; there chiefs were selected principally on the grounds of their efficiency, and their legitimacy in the eyes of the people they ruled came only as a secondary consideration. But in a British administration, where policy was to administer the 'natives' through their own rulers, his approach was out of place. He sought agents for carrying out his orders, people who would do what they were told, rather than operating through traditional heads of Native Authorities which he could develop into increasingly efficient units of local government. Unfortunately, in a protectorate where the latter was general policy (and had been the general guideline in Borgu since its occupation by the British) he was the purveyor of ideas which would have short shrift at Headquarters if they were to fail. While the British were sometimes prepared to support the appointment of chiefs who had no traditional legitimacy in the interests of efficient administration, they were not prepared to back up their rule with force.

That Clarke could have recommended his reforms with such

confidence stems partly from his own arrogance, partly from his lack of knowledge of Borgu. This is made clear by the way in which he dismissed the petition to the Resident drawn up anonymously on behalf of the people of Yauri and Bussa against him. The petition listed a number of complaints and accusations, including some fantastic ones, such as the fact that Clarke had four wives. The full petition, which Clarke described as 'a tissue of lies from beginning to end',[52] together with Clarke's reply is reproduced in an appendix, for though it is clearly prejudiced in favour of the recently deposed Sarkin N'Gaski, the reader will see, in retrospect, that if Clarke had been prepared to take it at all seriously he might have learnt from it. In particular it criticizes the power which both Aliu, Sarkin Yamma, and Abba, the Political Agent (or chief interpreter and informant on local affairs to the District Officer), had obtained under him. It also points out clearly that things were not well in the area:

'The people of Yauri and Bussa are not at ease. When the big white man "Giwa"* [Major Sharpe] and Laramir [Captain Larymore] were here, we were happy. We beseech the Governor to give us peace that we may cultivate our lands: we ask only to be allowed to rest in peace.'

Clarke dismissed the petition, and Blakeney, his Resident at the time, concurred in his comments to the Lieutenant-Governor on the petition. Nevertheless, as it turned out, Sarkin Yamma and Political Agent Abba, against whom the petitioners complained so bitterly, were to be seen by the people of both Bussa and Yauri as chief villains in the administrative reorganization that Clarke and Hamilton-Browne proposed for their ostensible good.

The main consequence of Clarke's patrol of Kaiama and West Bussa, which was meant to have done a great deal to strengthen the Native Administration there, was a series of recommendations for depositions of chiefs in the emirates made through Hamilton-Browne. Jimi, the Emir of Kaiama, 'to whose incapacity and weakness I attribute the present trouble in Kaiama Division' was to be replaced by Mashi, Sarkin Yashikera, as Acting Emir on a salary of £15 per month. The District Heads of Ilesha, Banara and Okuta were also to be deposed since they undoubtedly 'took advantage of the weakness of the Emir in encouraging the "talakawa" in disobedience and refusal to pay 1914 tribute'. This recommendation was sent to Zungeru on 11th March 1915.[53] On March 16th, Hamilton-Browne reported to Zungeru that the Emir of Kaiama had come into Yelwa with little over £100 in taxes, saying that he was

* Elephant.

unable to collect more. This was the first time in Kaiama's history since British occupation that it had failed to pay its taxes. 'Such a man, in my opinion, is unfit to exercise authority and is useless to us as well as a danger to progress in one of the most backward, if not most backward, districts of the protectorate. The Borgawa are an indolent drink-sodden people, and need a strong man to rule over them. Whatever the late Emir was, he was certainly that.'[54] Again on March 25th, to strengthen further his case for deposition of the Emir of Kaiama, Hamilton-Browne quoted Clarke's opinion of him in a letter to the Acting Lieutenant-Governor:

'He is generally under the influence of drink, smuggled in I am afraid from the Southern Provinces. It is impossible to discuss anything with him. He simply sits there looking like an ox, and has not the haziest notion of the responsibilities of his position which he looks upon only as a means of extorting money, girls, etc.

'He has reduced the Emirate which was in a comparatively high state of efficiency to which the late Emir brought it, to a state almost of anarchy.'[54]

A week earlier Hamilton-Browne had also sent in a recommendation for the deposition of Kitoro Gani. His charges are worth quoting in full. Sarkin Bussa, he wrote:

'is inefficient and unreliable and is unfitted for the post of Emir of Bussa. He is continually up to "munafiki"* and his loyalty could not be relied upon in an emergency. He works against the district officer and those District Heads whose appointment were influenced by the Resident. He is in fact one of the "old school" and is I am afraid quite incapable of improvement.

II. From the time Sarkin Bussa was appointed up to the present date he has not only been a failure from an administrative point of view but he has constantly and purposely obstructed the work of European officials and hindered that of the rest of the Native Administration.

III. In the years 1903-4 Sar. Bussa succeeded in encouraging the people of Agwarra village, N'gaski District to migrate to Borgu. He informed these people that they would be free from doing carrier work and work in Government buildings if they crossed the river. By degrees he induced a number to emigrate. A short time after the matter became serious. These Kamberri refused to pay tribute to Bussa, at the same time refusing to return to N'Gaski in order to avoid work.

---

* 'Munafiki'—hypocrisy, dissembling. It was used by the Political Officers to mean 'intrigue' or 'up to his old tricks'.

THE DEPOSITION OF KITORO GANI

In the end Assistant Resident Howard was sent by Mr. Kemble, A[ctin]g. Res. Borgu, to stay amongst them until they consented to nominate a Headman and obey Sar. Bussa.

IV. To the present time an open quarrel exists between Bussa and the Chiefs of Yauri and N'Gaski caused at the time of the building of the Jebba–Zungeru Railway (Borgu being exempt from labour demand)* by Bussa sending messages to Gungawa asking them to bring drink to him and allowing these "talakawa" to sit down and drink with him. Having ingratiated himself with these means he invited them to immigrate to Borgu by all sorts of rash promises.

The result was that a wave of immigration swept from Yauri, N'Gaski and the Islands to Borgu. Two islands north of Yelwa became depopulated. Res[ident] Kon[tagora] ordered Bussa to publicly apologise to N'Gaski and Yauri on account of his actions. For a time he reformed but has since recommenced his intriguing.

V. About two years ago while Sar. Bussa was in the Kunji District he got drunk with the people of Agwarra. He then advised the people to shoot the D.H. Mr. Boyd arrived unexpectedly in the district and the disaster was averted.

VI. While in Yelwa, this time, the S. Bussa was reprimanded by Mr. Dwyer for his drunken habits. He promised that he would put a stop to the manufacture of native liquor. On his way back to Bussa he called for a drink at every village he came to. Mr. Dwyer reports that he is drunk every night and very nearly every day.

VII. He has been dealt with very leniently, although a few years ago his deposition was sanctioned on the grounds of drunkenness. He was given another chance by Major Sharpe but he has made no improvement and his Sarakuna are openly ashamed of him.

VIII. Kiotedi, the present Chief's brother is as useless and drunken as the Sar. Bussa himself: he cannot therefore be considered for the position.'[56]

Hamilton-Browne completed a hat-trick by recommending the deposition of Jibrilu, the Emir of Yauri, who was inefficient and allegedly mentally incapacitated, and his replacement by Aliu, Sarkin Yamma, who had been acting for him. (See above, pp. 97–8.)

Aliu, Sarkin Yamma, was the son of Abdullahi of Jabo in Sokoto. His father died when he was still young and he was brought by his mother to Yelwa. There he lived in the house of the reigning Sarkin Yauri,

* Which was untrue.

Abdullahi Abershi. When Jibrilu succeeded Abershi as King of Yauri, Aliu not only continued to live in the palace, but was appointed Tukura in which capacity he acted as a 'confidential messenger' between the Emir and the Assistant Resident at Yelwa. It was quite normal practice for the kings of Yauri, as with the kings of Bussa, to use as their administrators people who were not indigenous or even who were slaves. The important point is that such people did not have authority in their own right, but only from the king who appointed them. This was in contrast to administrators who came from the royal family or from other noble families.

Aliu proved so efficient that he was given the title Sarkin Yamma in 1912 at the time of Clarke's administrative reforms and put in charge of the lands of the West (Yamma). Such a situation would have been acceptable to the King and people of Yauri only if Aliu had acted as administrator for the King in fact as well as name. It became increasingly clear that he was more the tool of Clarke than of Jibrilu, and was conspiring with Political Agent Abba to exploit his favoured position with Clarke to gain higher office. In a confidential report on Aliu, Clarke wrote in early 1915 that he had 'the respect and confidence of the whole countryside. Dan Galadima, the heir to the Emirate of Gando, has given Aliu (Sarkin Yemma) his daughter in marriage. The promotion of Sarkin Yemma would be popular locally and would have the approval of the Emirs of Sokoto and Gando.'

But as L. Blake, District Officer for Yauri, wrote in 1918, admittedly with the advantage of hindsight,

'I have no hesitation in saying that there is not a word of truth in this statement and Mr. Clarke must have been vastly ignorant of the feelings of the people of this Division when he foisted on them an outsider who had no claim to the title of Sarkin Yauri. A more unpopular appointment could not possibly have been made. As Sarkin Yemma he was disliked and feared by all and as Sarkin Yauri he has abused his powers and treated the people unjustly.'

A note on this in the margin says: 'Extract to Mr. Clarke's personal file.'[57]

It was on this basis, however, of Clarke's confidence in Aliu, Sarkin Yamma, that he made the startling recommendation that the emirates of Bussa, Kaiama and Yauri be amalgamated and placed under him. The emirates of Bussa and Kaiama would thus be abolished and their constituent districts be made districts of the proposed Greater Yauri. Hamilton-Browne, advised by Clarke, felt there would be no problem

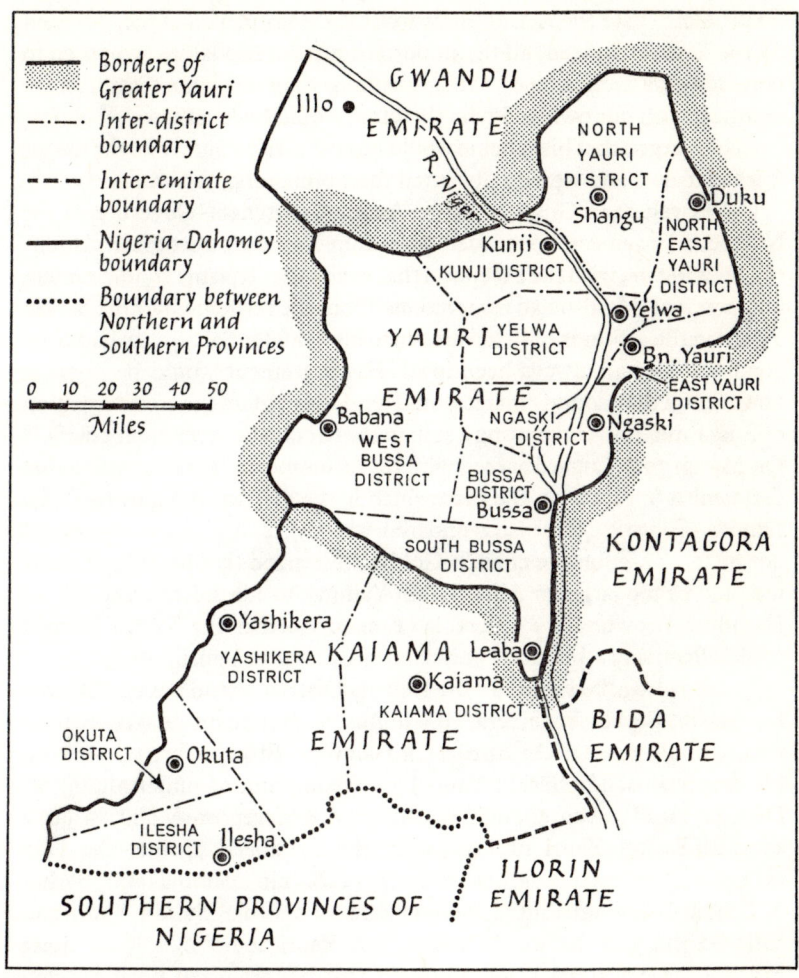

Map 7: Greater Yauri Emirate, 1915

here. The District Head of Bussa, Turaki, and the District Heads of Aliyara and Kunji were all supporters of Sarkin Yamma. He did not mention this, but it was clearly in view, that in Kaiama there would be no problem since the Acting Emir would be Mashi, a chief hand-picked by the British. Indeed, all the important district headships would go to non-Borgawa men 'who owe their positions to us and whose interests are identical with our own and who therefore would be loyal to us'.[58]

Clarke urged that his scheme would be best carried out while the troops were in Yelwa and would only entail their remaining two weeks.[59]

On March 23rd Goldsmith, the Acting Lieutenant-Governor of the Northern Provinces, forwarded Hamilton-Browne's recommendations to Lagos *in toto*, with the exception that he felt that Kaiama should remain independent. He also had reservations about the retirement of the Sarkin Yauri on the grounds of ill health, since his confidential reports had been good and he had always been loyal. His retirement would be justified however on the grounds that it would tend to facilitate the administration of Bussa and Yauri by putting a stop to the friction between their chiefs.[60] On March 30th Lugard agreed with his recommendations but asked that Goldsmith 'indicate on the map which is the district of Yauri (is it the same as Yelwa?)'. He also wondered whether Yauri and Bussa would not be too large for one chief.[61] Goldsmith replied that he did not think it would be too large for Aliu, Sarkin Yamma, to administer, but did ask Hamilton-Browne for a report, later, as to whether the Sarkin Yamma could effectively administer and control Bussa and Yauri.

Lugard also asked whether the Kaiama District would not be too large for Mashi, Sarkin Yashikera, to administer. But again he was assured that it would not be. On April 15th Hamilton-Browne further built up his case against the Sarkin Yauri by accusing him of undermining his District Heads even though in the past well reported on.[62] Clarke accused Sarkin Yauri of instigating the Kamberri against the Dan Galadima,* of planning the murder of Sarkin Yamma and Sarkin N'Gaski. Clarke attributed these actions to a stroke Sarkin Yauri had suffered the year before. 'Though Sar. Yauri sometimes looks quite rational there appears to be no doubt that his brain has been affected since his stroke and he is quite unfit to administer the Emirate . . . jealousy of his District Heads has become a mania with him.'[63]

Approval was given for the deposition of Kitoro Gani and Jimi in

* The Dan Galadima was a senior office-holder or councillor who was also a district head.

April, and the Sarkin Yauri was retired. Kaiama was placed under Yashikera, while Bussa was amalgamated with Yauri under Aliu, Sarkin Yamma, as Wakilin Sarkin Yauri.* Hamilton-Browne even proposed to abolish the name Bussa and designate the emirate simply as Yauri Emirate, retaining however metropolitan Bussa as Bussa District.⁶⁴

For Hamilton-Browne, the scheme would solve a host of problems: the insufficiency of European staff to post a political officer to Bussa; the replacement of an inefficient emir, for whom there was no apparent capable successor, by the dynamic Aliu, Sarkin Yamma of Yauri; the lack of progress in the Bussa emirate; and finally it would give room to Yauri farmers to expand across the Niger since they would no longer be stranger farmers in the Bussa emirate but merely immigrating into districts of the Greater Yauri.⁶⁵

Hamilton-Browne then put forward his detailed proposals for the administrative reorganization of Yauri and Bussa. Kitoro Gani would be settled at the village of Gulbin dan Zaki with a small sum to enable him to take up farming. He would be given £2 a month until the end of 1915 to enable him to live pending the planting and harvesting of his crops. The office of Kiwotede of Bussa, or heir apparent, would be abolished. The funds saved from the salaries of Kitoro Gani and his half-brother, the Kiwotede, would be used to increase Sarkin Yamma's salary. In the dismantled Bussa emirate, the Kunji District would remain under its Fulani district head, whose salary would be increased by £3 a month. Agwarra District would be abolished since it was populated by people from the N'Gaski district of Yauri who, Hamilton-Browne alleged, had been induced to emigrate there by false promises from the Sarkin Bussa. Bussa District would continue to be administered by Turaki, who would have his salary increased by £3 a month. Leaba District would continue to be administered by Ajia, and Wawa District would be abolished and included in Leaba. Thus the Sarkin Wawa would become subject to Ajia, whose salary would also be increased by £3 a month. West Bussa, under Aliyara, would take its chief's name, and he would similarly get a pay rise of £3 a month.⁶⁶

Hamilton-Browne, fearing that if the Sarkin Yauri were allowed to stay in retirement in Yelwa he would undermine the authority of Aliu, Sarkin Yamma, wrote to Goldsmith on April 29th that he was going to Yelwa to see things for himself. He was clearly determined that the Sarkin

* Wakilin: used in this context to mean Acting Emir of Yauri, rather than the Emir's Deputy, since Aliu actually took over from the Emir.

Yauri should be deposed rather than just retired:

'If on arrival at Yelwa I find that a criminal charge can be proved against Sar. Yauri I will proceed against him. I should not be averse to seeing a clean sweep made of the whole reigning house of Yauri. I am not satisfied that the amount of migration from districts under the headship of his relations is due entirely to "Munafiki".'[67]

When he arrived in Yelwa he was met by both Sarkin Yauri and Aliu, Wakilin Sarkin Yauri, at the Malendo river. He told Sarkin Yauri he did not want to be accompanied by him into the station and ordered him to go back. He would see him later. In his subsequent interview with him he informed him 'that owing to his attitude of continuous effort to undermine the authority of his D.Hs. by secret means and his failure to render that assistance to the District Officer which he had the right to expect . . . it became necessary to appoint a Regent and that he must be prepared to leave to the Wakili all important matters. . . . Without mincing matters I told him that both the Governor and myself attributed his actions not so much to his own intentions as to the unfortunate state of his mind caused by the disease from which he was suffering. It was a somewhat delicate subject to touch on, as his recent paralytic stroke is due to advanced syphilis.'

'I then asked him whether he had anything to say to me and beyond the one sensible remark that he was now in a better state of health he indulged in a long rambling, disconnected flow of words.'[68]

Hamilton-Browne was reprimanded by Goldsmith for using the Governor-General's name without permission in his conversation with Sarkin Yauri. But he had his way, and Jibrilu was deposed on the grounds of mental incapacity. Aliu, Sarkin Yamma, then became Emir without any hereditary claim to the title.

The proposals made by Hamilton-Browne on the advice of Clarke were now complete. Clarke was the evil genius behind the whole scheme, for Hamilton-Browne relied entirely on his advice, having never visited Bussa, Kaiama or Yelwa before he put forward his drastic recommendations. Both men were extraordinarily confident in the effectiveness of their reorganization, and without inkling of the troubles which were to flow from it. In this they were able to take confidence from Captain Waters, the Commander of the Patrol, who wrote from Yelwa on 26th March 1915:

'It is very improbable that this proposed amalgamation of the Districts named will lead to any trouble. . . .'[69]

1. Garuba, King of Wawa, 1901. *From* Le Niger *by Capitaine Lenfant, Librairie Hachette, Paris, 1903.*

2. The King of Bussa, Kisan Dogo, comes to greet Capitaine Lenfant at Malali, 1901. *From* Le Niger *by Capitaine Lenfant, Librairie Hachette, Paris, 1903.*

3. The King of Bussa, Kisan Dogo, in 'Palaver' with Capitaine Lenfant near the jetty of Malali, 1901. *From* Le Niger *by Capitaine Lenfant, Librairie Hachette, Paris, 1903.*

V · SABUKKI'S REBELLION

1. The Taking of Bussa

On 13th June 1915, Hamilton-Browne arrived at Yelwa on his first visit to that town. On the 16th traders brought news that a rebel army led by Sabukki, half-brother of the deposed Emir of Bussa, had occupied Bussa, killing the son of Aliyara and driving Turaki and other members of the Native Administration out of the town.

In the evening these reports were confirmed by Kijibrim, the Kiwotede of Bussa, also a half-brother of Kitoro Gani, who had fled from the rebels with the chiefs of Kagogi and Malali. The Kiwotede told Hamilton-Browne that Sabukki had been backed up by the towns of Shagunu, Yambushidi, Sansani and Samba-Biu. Other towns like Kagogi and Ganikassai had been forced to join him out of fear. Bussa itself had thrown in its lot with the rebels who had been invited in by the deposed Alkali's faction.[1] Hamilton-Browne immediately sent Clarke off with seventeen Northern Nigerian Police to investigate the seriousness of the report.[2] As a precaution he called in the W.A.F.F. detachment from Zuru to Yelwa. The problem was that Zuru was in a disturbed state itself, so he had to order all available police in Kontagora to go to Zuru. On top of that, there was not only a shortage of troops because of the W.A.F.F. campaign in Kamerun, but there were a number of other disturbed areas in Nigeria at this time, including Geli in Kontagora Province itself, making similar demands on the army's resources.[3] Indeed the Secretary of the Northern Provinces telegraphed Hamilton-Browne: 'You are aware that at the moment troops cannot be spared to settle local disturbances. Please proceed with utmost caution keeping that fact in view.'[4]

Hamilton-Browne, who had been persuaded that Sabukki had started his operation from Naganzi in French Borgu, asked that the French authorities in Dahomey be appealed to for co-operation and telegraphed the Resident at Nikki about the situation.

REVOLT IN BUSSA

What actually happened in Bussa did not begin to be understood by the British until Clarke arrived there with his patrol. Indeed it is not certain on which day of the month the rebellion actually took place. It seems probable that the rebels actually attacked Bussa on June 14th, though Gani of Bussa subsequently gave evidence that 'on or about 11th June he saw Bokko of Puissa leading a section of Sabukki's army at the attack on Bussa'.[5] The British were never to be sure how the rebel army was raised by Sabukki.

According to informants in Bussa, the outlawed Sabukki met clandestinely with some of his brother-princes to plot the rebellion.[6] They were all deeply worried by the presence of Turaki the slave as effective ruler of Bussa, now that Kitoro Gani was in exile. They were even more worried by his ambitious nature which they feared might deprive them of the succession. These fears were heightened by the way in which he enjoyed all the styles and perquisites of the kings of Bussa except the name. They also resented the way in which princes of the blood had been excluded from all positions of power in the former Bussa emirate. Only Kijibrim, the Kiwotede, still had any position in Bussa. The district headships of metropolitan Bussa and West Bussa were in the hands of *Wete Futani Gerede* or royal slaves—Turaki and Aliyara Bisalla respectively. Another royal slave, Sabi Zakara, was in charge of Agwarra. And while Ajia Umoru, District Head of Soutir Bussa was not a slave, he was also not a royal. Their resentment of the power of the new men was shared by the representatives of 'the owners of the land', such as the Bakarabonde, who were also deprived of their traditional position by the presence of a slave as their ruler.

As a result of his discussions with his fellow princes, Sabukki together with at least four other brothers—Layan Gaba, Sabi Kushi, Dodo Lilai Gbakashe and Garba Godo—left Bussa for Zali, in West Bussa, where they gathered up their forces. Thus the disturbed area which Clarke had patrolled, and which he thought had been pacified, became the main recruiting-ground for Sabukki's forces. There resentment of the increase in taxes and the rule of Aliyara Bisalla brought forth willing recruits. Sabukki obtained his soldiers mainly from Bargu, the name by which the present Babana and its neighbouring areas were formerly known. Other soldiers came from Shekwana, Kuta, Patengi, Vera and Kankaye. Some troops were raised in the towns of Niganzi, Thumbu and Thumbu Baba, across the border in French territory, where the Borgawa were becoming increasingly hostile to the French authorities because of heavy taxation, forced labour and compulsory recruitment for the French army. Sabukki's forces were also joined by men from the towns of Kainji, Zambara, Musina and Shebenna, Shagunu, and Garafini close to Bussa itself. Local informants say the army that marched on Bussa numbered about 1,000, though the British records of the day put it at between 500 and 700. Even if the lower figure is accepted, an army of 500 was quite substantial for an emirate numbering less than 11,000 people.[7]

The army, on foot, with a few leaders mounted, marched on Bussa armed with bows and the poisoned arrows for which Borgu soldiers were notorious. The evening before the attack they camped at Munai, three miles north of Bussa.

Turaki had had ample warning of Sabukki's impending attack on Bussa. Shortly beforehand, he had heard that Sabukki had returned from French territory and had established himself at Zali, in West Bussa. He had tried to effect his arrest, but found him entrenched there with a large following. He therefore returned to Bussa and gathered together the leading men of Bussa, including the Kiwotede, and made them swear an oath of allegiance to him. He was also joined by the District Heads of West and South Bussa, presumably because their own district headquarters were unsafe. Finally, as a last resort, according to the present Emir, he sent emissaries to negotiate with Sabukki. To this mission Sabukki gave the following conditions for peace:

(1) That Turaki should give up the District Headship of Bussa.
(2) That Turaki, as well as Aliyara, District Head of West Bussa, and Ajia, District Head of South Bussa, should leave Bussa.
(3) That the exiled Emir should be reinstated, or else another member of the royal family should be appointed to the Emirship.[8]

These conditions not unnaturally were refused, since Turaki had no authority to make such concessions without the sanction of the British administration. At Bussa, therefore, an ill-prepared Native Administration assembled to face Sabukki's forces, having sworn on a *tsafi** to support Turaki. The rebels marched on Bussa, killing the Alkali and three District Mallamai, or tax-collectors, en route at Shagunu. Although Turaki disposed of some twenty horse and had put the town on a war footing, the rebels had little difficulty in taking it, for they had the support of the majority of the townspeople, and in particular the followers of the ex-Alkali Isa, who, however, was not in Bussa at the time. Sabukki

* fetish.

headed the army when it entered the town. In his hand he held a 'fetish stick' which he said would give his followers protection in battle. According to one witness he ordered his army to loot all the goats and sheep. There was almost no resistance and Turaki and his chiefs took flight.

Sabukki now controlled the ancient capital of Bussa, and had the support of most of the surrounding towns and villages, though it was reported that Wawa remained loyal to the British-imposed Native Administration and Kaiama was half for and half against. In Kaiama Wuru Suku Suku led an armed rising against Mashi, the Acting Emir,[9] who was at the time absent in Yelwa. This same Wuru Suku Suku had raised an armed disturbance against Mora Tasude, but the late Emir had been too strong for him and had driven him out. He now seized the opportunity to bring Kaiama men out in rebellion in sympathy with Sabukki and in reaction to Clarke's recent patrol.

Sabukki's forces pursued Turaki and his supporters south past Wawa. At Malali, the Kiwotede Kijibrim managed to cross the Niger with the aid of the Chief of Malali, who accompanied him to Yelwa, together with the Chief of Kagogi whose town had come out for the rebels. At the crossing the Kiwotede saw their pursuers kill Wuru, the son of Aliyara, District Head of West Bussa, and wound another man. There they parted company with Turaki and Ajia, the District Head of South Bussa, who were trying to get to Jebba, downstream. At Leaba, Turaki and his companions took canoes, which, tradition has it, they even paddled with their hands. They were followed across the Niger by the rebels and had to hide in the bush all night. The rebels finally caught up with Ajia Umoru at Kania in Mokwa District of Niger Province. There they killed Ajia by shooting at him with arrows. When asked why they had done this by Chado, the Village Head of Kania, they told him because the 'White Man had deprived the former Sarikin Boussa of his rank and had installed a slave in his place and that the people of Boussa did not want a slave as their Sariki'.[10] Chado tried to stop them but they said they would kill him if he did. He had them followed to the Niger as far as Leaba where they crossed. Chado reported that another man called Twaki, clearly Turaki, was with Ajia, but he had escaped and was said to have gone to Zungeru. Turaki made his way to Mokwa where he was lent 3/- which he used to go on to Zungeru where he reported the rebellion to Headquarters. From there he made his way back to Kontagora. It is not clear from the records where Aliyara Bisalla was killed, but informants in Bussa say that it was at Kania near Leaba where Ajia was murdered.

Sabukki now controlled Bussa, its surrounding towns, and of course West Bussa where the revolt was raised. Only Wawa seems not to have come out on his side. Informants say this was partly because the people of Wawa considered it a purely local affair, partly because memories of the dire consequences that followed involvement in Bussa's affairs at the time of the French occupation were still vivid. Other informants, however, say that Wawa people did take part in the revolt, and that they were considered to have remained neutral only because when Clarke asked Kantama, the Chief of Wawa, whether they had assisted Sabukki, he replied no. The present Emir of Bussa states categorically that the people of Wawa refused to let Turaki and his followers enter the town when he was fleeing from the rebels.[11]

The British had thus lost control of most of the former Bussa emirate, while their situation in Kaiama was precarious.

2. The Second Borgu Patrol

On 17th June 1915 the W.A.F.F. detachment at Zuru received Hamilton-Browne's request that all available troops be sent to Bussa to rendezvous with Clarke and his Northern Nigerian Police. On the morning of the 18th at 6.30 a.m. Colour-Sergeant Kerry and 25 rank and file left for Bussa, meeting Clarke and his 17 Police at West Gaski on June 21st.[12] Meanwhile Hamilton-Browne argued the necessity of sending the troops to Bussa. 'I consider the ordering out of troops to prevent the murder of those whom we have appointed justified under the circumstances,' he told Zungeru sharply.[13] It was not until June 22nd, the eve of the entry of Clarke's force into Bussa, that Goldsmith, the Acting Lieutenant-Governor, finally relented and asked for permission from the Governor-General to send the Zuru detachment into the disturbed area. On the 23rd Lugard gave his approval, as Clarke was battling with the rebels. This approval was passed on to Hamilton-Browne the same day, with the rider that the information supplied by the Resident of Niger Province seemed to suggest that the trouble was caused by the installation of Ajia Umoru as Sarkin Bussa. Goldsmith, apparently ignorant of native affairs in Bussa, expressed the hope that this was not the case!

Hamilton-Browne replied the next day that no Sarkin Bussa had been appointed, and showed his own ignorance by saying that he did not know who Ajia Umoru could be. 'He has received no appointment under the amalgamation with Yauri.'[14] The poor Ajia was of course the recently murdered District Head of South Bussa.

Hamilton-Browne had returned to Kontagora on the 18th, reporting to Zungeru that 'no useful purpose was to be served by remaining there'. The Secretary of the Northern Provinces noted in the margin of this report: 'This fighting at Bussa was sufficiently serious for the Resident himself to proceed to the centre of the disturbance.' To cap this, Hamilton-Browne also requested permission to go on leave, to which Goldsmith replied: 'As Resident in charge of a Province you would not desire to leave your Province in an unsettled state. If Clarke is able to arrest Sabukki and other ringleaders and can report Bussa district quiet there will be no reason to further postpone your leave.'[15]

Meanwhile Clarke, at the head of the Zuru detachment and the Northern Nigerian Police and accompanied by his Political Agent, Abba, and Aliu, Sarkin Yauri, reached Bussa having crossed the Niger at Warra under cover of darkness. There they met considerable resistance. Ten of the rebels were killed before they retreated to Garafini. During the occupation of Bussa, an incident took place that was to cause Clarke no little trouble later. The W.A.F.F. detachment and the Police had considerable difficulty in tracking down the rebels in the abundance of long grass and other local cover. As they advanced on Bussa, Clarke told a mounted party of Yauri horsemen and mounted native police (who would have the advantage of height in the long grass) to try to track down Sabukki and other ringleaders. One rebel, who took cover in the grass near the town wall, was passed over unobserved and when the advancing line of soldiers was at a safe distance he got up and made a dash for the bush. He was thereupon captured by the Yauri horsemen and taken before Aliu, Sarkin Yauri, who, after questioning him, decided he was not one of the ringleaders but a *dogari** and released him. At that point, the Kiwotede Kijibrim rode up and shouted that the man was one of the leaders of the Shagunu rebels who had killed the Alkali of Bussa and the Assessment Mallams. Thereupon he made a dash for the bush, and was shot, apparently by Aliu, Sarkin Yauri.[16] The dogari was apparently a brother-in-law of Sabukki. Clarke makes references to fuller accounts elsewhere, which unfortunately I have been unable to trace. In later correspondence Dwyer, as Acting Resident, said Aliu killed him. Clarke

* Native Authority policeman.

SABUKKI'S REBELLION

seems to accept this when he says, 'The affair was perfectly open and S. Yauri was simply doing his best to help me.' For the row that boiled up between Clarke and Dwyer over this, see below, p. 135 ff..

The same day Clarke pursued the rebels to Garafini where his troops were shot at with arrows by rebels on canoes in the middle of the Niger. In Garafini, as at Bussa, the British force met with considerable resistance and nine rebels were killed. In his report on the Patrol, Colour-Sergeant Kerry wrote: 'If the troops had taken a defeat the whole of Borgawa would have been up in arms, as they were all ready to take up arms.'[17] The Patrol was unable to catch any of the ringleaders and it was reported that Sabukki, Sabikushi, Mama and Sukki had fled to French Borgu. Hamilton-Browne, therefore, asked Zungeru to arrange for their extradition on the charges of murdering Woru at Bussa and conspiring to murder the Alkali of Bussa, two District Heads and three Assessment Mallamai.

From Garafini, Clarke's force marched to Wawa on the 24th. On the 25th the balance of the Patrol consisting of one corporal and three soldiers arrived in Bussa from Zuru. There they were met by a group of rebels armed with bows and arrows singing their war-cry. They killed one man, whereupon most of the people fled to the bush. This seems to have brought an end to troubles in Bussa, for Hamilton-Browne was able to report on July 1st that all was now quiet; Kiwotede had returned to Bussa and people were returning 'repentant'.

From Wawa the Patrol marched to Kaiama by way of Kali. On the 27th Clarke entered Kaiama together with Aliu, Sarkin Yauri, even though Kaiama was not under the latter's jurisdiction. Although Wuru Suku Suku had led people against Mashi, the Zaberma placeman Emir of Kaiama, the Patrol was offered no resistance, the ringleaders having fled across the border to Kishi in Southern Nigeria. Clarke ordered the Chief of Kishi to give up the rebels. He refused, writing that 'he takes no orders from Europeans but only from the Alafin of Oyo, his overlord'.[18] Campbell-Irons, acting for Hamilton-Browne, who was preparing to go on leave on July 17th, reported to Zungeru that he had wired the Commissioner at Oyo about the situation. Zungeru then requested that the Deputy Governor in Lagos ask the Commissioner in Oyo Province to detain the five men till warrants for their arrest arrived.

This shows nicely how the two groups of provinces, the Northern and Southern, though formally amalgamated, were still like two different countries. Indeed, the formalities for extraditing the rebels from the

Southern provinces to the Northern were similar to those the Northern provinces had to follow to extradite rebels from Dahomey. In both cases they could not deal direct, but only through Lagos. A minute on Clarke's report that he had written to the Chief of Kishi in Arabic to tell him to give up the rebels, reads 'This should never have been done—the letter should have been written to the Commissioner Oyo.' Clarke also reported that a large number of people had crossed the border, where, he pointed out, there was no taxation. This was confirmed by the Alafin of Oyo, who reported 1,000 Bariba from Kaiama crossing to Kishi, and that there were probably more coming.[19] This again pointed to a difference between the Northern and Southern provinces, though Lugard was to introduce taxation in Oyo in 1918. Clarke also added that if these fugitives returned to Kaiama he would overlook their share in the recent disturbances, on which Hamilton-Browne minuted just before he went on leave, 'Mr. Clarke has no powers to overlook any offences, the Resident himself has no such powers.'[20] Clarke stayed in Kaiama with his patrol from June 29th to July 20th waiting for the Oyo authorities to hand over the ringleaders of the Kaiama disturbances. Eventually an arrangement was made for him to meet with the Commissioner of Oyo on the boundary near Kishi, as though they were representatives from two different states.

On July 21st the Patrol moved off in daily marches to Gberia, Mori, Moshi and Ilesha, where they spent two days before crossing to Igboho in the Southern provinces on the 27th. The following day Clarke met the Acting Commissioner of Oyo Province, equivalent in rank to a Resident of a Northern province, and together they marched to Kishi. There on July 29th six ringleaders of the Kaiama disturbances were handed over to Clarke by the Acting Commissioner.

On the 31st the Patrol returned through Gberia to Kaiama which they reached on August 1st. On the 3rd they marched northwards through Bera, Kali, Wawa, West Gaski and Jingima to Yelwa which they reached on August 9th. This marked the end of the 2nd Borgu patrol, which was disbanded, the soldiers returning to their base at Zuru. There had been no casualties among the troops, for, as Colour-Sergeant Kerry put it, the arrows of the Borgawa were 'extraordinarily devoid of aim'.[21] Only 150 rounds of ammunition were expended, and no stock was captured.

Sabukki and the other ringleaders of the rising were still at large and were believed to have crossed into French Borgu. In Dahomey, the authorities were sufficiently concerned by the reports of the rising sent them by Hamilton-Browne to take precautions along the frontiers against any repercussions among the Dahomeyan Borgawa.[22] Governor Noufflard of Dahomey instructed the Commandant de Cercle of Borgou to do his best to prevent the rebels crossing the frontier. A recruitment campaign was immediately announced along the frontier in the Naganzi area, to discourage rebels crossing. The French intelligence service reported that the main cause of trouble in the Kaiama area was the installation of Mashi as Emir of Kaiama. In the Bussa area, their sources informed them, the cause of the rising was the sequestration and severe punishment of several 'Chefs de Canton'. The situation in the Cercle of Borgou remained good and 'notre politique d'ailleurs ne cesse de la maintenir en cet état sinon l'améliorer'.[23]

On July 14th Ferlus, the Commandant de Cercle of Borgou, received a message from Clarke at Kaiama saying that he and his patrol were at Ferlus's disposition should he consider a common action necessary. Ferlus replied that one of the rebel leaders had been seen with seven men and four women at Naganzi in French territory where he had relatives. This had been about a month before, and they had left in the direction of Cabe, some 30 miles east of Naganzi.

Ferlus reported to his Governor that the Commandant at Nikki reported that British troops had fired on rebels at Chakanda, near the Dahomeyan frontier, killing one, wounding two and taking two as hostages. There is nothing in Colour-Sergeant Kerry's report concerning this action, though the Acting Resident of Kontagora reported it to Zungeru on August 19th, recommending the lance-corporal who led the attack, Hassan Sankara, for promotion.[24] Furthermore, the Commandant at Nikki reported that some thirty refugees from British Borgu had crossed the border to the village of Alafirarou.[25] On July 16th Géay, the Commandant de Cercle of Kandi, telegraphed the Governor confidently that the Bussa affair was purely local in character 'and can have no influence on the French population'.[26] Earlier, the Governor had gained permission from the Acting Governor-General at Dakar (Clozel) to send troops, if necessary, to stop rebels in the Naganzi area crossing over the frontier or push them back. By July 29th, he reported that though some rebels did cross there was no need to use the troops. Now, contrary to Géay, the Governor admitted that the rebellion in British Borgu could have repercussions on the French Borgawa, and it was for this reason he had not used troops, 'for fear of provoking the mistrust of our own troops'.[27] The French authorities succeeded in capturing only one of the rebel leaders, one Bogo-Yaru, who was seized by the Chief of Segbona and imprisoned at Kandi. After protracted procedural negotiations via Lagos and Porto Novo for his extradition, witnesses and policemen were allowed to cross the frontier to identify him and take him back to Nigeria for trial, where he was given two years in jail.

The French authorities found the Bussa rebellion and its apparent lack of repercussion on their Borgawa subjects the occasion for smug self-congratulation, which rings hollow in view of the large-scale revolt which was to occur in Dahomeyan Borgu a year later.

'Cette querelle', Noufflard reported to the Governor-General in Dakar, 'laisse parfaitement indifférentes les populations des cercles du Moyen-Niger et de Borgou. Elle n'affecte aucun caractère religieux et je dirai même qu'elle a fait ressortir, aux yeux du roi de Nikki et du Chef du canton Segbana notamment, la supériorité, dans ce cas en particulier, de nos méthodes de politique indigène.'[28]

In Nigerian Borgu, the British administration now had to try to pick up the pieces of the rebellion.

3. The Aftermath

Not surprisingly, the administration of the Northern provinces looked for someone to blame for the rebellion. Goldsmith, the Acting Lieutenant-Governor, wrote a minute to the Secretary of the Northern Provinces on 12th July 1915:

 'This outbreak has come as a surprise to me. Early in the year the Resident received approval for a military patrol which escorted the Political Officer and toured the District for a month. The Resident then reported the district as quiet and no mention as far as I can remember was made of Sabukki or his intriguing. [This is correct— M.C.] No sooner have the troops left the Province than the Resident reports the return of Sabukki and serious fighting. From the Resident's telegram dated 1.7.15 he states that "this rising is not of recent growth but has been fomented for years." If this is so Res. Kontagora appears to have been kept in ignorance of what was going on in his Province? I do not remember any report being received in Headquarters which hinted at Sabukki's [illegible] or attached any importance to influence he exercises in the Bussa district as likely to lead to serious trouble.

'Maj. Hamilton Browne has now been in the Kontagora Prov. for 3 years and this disturbance leads me to think that he has not kept in as close touch with the N.A. in Bussa as he might have done. I should be glad to know if he has yet toured the disturbed district and visited Bussa, and if so, what was the period and object of his tour and what were the results achieved.'[29]

Later, however, he was to eat his words when he minuted on Hamilton-Browne's annual report for 1915.

'I anticipated that the change might produce unrest but the Native Administration of these districts *was about as bad as it could be and action was called for*. It would be a confession of weakness on the part of Government to avoid necessary reforms on account of anticipated disturbance. It is seldom that administrative changes of this nature can be introduced without creating some discontent. The new Emirate requires the close attention of the Resident and all the support and guidance he can give to Sar. Yauri.'[30]

Hamilton-Browne, himself, justified his actions:

'Progress and development were impossible under the old regime, in fact practically none had been made; added to which the staff of the Province does not admit of a Political Officer in the old Borgu Province. Also there is not one of the ruling family who is not tainted with the disqualification of drunkenness, with the possible exception of the ex-Emir's son at School at Birnin Kebbi.

'It might have been feasible to have put him in mind had it been possible to find able advisers during his minority but none were forthcoming and so I had reason for recommending the amalgamation of Yauri and Bussa.

'That this change has led to disturbance cannot be refuted but I am convinced that it will make for ultimate progress provided the authority of Yauri is backed up by us.'[31]

This firm resolve was abandoned during the early months of 1916. With Sabukki at large there was still the danger of further trouble. Hamilton-Browne had firmly predicted: 'His public execution in Bussa will put an end once and for all to any possibility of a recrudescence of this trouble.'[32] But efforts to track him down were in vain. Despite Hamilton-Browne's pleas for additional political staff, none was available because of the exigencies of the War. Bussa and Kaiama had to be administered at a distance from Yelwa. So, if the people were not to be provoked again, some compromise would be necessary. To ensure closer supervision of Kaiama, Hamilton-Browne even proposed that it be included in Ilorin Province.[33]

Furthermore, the Bussa districts had lost two out of their three District Heads in the rebellion. Only Turaki, hated by the people, remained.

The administration started to try to discover in depth what the causes of the revolt were. Their ignorance of the state of affairs in Borgu at the time it happened is highlighted by Goldsmith's criticisms of Hamilton-Browne who, in 1913, had written to Zungeru for permission to remain as Resident of Kontagora Province: 'Apart from private considerations, I have become deeply interested in the development of this Province and am engaged in reassessment work from which I anticipate considerable results.'[34] The results were now well known. The causes of the rebellion, of which Hamilton-Browne's ignorant administration was one, were less clear. In retrospect the administration came to see them as falling into a number of categories, which we will take one by one.

(a) *The administrative reorganization of Bussa*

It is clear that even the abolition of the Kofa system and the division of Bussa into districts, prior to its subjection to Yauri, had not been popular, especially as it was associated with more efficient tax collection and a higher incidence. The princes of Bussa clearly resented the power given to Turaki, Aliyara and Ajia as district heads. This resentment was of course increased to boiling-point when Kitoro Gani was deposed and, as far as Bussa was concerned, power was concentrated in the hands of Turaki in metropolitan Bussa, Aliyara in West Bussa and Ajia in South Bussa. None of these was a native of Borgu, and two of them, Turaki and Aliyara, were slaves, whose rule was acceptable if they were agents of Sarkin Bussa but not as district heads in their own right subject only to Yauri, a foreign ruler.

(b) *The deposition of Kitoro Gani*

For the British, Kitoro Gani was an incompetent drunkard, and even after the rebellion they dismissed the idea that his deposition was a cause. Fergus Dwyer, Acting Resident of Kontagora, wrote categorically in 1916: 'The deposing of the Emir was not the cause of the disturbance.'[35] But given the difficulties the Kiwotede Jibrim had in ruling as Emir, even though he was heir apparent, after the dismissal of Turaki, and given the popularity of the decision to restore Kitoro Gani in 1924, it seems clear that his deposition was one of the causes of the revolt. In the first place, though Kitoro Gani was far from being universally popular with his people, there was no concept of deposition of Bussa kings in pre-colonial times. Secondly, he had been supplanted by a slave, Turaki, and then by Kijibrim, who though he was heir apparent was disliked by the people for his support of Turaki. If another brother had been chosen, the situation might have been accepted by the people. Thirdly, the religious significance of the kings of Bussa for their people must not be forgotten They had a divine status and the present Emir of Borgu records that when Kitoro Gani went into exile not only did many people follow him, both to Dukku and later Ilorin, but that a policeman who accompanied him died as a result of mocking him. On their way to Dukku, when Kitoro Gani knelt by a stream to drink, one of his escorts laughed and said how shameful it was that the King of Bussa should be seen publicly drinking without assistance. Immediately the policeman's horse went wild and threw him so that he broke his neck and died on the spot.[36]

(c) The subjection of Bussa to Yauri and the loss of Bussa lands
The subjection of Bussa by the British to Yauri was, in view of the rancour existing between them at the end of the nineteenth century, tactless, to say the least. It was bad enough being placed under a neighbouring state, which some Bussa traditions hold had in early times been subordinate to it. (See page 37.) It was worse still being subjected to the interloper Aliu, Sarkin Yauri. From the point of view of the Bussawa, the administrative reorganization that took place in 1915 had been largely the result of scheming by Aliu, with the connivance of Turaki and Aliyara, to deprive them of their lands. In this fear they were justified, for large tracts of their land were integrated into Yauri districts and lost to them for ever. The administration seemed at this time to be quite insensitive to Bussa's concern over its land. Even after the rebellion, the Acting Resident of Kontagora, Fergus Dwyer, who otherwise was very critical of the policies pursued by Clarke and Hamilton-Browne, advocated the transfer of Bussa islands to Zugurma* in the Kontagora Emirate. On 24th December 1915 he recommended that all those islands south of Bussa which had been occupied by Zugurma farmers, even though they had belonged to Bussa in pre-colonial times, be placed administratively under Zugurma since this would prevent 'the cropping up annually of trouble through the Native Administration of Boussa (now Yauri)

* Zugurma is sometimes written Zuguma.

sending Tribute Collectors into Zugurma District of Kontagora for the purpose of collecting Tribute from the island people who are farming Zugurma land'.[37] He did however express reservations about the island of Potashi because it was clearly a dependency of Wawa, but even then, with the exception of the very old, its people all farmed in Zugurma. When Hamilton-Browne returned from leave he was asked to comment on these proposals. He recommended that Potashi, the largest of the islands, should be handed over to Zugurma, but he was not prepared 'at present to recommend that all the islands south of Bussa should be included in the Kontagora Emirate'.[38] Lugard approved the transfer of Potashi to Zugurma in April 1916.

(d) *Aliu, Sarkin Yauri*

Clearly subjection to Aliu, Sarkin Yauri, was a major grievance of the Bussawa. He was high-handed in his dealings with his Bussa subjects and even went so far as to remove the symbols of authority of the Bussa kings, the Gangan Kisra and the state trumpets, to Yauri. He took an active role in the Patrol sent to suppress the rebellion. He even entered Kaiama with the Patrol, despite the fact that he had no jurisdiction over this emirate. Indeed Temple, Lieutenant-Governor of the Northern Provinces, in November wired Dwyer to ask: 'Is Kayama in any way under Sar. Yauri and if not why did the latter accompany the patrol to Kayama.'[39] Dwyer replied that Kaiama was an independent emirate and that Aliu had had no concern with the work of the Patrol.[40] This did not satisfy Temple who asked again why Aliu had accompanied it to Kaiama.[41] Asked for an explanation, Clarke did not mention that Aliu had entered Kaiama with him, but merely said he had taken Aliu along with him to re-assess Wawa District whilst he was in Kaiama. Backing up Aliu, Clarke wrote: 'His services were invaluable and the reorganisation after the disturbances does him great credit.'[42] This did not satisfy Dwyer, who had little time for Clarke, and he wired him for a full explanation of Aliu's presence in Kaiama. Clarke finally replied on December 6th: 'I have the honour to inform you that I took Sarkin Yauri on to Kaiama as a precautionary measure until I ascertained the movements of Sabukki's band. As soon as Sabukki had been located he returned to Wawa and carried on with the re-assessment.'[43] On this Temple commented: 'It was most unwise of Mr. Clarke to take the Sarikin Yauri to Kaiama.'[44]

Dwyer now wrote to Temple that he personally would never have

SABUKKI'S REBELLION

recommended the promotion of Aliu to the position of Sarkin Yauri had he been in Kontagora Province at the time. He now took the occasion to write a damning report on Aliu and, by implication, Clarke who had pushed him into his present position. Dwyer told Temple that he had first met Aliu when he was a mere boy in 1903.[45] At that time he was acting as Zagi (one who runs in front of a very important person when mounted on a horse) to Abershi, Sarkin Yauri. Dwyer had been surprised to see a light-skinned Fulani rather than an indigenous Yauri occupying the position of Zagi to the King of Yauri. This prompted him to make enquiries about Aliu. He wrote:

'The boy was brought to Yelwa by his father and mother; they having been, practically speaking, driven out of their village, in the Sokoto Province, on account of the fact that the child, when born, had a malformation of the right side of the face and that the child was looked upon at that time as "maita" [one cursed by witchcraft, or a witch]. On their arrival at Yelwa the father and mother had no food or money and were destitute. The old Chief was told the story and he, through charity, gave the man and woman a hut in his compound to live in, and supplied them with food. Shortly afterwards the father left Yelwa on some pretext and has never been seen or heard of since.

'The mother and the baby were permitted by the Chief to continue to live in his compound and received, as charity, food and house room. When the baby had become old enough to run about, he was the butt of the town, as far as the children were concerned, and was soundly slapped by the small boys and girls every time he came outside the compound. Later after some years (1903) the Chief of Yauri died and the man who has recently been deposed, was appointed.

'The newly appointed Chief, after a year or so, appointed or promoted the man Aliu from Zeggi to that of Tukuran Gari. He also became Jangali Collector on account of his Fulani extraction. From Tukura he was made Sarikin Yamma and recently he has supplanted the Chief of Yauri by being promoted Sarikin Yauri, and has been given all the Sarikin Yauri's horses, property, house and title.

'From what I personally know of the man he has, through Mr. Clarke, District Officer Yauri, deliberately schemed to obtain his present position, making claims to Borgu Lands, for Yauri, all of which claims were absolutely unfounded.

'You will notice that Mr. Clarke states in his letter dated 6.12.15

that "as a precautionary measure". I can well understand this. Yauri and Borgu for a number of years, have been open enemies. . . .'

Dwyer continued, incorrectly, that Yauri had been a dependency of Kontagora under British rule. This had in fact not been the case; indeed for a brief period of three months Abershi, Sarkin Yauri, was made Emir of Kontagora by Lugard.

'In 1914 [Dwyer continued] when I returned to Kontagora I found that Yauri was independent of Kontagora, and that Sarikin Yamma of Yauri (now Sarikin Yauri) had crossed the Borgu-Yauri Boundary (the Niger) and had made a road to Puissa on the Western Boundary of Bussa's Territory, and had been encouraging the Gungawa (islanders) to farm Bussa land. I explained to Resident Kontagora, Major Blakeney, that such a state of affairs was out of the question and that trouble was certain to be the result if the Yauri Native Administration were not kept within their own territory.

'When I went to Yelwa to take over charge of that Division in 1914, I discovered that Mr. Clarke, District Officer, had encouraged the crossing of the Boundary Bussa-Yauri, and that Yauri Tribute Collectors had been in the habit of entering Bussa territory for the purpose of Tribute Collection. Matters had gone so far that it was next to impossible to separate the farms and farmers. The crossing of the Boundary was due chiefly to the man Aliu Sarikin Yamma, now Sarikin Yauri; he having put forward to Mr. Clarke unfounded claims to the right of Yauri subjects to farm Bussa lands.

'In 1915 I went on leave, and on my return in 1915 learned that Bussa had been deposed (and rightly so) and that Yauri had also been deposed in one sense and not in another; that Aliu Sarikin Yamma, the one time Zeggi to Sarikin Yauri, had not only been promoted to the title of Sarikin Yauri, but had been placed in charge of Bussa Territory which included the islands as far south as Badjibo.

'I could, at once, knowing the history of the people concerned, understand the cause of the recent disturbance and more thoroughly do so when I learned that Turaki, a slave to Ex-Emir Bussa, and under him a District Head, had been selected as Yauri's representative at Bussa. Of course, the relations of the Ex-Emir Bussa objected to their Emirate being included in that of Yauri and also objected to the presence of Turaki at Bussa as the representative of Yauri.

'The attack on Bussa by Sabukki and the murder of the several people and the subsequent Patrol and present unrest in Bussa is the

The nephew of the King of Bussa and his entourage before the Graphophone, 1901. This is the nephew whom Capitaine Lenfant describes as the heir to Kisan Dogo. It is therefore possibly a photograph of Kitoro Gani. *From* Le Niger *by Capitaine Lenfant, Librairie Hachette, Paris, 1903.*

Repairing the Bussa Residency, 1906. *From* A Resident's Wife in Nigeria, *by Constance Larymore, George Routledge and Sons, London, 1908.*

6. The Emir Jibrim, photographed in February/March 1922. *From* The Voyage of the Dayspring *by A. C. G. Hastings, John Lane, The Bodley Head Ltd., London, 1926.*

direct result of Aliu the Sarikin Yauri's scheming and false information given by him to Mr. Clarke, District Officer in charge of the Yauri Division. . . .'

Dwyer concluded his remarkable indictment of Clarke:

'As I have said I can well understand Mr. Clarke's words "As a precautionary measure". He now understands, I feel certain, the mistakes which the man Aliu (Sarikin Yauri) has led him into, and understands that this man's life is not worth very much if he attempted to visit the Bussa territory unaccompanied by an European.

'If Aliu had not been given this position, . . . instead of a state of chaos, Bussa and Kaiama would have been comparatively prosperous and peaceful.'

Dwyer ended his letter with a list of acquisitions made by Aliu at the expense of the deposed Kitoro Gani, and reported that he had applied for Clarke to go on leave and was placing Diggle in charge of Yauri. Despite his misconception about the relationship between Yauri and the Emir of Kontagora, his cogent analysis of the problems caused by the elevation of Aliu to the position of Chief of a greater Yauri should have ensured the immediate separation of Bussa from Yauri and the deposition of Aliu himself. But, for the time being, the administration in Zungeru did nothing.

(e) Unsympathetic administration

At a more general level, the early docility of the Borgawa had been tried sorely by the British administration, as we have tried to suggest. Periods of minimal interference by district officers would be succeeded by short bursts of interventionist administration culminating in that of Clarke whose wholesale depositions of *sarakuna* contributed greatly to the discontent in Borgu and help to explain the support Sabukki obtained in Kaiama, even though this was not incorporated into Greater Yauri. Generally the political administration showed little understanding of the Borgawa and tried to make a northern emirate-style administration work in a state of very different political traditions. At one level Kitoro Gani was considered by the British as having the status of a first-class emir; at another he was a chief treated with contempt, since he did not have the powers to carry out what the British wanted. Furthermore he resented his constantly diminishing position, with land being taken away, and with, in his eyes, a comparative upstart, Kaiama, being placed on a footing equal to his own.

(f) Taxation

It is clear that the increase in incidence of taxation and the stricter enforcement of it did much to exacerbate unrest in Borgu, both in Bussa and Kaiama. Significantly the District Mallamai (tax assessors) were a prime target of the rebels.

All these factors combined to give Sabukki, a prince who had the right to succeed to the throne, the support he needed for his rebellion. It seems clear that his rebellion was mainly focussed on ridding Bussa of an unpopular native administration, albeit a British-imposed one. There were, of course, no immediate representatives of the British, either in the guise of a political officer, or of Police or W.A.F.F. soldiers, for him to attack. I can as yet find no evidence that a motive of the rebels was a desire to return to independence—which was, however, a theme in the rebellion of the Dahomeyan Borgawa the following year.

Over the succeeding decade the British administration were to admit tacitly or overtly that the above were the causes of the rebellion and took steps to rectify a situation which, they were to admit, was largely of their creation.

Clearly, to govern Bussa effectively, the demands explicit and implicit of the rebels had to be met: these were

(1) The removal of the slave District Head, Turaki.
(2) The restoration of Bussa's integrity, and administrative separation from Yauri.
(3) The demand that Bussa's lost lands be restored.
(4) The restoration of Kitoro Gani, or at least the placing of a prince of Bussa on the throne.

Implicit in all these was the need for a change in the general approach of the British administration. High-handed methods, particularly those of Clarke, had shown themselves ineffective. The need now was for sympathetic administrators, with a light-handed touch.

It took more than a decade for the British to meet these demands. As late as 1926 the Hon. H. B. Hermon-Hodge, Resident of Ilorin Province, could still write of Borgu:

'I do indeed feel that some reparation should be made to Bussa for the sufferings and sacrifices which have reduced a proud and comparatively populous race to a soured and sporadic handful.'[46]

VI · TWO MURDERS IN BUSSA

1. Turaki's Revenge

Turaki returned to Bussa from Zungeru and resumed his functions as district head. Having survived the rebel attack, his position was greatly enhanced by the swift punishment visited on the opposition by Clarke's patrol. He was also very bitter against the rebels, who had not only tried to remove him, but had killed his brother, Dowdu Bindiga, in the process. From his new position of strength, protected by his own Native Authority Police and two Northern Nigerian Police left him by Clarke, he determined to take revenge on any rebel involved in the deaths of his friends and officials who came his way. And in so doing he overplayed his hand.

Some time soon after his return to Bussa, one Gani of Kagogi came to Bussa to sell honey and tobacco to obtain cash to pay his taxes. He had been sent to Mallam Isa, the ex-Alkali of Bussa, to arrange the sale. Soon after he left Mallam Isa's house he was spotted by Turaki, who thought he was one of Sabukki's followers. Although Turaki's first instinct, so he later said, was to leave him alone, his district mallam, Matakure, advised him to seize him. So he ordered two dogarai, Mohamma and Bisheru Gamzo, to catch him and take him away so that he could question him about Sabukki. By this time a large crowd had gathered, including Mallam Isa and Yakubu, the ex-Galadima of Yauri. Both of them told Turaki to release the prisoner, since he had had nothing to do with Sabukki. While Turaki was arguing with Mallam Isa and Yakubu, the village head of Kagogi, Zakara, ordered the two dogarai to catch Gani of Kagogi and tie him up and place him in the sun and let him die.[2] This the two dogarai did with a vengeance, beating him all the way to their house where they kept him prisoner.

About noon, when Turaki's drummer Gemmu went to the dogarai's house he found the victim lying on the ground in the sun with his feet so tied that his toes nearly touched the front of his shins. His arms were tied behind his back at his elbows while his hands were tied by their wrists in front of his body. Gemmu, thinking it very likely that the man might die in this condition, went to Yakubu, the ex-Galadima of Yauri, to tell him what was happening. Yakubu then sent his mijindadi,* Garuba, to order the man's bonds to be loosened. When Garuba, who was accompanied by Gemmu, got to the dogarai's compound, he found that the victim's arms from his shoulders to his wrists were nothing but raw flesh. He was also covered with dust as a result of rolling about in agony in the sun. Garuba ordered the dogari Mohamma to loosen the victim's bonds, but he refused to do so until he had finished eating. When, eventually, Gani was released from his bonds at about 4 p.m. he was not surprisingly unable to stand or speak. The cords with which he was bound had cut deeply into his flesh. When the wife of the owner of the house brought water for him in a calabash, he was unable to drink it. Turaki's drummer, Gemmu, then helped the victim into the shade and held the water to his lips.

At this juncture, Turaki entered the compound and seeing the victim told Garuba and Gemmu: 'I will now question him about the whereabouts of Sabukki. Perhaps he will now speak.' Turaki then cross-examined him, after which he left.[3]

By evening the victim, who had not been tied up again, was still too weak to stand, and his joints were cut and badly swollen. It was in this state, lying outside Dogari Mohamma's hut, that the owner of the compound, also called Gani, found the victim on his return from his farm. The next morning, as Gani, the landlord, was preparing to go to the farm again, Mohamma cried out that the prisoner had escaped. Gani saw signs of blood where the victim had lain the night before, but no signs of his escape route.

In the evening, about 6 o'clock, Gani of Kagogi was found by a friend, the Badaburude (Badabuli), the official in charge of burials at Bussa, lying on the road to Zale, about 400 yards from the dogarai's lodgings. At first he thought him dead, but then saw that he was breathing. Gani then asked him how to get to Munai, but the Badaburude was too frightened that he might be taken as a friend of Gani to reply.[4] The Badaburude returned to his house but said nothing because of his fear of the consequences. However, the next morning when he saw Mallam Isa searching for the body, he pointed to the place where he had found Gani of Kagogi,

* Mijindadi (Majidadi) = Chamberlain, Head of the Household.

TWO MURDERS IN BUSSA

but was too afraid to go with Mallam Isa to see if it was still there. When Mallam Isa reached the spot Gani was no longer there.

That evening, Mazandawa, another friend of Gani, found him near a marsh on the Zale road. He was by now in a terrible state. Gangrene had set in and his flesh stank. His legs, arms and face appeared to have been burnt. He was bleeding and was covered with wood ash which some of the witnesses said had been rubbed into his wounds by Zakara, Sarkin Kagogi. He was able, however, to tell Mazandawa that he had been dragged there, though when he was asked who had dragged him he did not answer. Mazandawa shouldered Gani of Kagogi to his canoe, and paddled him up river to Shagunu where he handed him over to Afwoingi, a native doctor, for treatment. By now his condition was clearly far too serious for any cure, and even before Afwoingi had returned from the bush with herbs with which to treat him, he was dead. The next morning the villagers buried him. Afwoingi did not report his death to Turaki, because he was too afraid of him. Nor did Mazandawa report the matter. According to him, Turaki had already shot one man but nothing had happened, so he thought Turaki had the power to do such things. Later, however, he told the Court, 'At Igwarra (Mr. Clarke) the Yelwa whiteman called me and asked me about Genni's death. I told (Mr. Clarke) the whiteman all about the death of Genni. He said he would see about the matter. When Mr. Clarke asked Turaki did he kill Genni, Turaki said I was a liar. That the man had escaped from custody.'

News of the death however spread quickly through the fear-ridden and deeply divided town. Aliu, Sarkin Yauri, said that he had heard about the death from the ex-Galadima, and had reported it to Mr. Clarke. This was presumably the source of the information which had prompted Clarke to question Mazandawa. But he did nothing about it, and Turaki and the others involved in Gani of Kagogi's death remained free.

Not long after this cruel murder, a woman was heard by Mallam Isa late one evening shouting that Turaki had caught a man and was going to kill him. He went outside his house to see what was going on and met Ajia, Turaki's younger brother, who told him that his brother wanted to see him. He hurried to Turaki's compound where he found a heated discussion taking place between Turaki, Zakara, Sarkin Kagogi and Imoru, a Bussa man. Lying at their feet was a prisoner, tied with a rope, whom Zakara was kicking and beating with his fist.

Earlier that day Turaki had caught the man, Gani of Wawa, who, he had been informed by Mashi, the Sarkin Kaiama, had been seen wearing the gowns and trousers of the murdered District Head of South Bussa. Imoru was pleading to no avail that they should not kill Gani of Wawa but send him to Yelwa to Mr. Clarke. Zakara then turned on him and accused him of treachery and supporting the opposition to Turaki. In Mallam Isa's presence Turaki shouted out that he was going to kill Gani of Wawa because he had murdered Ajia, the District Head of South Bussa, and his own brother, Dowdu Bindiga. Other important men, summoned by Turaki, arrived, among them the Liman of Bussa and Kissoin, a brother of Kitoro Gani. Both of them protested against Turaki's decision to kill Gani of Wawa and urged that he be sent to Yelwa. But Turaki would not listen to them. The Liman then asked Matakure, Turaki's district mallam, what the orders from Yelwa were. Matakure replied that Aliu, Sarkin Yauri, had told Turaki that if Gani of Wawa were caught he should be killed. Turaki confirmed that this was so, both to the Liman at the time and during his trial.[5] He even went so far as to say that both Aliu and Clarke had given him a list of rebels who were to be shot on sight. Aliu denied this at the trial. Clarke was on leave in England so he could not be questioned on this allegation.

While these heated exchanges between Turaki and the leading men of Bussa were taking place, Zakara, the Sarkin Kagogi, was beating the prisoner with such energy that his hand was too sore to use for over a month.

Turaki, disregarding all contrary advice, called upon the two policemen left him by Clarke, Mainassara Argungu (no. 2806) and Daudu Darbai (no. 3852), to bring their rifles and shoot the prisoner. He was taken away by Zakara, followed by the policemen with their rifles. The crowd heard two shots in succession, after which Zakara returned to announce his death. Turaki then turned to the crowd and told them: 'You see what has happened. Anyone who fights with me I have the power to kill them.' The crowd, most of whom were very angry at what Turaki had done, but too afraid to react, then dispersed.

In the morning the naked corpse was seen by Mallam Isa lying in the place of execution, not far from the old Residency. That day, on the instructions of the Beresumi, a relative of Gani of Kagogi, who had been present when Turaki ordered the execution, the corpse was buried by the Badaburude, the official grave-digger. As he prepared the corpse for burial, he saw two bullet wounds, one through the victim's neck, one through his chest just above the heart. The next morning, according to his own evidence and that of other witnesses, Turaki instructed his district mallam, Matakure, to write and tell Abba, Clarke's political agent in Yelwa, what had happened. Matakure agreed that he had written a letter to Abba, but stated that it was not about the death of Gani of Wawa but about a present of one hundred yams for Abba and ten yams for the Mijindadi of Turaki. Abba confirmed to the Court that this was the subject of the letter. It was only later that he and Aliu, the Sarkin Yauri, received news of Gani of Kagogi's death. Both of them had reported it to Clarke, but Clarke was not in court to confirm or deny this.

First news of the death of Gani of Wawa reached Fergus Dwyer, Acting Resident of Kontagora, in October, when the two policemen who had been seconded to guard Turaki returned to Provincial Headquarters. On October 14th he wrote to Clarke for a full report on the subject.[6] Eight days later Clarke telegraphed, 'I cannot understand why Police did not report to me. They came through Yelwa, en route Kontagora.' It was not until December 9th that Clarke sent in a report on his investigation into the affair and asked that the two policemen be sent to Yelwa to give evidence. Dwyer did not send them but telegraphed that he was informed by native sources that Turaki was still at large in Bussa and that although Clarke had recently spoken to him he had not arrested him. 'This is a serious matter and I require your explanation of your action taken. The fact that the Bussa people and people of the surrounding villages ran away on the recent approach of yourself and staff does not in any way exempt Turaki from arrest and trial before your court.'[7]

This reprimand however had crossed with a telegram from Clarke saying he had completed collection of taxes with Turaki and had sent him to Yelwa to await the arrival of the two policemen. On the 14th Dwyer ordered Clarke to arrest Turaki as well as the dogarai involved in the murder of Gani of Kagogi about which he had now also heard, and send them and the witnesses to Kontagora. Clarke did not reply until December 23rd, for he had by now left for Kaiama where Dwyer's telegram eventually caught up with him. He telegraphed in reply that he had passed on Dwyer's instructions to Sarkin Yauri. Dwyer despatched another telegram that day asking where the dogarai were.

By now Dwyer had completely lost patience with Clarke. Here was an officer who was apparently delaying bringing to justice a man accused of involvement in two murders of which he appeared to have had knowledge for some time. Furthermore, Dwyer had written him at length about information he had received that, during the occupation of Bussa, Aliu, the Sarkin Yauri, had murdered a dogari, again called Gani, this time Gani of Bussa. According to Dwyer's sources of information the dogari had come out of the old Residency and prostrated before Aliu, the Sarkin Yauri, in salutation. Aliu then ordered him to stand up and walk away, whereupon he shot him in the back and killed him. This accusation, and Clarke's failure to do anything about it, together with his apparent failure to arrest Turaki, and the allegation by Turaki that Clarke had given him twenty trade guns, formed the subject of a bitter complaint by Dwyer against Clarke to the Secretary of the Northern Provinces at Zungeru. The result was that Clarke, who was due to go on leave, had to postpone it while he answered these complaints. As to the allegation against Sarkin Yauri, Clarke repeated what had actually happened during the occupation of Bussa. As to the complaints about his failure to arrest Turaki, he sent in copies of his letters and telegrams to Dwyer to show he had in fact instructed Aliu, Sarkin Yauri, to send Turaki to Kontagora.

Clarke was eventually given permission to go on leave on January 17th by the Lieutenant-Governor, but instructions were left for Major Hamilton-Browne that on his return to Kontagora from leave he was to inform him which of the two officers was telling the truth. To this Hamilton-Browne replied in February: 'The charges brought against Mr. Clarke by Ag. Resident Dwyer are very serious, nor do I like the spirit which seems to exist between these two officers.' Later he told the Lieutenant-Governor that he found it difficult to say which of them was in fact telling the truth. However as a result of it all, Clarke, by now a lieutenant-commander in the Royal Naval Reserve, was sent a mild reprimand while on leave in London, by the Secretary of the Northern Provinces, on 2nd May 1916:

'I am directed, with reference to my Conf. letter to you at Zungeru no. 183/1916 of 9th Jan. 1916, to inform you that HH the Lt. Gov. although recognising that you have done good work in Yauri District, is not satisfied that you investigated with as much care as was called for the alleged crimes referred to in my letter above mentioned.'[8]

2. The Three Trials of Turaki

Meanwhile on 20th January 1916 Fergus Dwyer had brought Turaki to trial together with Zakara, Sarkin Kagogi, and the two dogarai,

Mohamma and Bisheru Gamzo, but not the two policemen. All four were charged with the murder of Gani of Kagogi, while Turaki and Zakara were charged with the murder of Gani of Wawa. The two policemen were not charged. The trial record is exceedingly difficult to follow because evidence was given at the same time on both charges, because both victims shared the same name and were not always distinguished by their place of origin and because there was also a great deal of hearsay evidence. Despite the confusing record, Dwyer judged that it had been clearly proved that Turaki was the author of the deaths of both men. Zakara was found guilty of having contributed to the death of Gani of Kagogi and having 'concurred with' the death of Gani of Wawa. The two dogarai were found guilty of contributing to the death of Gani of Kagogi. However, because evidence was adduced that Aliu, Sarkin Yauri, had instructed Turaki to kill any rebels, Dwyer judged them all guilty of manslaughter rather than murder:

'Although Turaki must have known that the orders given him by Wakilin Serakin Yauri, if they were given, were illegal he according to Native ideas was bound to obey them. I do not consider that Turaki, Zakara, Mohamma and Bisheru are guilty of murder but that they were acting under excitement, had no personal grudge against the deceased person. That the evidence tends to prove that the Wakilin Yauri had given Turaki instructions to kill any persons arrested by him who were members of the opposition party.

'The fact that the Govt. Police were used as Executioner in the case of Gani of Wawa, makes it even more certain that Turaki in his own mind was merely carrying out what he considered to be his duty.'[9]

On January 29th, Dwyer sentenced Turaki to fifteen years imprisonment, Zakara to ten and the two dogarai to two years each.

Confirmation of sentence was withheld by the Lieutenant-Governor, on the advice of the Legal Secretary L. S. Tew, who considered that separate retrials should be ordered for each case, to avoid the many confusions of Dwyer's joint trial. Hearsay evidence should also be excluded. He did not feel there were enough grounds for bringing Aliu, Sarkin Yauri, to trial but he advised that the two policemen should be brought to justice.[10]

The retrials were held before Major Hamilton-Browne during March. In the case of Gani of Kagogi, Turaki and the two dogarai were found guilty of manslaughter while Zakara was freed since his guilt was not proven. Turaki was given ten years imprisonment, and the dogarai five each, three more than they had received from Dwyer for the same crime.

In the case of the murder of Gani of Wawa, the two Northern Nigerian Policemen, Mainassara Argungu and Daudu Darbai, were joined with Turaki and Zakara. Aliu, Sarkin Yauri, was called in evidence. Where Turaki had said nothing in his defence at the new trial for the murder of Gani of Kagogi, he openly admitted ordering the police to kill Gani of Wawa:

'I have nothing to say than that the Police had nothing to do with the killing other than carrying out my orders which I received from Mallam Matakure who got his orders from Sar. Yauri that if Gani of Wawa one of the murderers of Aliyara (District Head) was caught he was to be killed. I told the Police that I had power to kill the man Gani. At the time when Aliyara was killed the man Gani of Wawa was taking a principal part in the insurrection and while I was escaping he attempted to kill me. When I caught him afterward I said you are the man who tried to kill me and who did kill my younger brother Daudu Bindiga and I am going to take you before my compound and call the principal men, Mallam Isa, Liman, etc., and Matakure said "Kill him." Such are the orders of Sar. Yauri. The principal men remonstrated and said do not kill but take him to Yelwa but I would not listen to them as I had my orders. I told the Police to take him away and shoot him. I told Zakara to go and assist them and he did. Gani of Wawa was taken away and shot by the Police and they came back and reported that they had done so. The fault if any is mine alone, the Police are not to blame.'[11]

The two policemen however denied any involvement in the shooting.

'*Mainassara Argungu* states I did not kill Gani of Wawa we were put by Mr. Clarke's orders to protect Turaki and to go with him wherever he went—when we returned to Yelwa none of our ammunition was missing.

'*Daudu Darbai* states I did not kill Gani of Wawa, Mainassara Argungu and I were posted at Bussa to go with Turaki wherever he went. At Yelwa Mr. Clarke counted our ammunition and found none was missing.'[12]

Zakara denied having anything to do with the killing, though in his evidence he implicated the policemen.

'*Zakara* states that when Gani of Wawa was caught I was called by N'Dawawa to come to Turaki but I never went there I merely followed the Police and N'Dawawa when they were taking him to the place of execution. I heard two shots.'[13]

Mallam Matakure flatly denied that he had passed on orders from Aliu, Sarkin Yauri, to Turaki that Gani of Wawa should be killed if he were caught. Similarly, Aliu, Sarkin Yauri, denied ever giving such an order.

The only problem facing Hamilton-Browne was to prove that the police had actually shot Gani of Wawa. The difficulty was that some twenty dane-guns* had been sent to Turaki from Yelwa and it was thought that these might have been used for the murder rather than the rifles of the policemen, who claimed they had used no ammunition. Clarke had admitted in correspondence that he might have permitted the guns to be sent. Sarkin Yauri confirmed that Clarke had given him authority to send guns to Bussa but said this had been after, not before, he had received news that Gani of Wawa had been shot. Hamilton-Browne therefore obtained permission to exhume the body of Gani of Wawa. Since no doctor could be spared for the examination, it had to be carried out by Clarke's replacement at Yelwa, P. R. Diggle, who found the body in such a state of putrefaction that he had the corpse boiled, and, on examining the cleaned bones, found no sign of damage by bullets. Hamilton-Browne, however, on the evidence of the Badaburude concerning the wounds on the body accepted that they were such as could have been caused by a small-bore rifle, and that it was possible for the bullets 'to have passed through fleshy parts of the body without having come into contact with a bone'.

He concluded his summing-up:

'Of all the accused Turaki alone elected to make a statement on oath and in it he admits that it was by his orders that the Police shot Gani and Zakara assisted them—He takes the whole blame upon himself. The other persons accused were allowed to confront Turaki but none had any questions to ask which in any way might lead me to believe that Turaki was speaking anything other than the truth. Under the circumstances and after considering the evidence of all the witnesses I have no other course than to find all four guilty of murder with a recommendation to mercy by the Governor General on the ground that in the case of Turaki he may have misunderstood Sarikin Yauri's orders about the treatment of any of Sabukki's followers who were caught. That in the case of the two Police that Mr. Clarke's orders

* locally made flint-lock gun.

that they were to accompany Turaki wherever he went amounted to their being under his orders. And in the case of Zakara a village head that it was practically impossible from his code to disobey an order issued to him by his District Head.'[14]

He then found the four accused guilty of murder and pronounced: 'You will be taken from this Court to a place of Confinement and thence subject to confirmation, to a place of Execution and there be hanged by the neck till you are dead.'

The sentence, passed on 20th May 1916, was confirmed by H. S. Goldsmith, the Acting Lieutenant-Governor, on May 30th. When, however, it was forwarded to the Governor-General for confirmation by the Executive Council it went with a recommendation for mercy, on the following grounds:

'It should be remembered that Turaki, a loyal District Chief, was endeavouring to assist Government to capture Sabukki—who was the cause of a serious disturbance in the Bussa District. Turaki was overzealous and apparently sought revenge for the murder of Aliyara and Daudu Bindiga (his younger brother) and there is little doubt that he exceeded the instructions of his Paramount Chief (Sar. Yauri) but I suggest there are extenuating circumstances.

'Zakara is merely a Village Head and carried out, according to custom, the orders of Turaki, his District Chief. As regards the two PCs. who were placed under Turaki's orders by Mr. Clarke (2nd D.O.). There is a good deal to be said, on their behalf, and it was a time of great excitement in the District, and the Political Officer should, on my opinion, have given them clear instructions as to their powers and their conduct while absent from European supervision.'[15]

On 17th June 1916 the Clerk to the Executive Council wrote to inform the Lieutenant-Governor of the Northern Provinces that the Governor-General's Deputy had commuted Turaki's sentence to twelve months, and those of Zakara and the two policemen to six months apiece. In the case of the first two, the commuted sentences were to run concurrently with those imposed for the manslaughter of Gani of Kagogi.

Turaki now began his ten-year jail term and Bussa was without a district head, as also were the other two Bussa districts, West and South Bussa. It was only after he had been arrested that the fact that he had been a slave came to the attention of the authorities, when Fergus Dwyer had sent in the Kontagora Annual Report for 1915.[16] 'By what officer was a slave made a District Head?' the Secretary for the Northern

Provinces had asked on 21st January 1916.[17] To this Hamilton-Browne, just returned from leave, replied that he had approved Turaki's appointment as District Head of Bussa on Clarke's recommendation, but the fact that he was a slave was not reported. Trying to exonerate Clarke he added: 'Mr. Clarke's position must have been a difficult one, on the one hand he had inefficient members of the old regime of Bussa and on the other men who would support the new regime under Yauri. Further this man Turaki thoroughly knew the people.' On this the Lieutenant-Governor minuted 'I am not altogether satisfied with Mr. Clarke's work.'[18]

The imprisonment of Turaki, the slave administrator, removed a major grievance of the rebels. It also gave the administration a chance to reconsider the organization of the former Bussa emirate which now, in 1916, had no district heads at all, little over a year after Clarke's reforms had gone into effect.

VII · FIRST REFORMS AND A SECOND RISING

1. The Exile of Kitoro Gani

Though Turaki was not finally convicted until May 1916, he had effectively ceased to be district head when he had been called into Kontagora the previous December. Kitoro Gani, however, though deposed was still living in Dukku in the Bussa area. Soon after the rebellion, Clarke wrote to Campbell-Irons, who took over as Acting Resident when Hamilton-Browne went on leave, and asked him to arrange for the exile of Kitoro Gani to a place sufficiently distant from Yelwa. The Lieutenant-Governor of the Northern Provinces, however, declined to deport Kitoro Gani, but added that, if it could be proved that he had been implicated in the rebellion, he could be tried in the Provincial Court. Clarke had complained at the time that it would be difficult to gather evidence against the deposed emir while Sabukki his brother was still at large, especially since the principal witnesses against Sabukki's earlier disturbance had been among the first murdered in the rebellion. He considered that while Sabukki and his lieutenants were at large no one would dare come forward and give evidence against Kitoro Gani. There had also been instructions that Kitoro Gani be placed on trial in the Provincial Court for his alleged part in the rebellion, but Clarke did nothing about it. When Dwyer took over as Acting Resident, Clarke again request Kitoro Gani's deportation, but Dwyer asked him whether he had enough evidence to proceed against him. Clarke was told by Political Agent Abba that Kitoro Gani had been visited secretly by Sabukki on two or three occasions before the rebellion. However Abba said his informants, even if subpoenaed, would deny all knowledge of these visits while Sabukki was still at large. So by January 1916, when Clarke went on leave, he had no evidence whatsoever that Kitoro Gani had been involved with the rebels.[1]

FIRST REFORMS AND A SECOND RISING

The only way Kitoro Gani could be legally deported was to charge him with a crime, and the evidence for the only crime he might have committed depended on the capture of Sabukki. But, as Hamilton-Browne was to write on his return from leave, trying to capture Sabukki 'in the unlimited Borgu bush with friends in every village is not any easy thing to accomplish'.[2] A few days after writing this, Hamilton-Browne heard that Kitoro Gani had gone to Yelwa in the absence of Diggle, the Assistant District Officer. He called Kitoro Gani in to Kontagora to explain why he had left his farm without permission, to which Kitoro Gani replied that a 'man' had come and told him that the Resident had sent for him. Hamilton-Browne asked that he be removed from the province at once for disobeying orders.[3] Temple, the Lieutenant-Governor, minuted the suggestion that Lokoja be the place for deportation. Tew, the Legal Adviser, replied that he would have to be brought before the Provincial Court first and dealt with under the appropriate section of the Criminal Code.[4] But on trying to obtain the necessary evidence for Kitoro Gani's alleged act of disobedience, it now appeared that he had gone to Yelwa in good faith. The two men who had come to him with the message had been arrested and there was evidence that one of them, Kolo, had on earlier occasions extorted presents from chiefs by making similar false statements. Hamilton-Browne now wrote plaintively to the Secretary of the Northern Provinces: 'I can only state my opinion that he has been guilty of communicating with Sabukki and that his presence in the Province is a danger and a hinderance [sic] to the peaceful settlement of Boussa under Sarkin Yauri. Would the sworn statements of the District Officers to this effect as well as that of Sar. Yauri and other persons be sufficient to warrant the Court making an order?'[5]

To this suggestion the Legal Secretary replied that they would need facts, not simply opinion, so the Secretary of the Northern Provinces asked 'why not keep Ex. Sar. in Kontagora for the present?'[6] On June 21st Hamilton-Browne wrote that he was having Kitoro Gani carefully watched to see if any persons attempted to see him secretly. He thought he had a case when two Bussa men were found in Kontagora, but unfortunately for Hamilton-Browne they could give satisfactory reasons for their presence.[7]

Eventually, though I cannot trace the exact date in the records, Kitoro Gani was in fact deported to Ilorin Province without coming before the Provincial Court. What is interesting is for how long the administration was prepared to sacrifice convenience to legality. But in the end convenience triumphed, for it was clearly impossible to install a new District Head in Bussa while Kitoro Gani was in the province.

Kitoro Gani's property was divided into three parts by a specially composed court comprising the Emir of Kontagora as president, the Emir of Yauri, the principal Alkalai and Councillors of the two emirates. They ruled that two parts go to Kitoro Gani, after any claimants who could prove extortion against him had been compensated. The third part would be paid to the Native Treasury.[8] Kitoro Gani then began a long exile in Ilorin, where as we have seen he was joined by a large number of his people, despite its distance from Bussa.[9]

2. The Appointment of Kiwotede Kijibrim as Sarkin Bussa

From the time of the arrest of Turaki in December 1915 till July 1916, Bussa was without a district head. Diggle, the A.D.O. based at Yelwa, was in charge of both Greater Yauri and Kaiama which meant he could give little attention to the recently disturbed Bussa District, let alone West Bussa and South Bussa which were also without district heads. With Turaki in jail, it was possible to appoint a new district head for Bussa. But the problem was, who? Of the eligible princes, there seemed to be only two candidates. A number of them, like Sabukki, were outlaws. And the two who had not come out on Sabukki's side did not fully recommend themselves. The Kiwotede, Kijibrim, who as heir apparent should have been the obvious choice, had the virtue of being intelligent in the administration's eyes,[10] but from the point of view of the Bussa people his apparent collaboration with Turaki made him an unpopular choice. The other candidate considered by the administration was Kissoin, who was the popular choice of the people of Bussa, but was tainted with the failing of drunkenness. While Sabukki was still at large, Hamilton-Browne considered that Kijibrim's task might be difficult. If Sabukki were to be captured, however, Hamilton-Browne said, he would have no hesitation in recommending Kijibrim. Another disturbing influence would be the ex-Alkali, Mallam Isa, whom Hamilton-Browne strongly suspected of being in league with Sabukki, 'though he is far too cunning to give one loophole for deportation proceedings. In the present state of affairs no witnesses could be found to give evidence against him.'[11] As an alternative Hamilton-Browne suggested that Sarkin Yauri be allowed to appoint one of his own men as district head. However,

FIRST REFORMS AND A SECOND RISING

Hamilton-Browne seemed to have learnt something from the rebellion for he added: '. . . I would wish, if possible, to put a Borgawa over the Bussa people. I think it would be politic to, so far, concede to their wishes.'[12] On July 19th, Goldsmith the Acting Lieutenant-Governor approved the appointment of Kijibrim, and suggested that the ex-Alkali might be sent in to Zungeru, or called to Kontagora for a few days 'while Kiwotede finds his teeth in his new office'.[13] Kiwotede was thus made District Head of Bussa, and settled down to the difficult task of administering his resentful subjects, many of whom considered him a traitor and would have preferred Kissoin. Hamilton-Browne tried to make things easier for him by bringing both the ex-Alkali and Kissoin to trial, so that they could be deported. Unfortunately for Kiwotede, Diggle's hope that he could find enough evidence against them, expressed late in July, proved vain. Anyway, the newly installed Kijibrim and Aliu, Sarkin Yauri, both felt that it was best to leave them alone.[14] While Kitoro Gani was safely in exile in Ilorin, Sabukki still lurked in the bush, a threat to both Kijibrim and the administration.

3. The Revolt in French Borgu and the Second Bussa Rising of 1916

At the end of November 1916, reports came in that Sabukki was once more in the vicinity of Bussa, this time at the head of a gang of highway robbers who had pillaged a caravan en route for Sokoto in the vicinity of Gidan Lalle. Further, the District Mallam, whilst attempting to collect taxes in Gidan Lalle, Kabe and Kano was told by the people that if either the District Officer or District Head tried to force them to pay the 1916 tribute they would kill them.[15] Only £3 out of £17 6s od for which Kano had been assessed had been paid, while Kabe had paid only £7 out of the £42 16s od for which it was assessed. The District Mallam told Diggle on oath:

'In all of these towns there is considerable unrest, a rumour being prevalent that five French Europeans have been murdered near Nikki. Moreover I saw the men of these towns making arrow heads and preparing poison. At Giddan Lalle they told me that if the District Officer or Sarkin Boussa came there, they would shoot them. When I tried to obtain a man from these towns to convey a letter to Sar. Boussa all of them refused to take it. I saw Sabukki at Kano. It was only with great difficulty that we obtained food at these towns.'[16]

145

The significance he attributed to events in French Borgu was supported by his companion on the tour of the Gidan Lalle area, one Maidanda:

'Everywhere in the vicinity the people [speak] of the rising by Borgawa near Nikki and of the murder of five French Europeans. Sabukki freely moves about near Kano.'

Up to September 1916, French-occupied Borgu had been quiet. The French were tied down by revolts in Holli-Kétou and in the Atacora mountains. These revolts had been triggered off by intensive recruitment for the army, forced labour, heavy taxation, and administrative reorganizations which took little account of the people's wishes with regard to who should be their chief or with which neighbours they should be grouped for administrative purposes. In September 1916, the Commandant de Cercle of Borgou, Ferlus, was attacked whilst on tour of his Cercle at a village called Bécou. There Bio Guèra, the chief deposed by the French in 1905, had recently returned and driven out Baguène, the French nominee who had replaced him, and who had now fled to the headquarters of the Administrative Sub-Division of Bimbereke. There he asked the French administrator, Duthoit, to expel Bio Guèra from Borgu. Ferlus, however, considered that Duthoit was too inexperienced to deal with this matter, and proposed, 'with his profound knowledge of the Bariba', to deal with it himself on one of his future tours. He let matters lapse for several months. Meanwhile Duthoit had been posted and the administrative subdivision of Bimbereke was in the charge of an official interpreter, Félix Vignon. Bio Guèra asked Vignon to come to Bécou so they could discuss his problems with Baguène. Ferlus agreed to this, and Vignon went to Bécou and informed Ferlus that all was well. He proposed that a new chief, a son of Bio Guèra, considered to be loyal to the French, be installed.

Meanwhile Ferlus advised the Governor that, unless he had orders to the contrary, he would leave Parakou for Nikki and Bimbereke. The next that was heard from him was a telegram of the 21st saying that he had been attacked at Bécou. At first it was not very clear to the administration in Porto Novo what had happened, for Ferlus sent in a series of confusing and contradictory telegrams which were obviously designed to cover up his own humiliating role in what became known as the 'affaire Bécou'. Only after a mission of inspection, under Inspector-General of Colonies 1st Class, Charles Phérivong, did the sequence of events which triggered off the Borgu revolt become clear.[17] Ferlus, in his original long telegram

FIRST REFORMS AND A SECOND RISING

of September 21st, reported that he and his party had fallen into an ambush. According to Ferlus he was attacked at dusk by 150 men with bows and arrows and he himself was able to return to Bimbereke only with difficulty. Replying to the Governor's telegram, he reported he had been badly grazed on the legs whilst escaping through the bush. On September 24th he asked for 50 soldiers or *gardes de cercle* and 2,000 cartridges. By September 25th 30 *gardes de cercle* from Porto Novo, Savé and Kandi with 2,000 cartridges were sent to Bimbereke, arriving there on September 28th.

In fact what happened at Bécou was different from the version given by Ferlus. After detailed investigations by the Phérivong mission (as a result of which Ferlus was reduced in rank) the actual sequence of events became clear.

Ferlus left Nikki with Baguène himself, *moniteur* (instructor) Ali Bachabi as interpreter, seven *gardes de cercle*, a line of porters and three 'caisses de fonds' belonging to the administration. He bypassed Bimbereke, going direct to Bécou where he arrived on September 17th. There he was installed in a hut belonging to Bio Guèra who welcomed him. The *gardes de cercle* were lodged with Baguène in a compound some 100 metres from his own hut. Ferlus did not forewarn Bio Guèra of his intentions but ordered him to come and see him. Meanwhile Baguène had begun to threaten the villagers. So at night Bio Guèra came to ask Ferlus to leave his house. The latter, however, was told by his cook that some people wanted to kill him. Ferlus in his report stated that he had sent for his guards and while he was looking for his revolver he was wounded in the nape of the neck by an arrow. Believing his life to be threatened, he took flight, half dressed, leaving his personnel to look after themselves, and abandoning baggage and money belonging to the Colony. Like many villages in Borgu, Bécou was 'fenced' by a hedge of thorns and he cut his legs scrabbling through them. It was established later that, given the place where he had put his baggage in the hut, it would have been impossible for him to have been hit by an arrow while looking for his revolver.

After the cowardly flight of Ferlus, the *gardes de cercle*, rushing out with fixed bayonets, got into a fight with Bio Guèra's men, who numbered some 15 and not the 150 reported by Ferlus. One porter and one *garde de cercle* were killed on the French side, while a brother of Bio Guèra was killed and several of his men wounded.

Ali Bachabi the teacher was, however, able to calm the situation by promising that if order was restored he would see that nothing happened to the village or to Bio Guèra. He retrieved all the baggage and funds, less 1,000 francs. He re-formed the party and left the village, conducted by Bio Guèra himself.

The next morning, at Kisra, the party was found by Ferlus who had spent the night in the bush. Ferlus took a horse and returned alone to Bimbereke that same day.[18]

Phérivong concluded that, had the promises made by Ali Bachabi been kept, the whole matter might have been settled. Bio Guèra himself remained at Bécou, and kept calm up to the time he either got news of the telegram sent by Ferlus to the King of Nikki warning him and his people to keep away from Bécou, because of the impending punishment of its inhabitants, or else got news of the arrival of the reinforcements demanded by Ferlus. Anyway, the promises made by Ali Bachabi were not kept and the revolt broke out. Communications were cut, bridges were destroyed and four 'cantonniers' were killed on the Niger road 5 kilometres from Bimbereke.

The French took no action against the rebels until October 23rd, for they had much greater troubles elsewhere in Dahomey. The Somba of Atacora to the north-west of Borgou were in open rebellion, as well as the Hollidjé to the south, both because of forced recruitment of their young men into the French Army.

The only action the French took was to order an enquiry into Ferlus's conduct by Administrateur en Chef Sassias on October 15th. He did not get to Parakou until October 23rd because of lack of transport. Meanwhile a small hut was burnt down by the rebels near the *poste* of Bimbereke. Monsieur Lefilliâtre, Administrateur en Chef, and head of the automobile service of Northern Dahomey, ordered the Commandant de Cercle of Moyen-Niger to go to Bimbereke, in the Cercle of Borgou (under Ferlus, now under investigation), to help capture Bio Guèra. Governor Noufflard of Dahomey cabled Lefilliâtre that he had no right to assume the position of Commandant de Cercle of Borgou or to call on the services of a neighbouring Commandant de Cercle. But the cable did not arrive in time.

On October 23rd, Bimbereke was attacked by followers of Bio Guèra and telegraph lines pulled down, so that Bimbereke was cut off from Kandi to the north and Parakou to the south.

From then till the 29th when 75 soldiers arrived from Cotonou, having fought their way through to Bimbereke, the post was in a virtual state of siege, lacking food and water and with no means to get them. The next day further reinforcements arrived from Atacora, itself in a state of revolt.

The Borgu rebellion had now spread beyond the Cercle of Borgou into that of Moyen-Niger, whose headquarters, Kandi, was itself menaced. Indeed the Commandant de Cercle of Moyen-Niger, Géay, could not get back to his headquarters even with the support of a detachment of 110 *tirailleurs*. The rebels attacked the column with such force that it was put to flight and had to return to Bimbereke with 3 killed and 8 wounded. By November 25th the situation at Kandi had so deteriorated that the Assistant Commandant de Cercle, while still waiting for Géay, requested the support of 150 *tirailleurs* from Zinder. Meanwhile Governor Noufflard, accompanying Commandant Renard with two companies of troops, arrived at Bimbereke and began operations to open the roads. One company (the 8th) was sent north to Kandi to clear that road, taking Géay with them. They met resistance everywhere, with 3 *tirailleurs* killed. Some 5,000 rounds were fired, to claim 7 or 8 rebel victims, though because of the density of the bush it was not easy to estimate accurately the rebel losses. The other company (the 7th) went south to clear the road between Bimbereke and Béroubay. They met similar opposition with one French sergeant killed. This caused a major delay, for the column was ordered to turn back to Bimbereke to give the French soldier a 'sépulture convenable'—the African *tirailleurs* were, of course, buried on the spot. They continued fighting the rebels village by village.

By December 14th there still seemed no prospect of submission but on the 17th Bio Guèra and his son were killed in battle. By the 29th the French considered the rebellion effectively finished.[19]

There now followed a long uneasy period in which the population was to be disarmed, and the terms of submission fulfilled. Meanwhile, across the frontier in British Borgu the situation had deteriorated considerably, and the British administration blamed the recrudescence of revolt on the situation in Dahomey, where the French had had to put down the Borgawa with a force that was huge by comparison with the modest patrol sent out by the British to suppress Sabukki's rebels.

An ultimatum was sent by Bussa to Gidan Lalle, Kabe and Kano as well as Shagunu on November 27th to the effect that if they did not pay their taxes by December 17th a collective fine of 10/- per head would be imposed on Kano, Kabe and Gidan Lalle and of 5/- per head on

Shagunu.[20] Hamilton-Browne sent a request on December 2nd to Zungeru for sanction for imposition of the fine and a force of 50 rank and file 'to levy distress' if the villages in question did not comply within 21 days. Non-compliance, he considered, was a foregone conclusion. The troops would be needed for a month. He reckoned the disaffected adult male population consisted of some 1,000 adult males, a considerable number in sparsely populated Borgu.

To back up the urgency for troops, Hamilton-Browne added a footnote to his request that he had just received reports of another caravan raid by an armed band of 60 men in the vicinity of the disaffected towns. Police had been sent to patrol the caravan route pending further action.

On December 11th, having received no reply to his earlier request, he wired Zungeru that large numbers of Fulani were crossing from Dahomey into Aliyara District because of the rising against the French in Borgou. Again, on December 12th he wired that Kijibrim (Sarkin Bussa) had reported that Sabukki, with a large following, had entered Shagunu and was preparing to attack Bussa. Diggle had left for Bussa with 8 police, whilst Hamilton-Browne was sending him 25 more from Warra. The situation, he stressed, required the immediate presence of troops and a force of 50 should proceed to Bussa at once. Sabukki, he reported, 'has committed several outrages on the caravan road and is much elated by the reported rising of natives on the French border caused by enforcement of conscription by our allies. Fulani cattle owners are crossing from Dahomey in terror which gives colour to the report'.[21] This he had backed up with a letter on December 11th expressing fear that if troops were not sent soon the whole of Aliyara District would get out of hand.

The Secretary of the Northern Provinces replied with a coded telegram: 'You should avoid conflict if possible as unlikely Native Troops will be available while reorganisation in progress but am communicating with Commandant.'[22] On December 13th the Governor-General approved the despatch of 50 rank and file to Bussa if the Commandant of the W.A.F.F. could supply them, given the war shortage of troops.

30 rank and file were sent from Zuru under the command of Lieutenant Whitworth. They joined Diggle and Aliu Sarkin Yauri in Bussa on Christmas Day. On the 27th they left for Shagunu via Kagogi. On the 29th they entered Kagogi and met 4 armed scouts, who immediately took flight. The next four days were spent in search of Sabukki among the Shagunu farms which covered a very large area. On only one occasion did they encounter a large body of armed rebels, but these dispersed

FIRST REFORMS AND A SECOND RISING

immediately shots were fired in the air. There were no casualties reported. In the ungwa* of Layan Gaba, one of Sabukki's lieutenants, they found several articles belonging to some of the Bussa Native Authority officials killed by the rebels in the 1915 rising. The troops collected the outstanding tax in kind.

From Shagunu the Patrol moved to Luma, Kano and Kabe where Diggle interviewed the chief men of the surrounding towns. 'I think it unlikely', he reported, 'that any of these towns will allow Sabukki to come and move freely about among them again.'

On January 8th they reached Gidan Lalle where, in contrast to the other towns they had patrolled, they found the poison trees completely stripped of all poison pods. They encountered no opposition, for the whole population had fled across the border (less than an hour away) with all their goods and chattels. Gidan Lalle, a kango,† consisting of a dozen or so broken-down huts, was burnt down as an example, a fact which Diggle 'omitted to mention' in his first report on the Patrol. On January 9th they reached Babana, and on the 10th Gaiye. Here Diggle told Lieutenant Whitworth he could return, as he considered there was no further need for troops.

The Resident then reported that the object of the Patrol, to capture Sabukki, had not been achieved. 'The fact that no resistance was met with was I think due to the crushing defeat of the natives at the hands of the French and the subsequent punishment that followed.'

The Lieutenant-Governor gained the impression from Hamilton-Browne's report that the Patrol had failed.[23] To this Hamilton-Browne replied at length, justifying the use of troops in scarce supply, regretting that he had conveyed the idea that the patrol had failed to effect any of its objectives, for such was not the case.

'Though Sabukki was not arrested his prestige in Shagunu has been destroyed not only there but in other disaffected towns.

'The caravan road has been cleared of the bands of robbers from French Country and once more opened to trade. Your telegram dated 8th February 1917 refers (complaint from Resident Oyo re cessation of trade).

'Taxes which disaffected towns refused to pay have been almost entirely paid. Any attempt by police or soldiers on foot encumbered with equipment to overtake lightly armed natives who had 600 to 1,000

* ungwa = hamlet.
† Kango = ruined or deserted hamlet.

yards start in bush country with which they were thoroughly conversant had little prospect of success.

'Added to this was the military situation which was no doubt taken into consideration by the officer commanding. The information in Mr. Diggle's hands was to the effect that some 250 French troops had been employed against some 3,000 armed rebels who after cutting the telegraph line and tearing up part of the Railway had seriously engaged the French. Splitting up the small force might have entailed serious consequences if any considerable portion of the French rebels were present. Resident Kandi's telegram to Executive Yelwa seems to point to this being the case.

'Mr. Diggle informs me that Sarkin Yauri wished to persue [sic] with his horsemen, but Lieutenant Whitworth was averse to such action being taken.'[24]

The question remained as to how the disaffected peoples should be punished. Diggle felt sentences of imprisonment on those principally concerned would be more effective than collective fines, especially as one of sufficient magnitude to compensate those who had suffered from the depredations of the highway robbers would be practically impossible to collect. However Hamilton-Browne still favoured a collective fine, the original imposition of which, in the event of non-payment of taxes, had been criticized by Lugard.

'If the Resident as I understand sent an ultimatum stating that a certain Collective Fine would be imposed unless his orders were obeyed, he acted beyond his powers.'[25]

To this Hamilton-Browne replied to the Lieutenant-Governor:

'I regret that H.E. considers I have exceeded my powers but considered my action justified by the latitude allowed me by Conf. Circular 92/16 of 8/6/16. These people are pagan and unless the fine is levied at the time when the troops are present it is unlikely that it could be collected after their withdrawal. I have instructed the Acting D.O. to hold an inquiry in accordance with the Ordinance but consider that he should be permitted to inflict a fine at once upon such towns as are proved to have harboured or assisted Sabukki or any of the gang of highway robbers and murderers. H.E.'s Minute in Con. Circular 92/10 dated 2.5.16 would appear to sanction the course provided your previous consent has been obtained.'[26]

However, Goldsmith felt that the imposition of a collective fine would not serve any useful purpose. It would be better to place the Native

FIRST REFORMS AND A SECOND RISING

Authorities of the towns concerned in the highway robbery on trial in the Provincial Court, not the Native Court.

The problem for Hamilton-Browne with such a procedure was that the towns concerned with the caravan robberies appeared to be in French territory. Evidence indicated that the towns of Bissashe and Gumji, both in Dahomeyan Borgu, had been responsible. While Hamilton-Browne was unable to pin responsibility on any town in Nigerian Borgu, the people of Kenubwe, near which the first caravan robbery took place, captured one Woru, son of the headman of Bissashe, and accused him of the robbery. He had apparently came to Kenubwe and made enquiries about the caravan route.

The caravan was attacked a few days after his visit on the road between Dakkara and Kenubwe, en route to Sokoto. Two men were killed by the robbers, while the brother of one of them, wounded in the back, watched him die. When some of the survivors arrived in Kenubwe and asked for help, men working in the farms were summoned by the alarm drum. They chased after the robbers, but failed to catch them. However, some of them recognized Woru carrying the loads, so when a few days later he returned to Kenubwe they arrested him. Given the poverty of Borgu in those days, the robbers made a large haul.

Details of the losses recorded by Diggle were[27]:

ISA OF BIRNIN KEBBI	Cash £7 Copper Rods £2.4.0		£9.4.0
SALLA OF BIRNI KEBBI	Cash £1		1.0.0
MAHAMA OF ZARIA	Copper Rods	£2.16.0	
	Cloth	£1.11.0	
	Cash	£10.0.0	
	2400 Kolas	£6.0.0	20.7.0
ISIAKA OF ZARIA	1316 Kolas	£2.12.0	
	Cloth	£4.0.0	
	Gown	5.0	6.17.0
AMADU OF KAGOGI	Beads	£2.0.0	
	Cloth	£2.10.0	
	Kolas	£2.10.0	7.0.0
ALIU OF ZAGGA	Cash	£9.0.0	
	2 Gowns	£1.0.0	10.0.0
UMORU OF SOKOTO			
AHMADU GOGOBIRI			
ABDU	Losses not known		
DAN KORIJE			
MAMA			
GAJERI			
	Total		£54.8.0

The known losses of this caravan came to about one-thirtieth of the annual tribute paid by Bussa and Kaiama emirates in 1914. No wonder Diggle felt it would be practically impossible to levy a collective fine that could compensate the traders, even if it could be proved that towns in British Borgu were involved. As it was, no evidence came to light about the involvement in the robberies of either Kenubwe or Gidan Lalle. Woru, however, was sentenced to five years imprisonment, but no one was convicted for the second robbery near Gidan Lalle, though some of the stolen goods were recovered from Gumji in Dahomeyan Borgu.

4. The Deposition of Mashi and the Imprisonment of Political Agent Abba

While the administration was facing renewed troubles in Borgu, two of its most hated agents there were brought to trial: Mashi, the Emir of Kaiama, and Political Agent Abba. Mashi, the Zaberma ex-soldier who had been raised from the district headship of Yashikera to the position of emir of Kaiama in 1915 on the deposition of Jimi, was tried on charges of embezzlement and given consecutive sentences of two and three years respectively on 24th November 1916. He was also convicted on a further charge for which he was given a year's imprisonment to run concurrently with the others. Furthermore, he was to be deposed.[28] When the sentence was sent to Lugard for confirmation, since it concerned an emir, he minuted on 13th February 1917:

'Five years imprisonment in addition to deposition is I think an excessive sentence, the more so that there are considerable extenuating circumstances—the influence of the Government Political Agent—poverty and the position of Serkin to maintain,—absence of a Political Officer &c. I agree to deposition and if the Court recommends deportation I concur in a year's deportation. I think this is sufficient punishment without any imprisonment, for the whole of the charges brought against the Serkin [sic.].'[29]

Mashi had meanwhile been in prison since 24th November 1916. Now that his five years sentence had been quashed, he was brought in to Kontagora to await deportation arrangements. It was then pointed out to Lugard that a point of procedure had been overlooked: a deportation order could not be made by a court even with Lugard's agreement but only by the Governor-in-Council. Mashi's deportation was thus delayed, though arrangements had been made to send him to Ilorin. When the Executive Council met it ruled that:

'Deportation can only be imposed where the accused man's continued residence in a certain place is a danger to the neighbourhood. There is nothing to show that this is so in the present case. H.E. advises that the case should be sent back for the Court to impose some term of imprisonment.'[30]

Accordingly, Mashi was sent before the Provincial Court in July 1917 and sentenced to a total of six months imprisonment on all three charges. Hamilton-Browne then recommended that since the accused had already spent 108 days in prison, and thus had only 72 more to serve, the sentence be reduced by this amount.[31] This was approved by the Lieutenant-Governor of the Northern Provinces on August 20th and Mashi was in fact released on September 3rd.

These intricate legal niceties were understood by Hamilton-Browne, but E. C. Duff, who took over from him temporarily in 1918, was clearly unaware of them. In May he cabled the Secretary of the Northern Provinces that Mashi's term of deportation had ended and that it was 'most undesirable' that he should return to Kaiama. Since Mashi was a Zaberma, he recommended that he be returned there.[32] In the absence of any action, and the presence of a certain confusion as to the whereabouts of Mashi together with strong rumours that he was about to return to Kaiama, Duff sent a letter reporting that the people of Kaiama would leave the town if Mashi came back.[33] By now, however, the Governor-General had the power to deport chiefs under the Deposed Chiefs Ordinance of 1917, and he ordered that Mashi should not return to Kaiama for another three years.[34]

It was only at this stage that Duff discovered that Mashi was not in exile in Ilorin but living in Bussa. As Lugard noted, Mashi 'appears to have been sent away from Kaiama without any proper authority'.[35] Where Mashi spent his three years' exile is unclear: but he never came back to trouble Kaiama.

A key, but shadowy, figure in the troubles experienced by Bussa during Clarke's administration was Abba his Political Agent and informant about native affairs. In Bussa Abba, and Aliu, Sarkin Yauri, are considered the architects of Bussa's woes. The Bussawa believe that Abba, a Kanuri from Bornu Province, through the information and advice he gave to Clarke, who was much influenced by him, was responsible for the removal of Kitoro Gani and the imposition of Turaki on them.[36] It was with his connivance that Aliu, Sarkin Yamma, became Sarkin Yauri and that the Bussa emirate was dismantled and subjected to him. The Bussawa also believe that Abba, hand in glove with Aliu, worked to persuade Clarke that land that was rightfully Bussa's be incorporated into the districts of Yauri. To him they attribute the loss of Rofia, Kunji and Agwarra.

It is a phenomenon of colonial rule of this period in both French and British West Africa that the political agents or government interpreters, because of their roles as intermediaries between chiefs and administrators, who often understood imperfectly or not at all the indigenous languages of the people they administered, gained power and prestige quite incommensurate with their paltry salaries. They were able to threaten chiefs that they would report their misdeeds, actual or fictional, to the Political Officer unless they compensated them. They were able to use their position as 'the eyes and the ears' of the Political Officer to extort money from ordinary people. They were able to present situations to him in a light that was advantageous to them, and the latter had little means of checking up on them.[37] It seems quite clear that Clarke did rely heavily on the advice of Abba, whom the present Emir of Borgu accuses of having delayed and suppressed letters, spread false reports and generally treated the chiefs of Bussa with contempt.[38] Unfortunately the record of the trial of Abba cannot be traced but it was with a sense of jubilation that the people of Bussa learnt of his sentence in December 1916 to twelve lashes and seven years imprisonment.

The question of Abba's pernicious role in the affairs of Bussa and Yauri seems first to have come to light in 1915, though the records are unfortunately incomplete. When an enquiry was made into the estate of the late Emir of Argungu, in Sokoto Province, the Resident of Sokoto found that Abba had been carrying on a lengthy correspondence with the Emir. In this he had demanded a present of a horse, saddle and bridle, and had even threatened the long-standing friendship between the emirs of Argungu and Yauri. In August 1916 he laid a formal complaint against Abba with Hamilton-Browne, enclosing copies of Abba's letters, and expressing the hope that, if Hamilton-Browne did not see his way to punishing him, at least he would dismiss him from Government service.[39] Later, he wrote that if Abba could do what he had done in Argungu in a neighbouring province 'it seems possible that this [sic] undesirable activities extend to his own Province'.[40]

There had indeed been hints that such was the case as early as 1913, when the recently deposed chief of N'gaski in the Yauri emirate, Umoru dan Aliu, wrote in Arabic to the Governor to complain against Abba:

'He always promise to give the Resident good report about me. Not knowing that he was deceiving me, I always give him anything he asked from me.'[41]

The deposed chief then went on to list the occasions on which Abba had taken money from him, adding that Abba 'has taken a lot of bribes in Yelwa province'. He further complained that it was because Abba and Aliu, Sarkin Yamma, had gone to 'the Whiteman' and 'misrepresented matters' that he had been deposed.[42]

At the enquiry into these allegations, held by Hamilton-Browne, Abba denied that he had ever accepted anything from the ex-Sarkin N'Gaski, though the latter had made several attempts to bribe him. In this he was supported by Clarke, who stated that during his whole experience in Yelwa Political Agent Abba had never attempted to cover up for the ex-Sarkin N'Gaski but 'had been instrumental in showing up cases of munafiki'.[43] Hamilton-Browne terminated the case:

'In conclusion it is my opinion that this complaint is the outcome of hatred towards P.A. Abba whom he naturally suspects of being instrumental in disclosing wrong-doing on his part. What Political Agent would be of any use to us did he not do so ?'[44]

However, while the Acting Chief Secretary to the Government agreed to close the case, he requested that Abba should be kept under observation and that the case should be noted in his confidential report.[45]

Little notice seems to have been taken of this advice by Hamilton-Browne or Clarke. In April 1916, however, Abba was indirectly implicated in the trial of the District Head of Kunji before the Judicial Council of Yelwa on April 15th for embezzlement. Sarkin Kunji, amongst other crimes, had recovered £2 owed by Abba for over a year to one Daudun Noma, keeping it for himself.[46] Shortly before this, Abba had been transferred to the Resident of Kontagora's staff, whether on normal posting or for disciplinary reasons is not clear from the records.[47] In October he was dismissed from the administrative service and held for trial on charges that were not detailed, but were a great many in number and extended beyond Yauri into the Kaiama emirate.[48] What is remarkable about his career is how completely he seems to have won the confidence of Clarke and how far he was able to wield power without being detected. It is only sad that the full extent of his crimes, which the trial record would reveal, is not available to us.

5. The Separation of Bussa from Yauri

The two rebellions had made it clear even to Hamilton-Browne that his administrative reorganization of Borgu had not been a success. While the December 1916 patrol was marching to Bussa, he put forward suggestions as to the reorganization of the Kaiama emirate which, at the time, was in an even worse state than Bussa, being without an emir or any district heads.[49] Mashi had not only been Emir of Kaiama, but had administered metropolitan Kaiama, so that the district headship of Kaiama was vacant too. In Kaiama itself the posts of Alkali and Treasurer were also vacant, since the incumbents had been tried and convicted along with Mashi. The District Head of Yashikera had committed suicide; the District Head of Ilesha had been convicted on a criminal charge.

There were thus no senior Native Administration officials in the Kaiama emirate and the District Officer in Yelwa, some 100 miles away, was, pending their appointment, effective Native Authority.[50] Hamilton-Browne could see no suitable successor for the Alkali and Treasurer of Kaiama. There was no successor immediately to view as district head of Yashikera. For Ilesha, he proposed the appointment of Abigoga, son of the district head who had ruled before the one recently deposed. There was no one suitable in Ilesha to fill the post of Alkali, so he felt inclined to get one from Sokoto or Kano. For Okuta he recommended Wuru Gendi. Finally, for Kaiama he recommended that Yerima Kura, a distant cousin of Mora Tasude, be district head but not emir. If he turned out well in this post, he could become Emir, even though he was old. On his death he could be succeeded by Gunu, one of the younger sons of Mora Tasude, who was eighteen years old and at school in Birnin Kebbi.

As an alternative, he suggested that they might make Emir one of the numerous younger sons of the King of Nikki living in the Kaiama emirate. This, he argued, would be acceptable to Okuta, Ilesha and men of the Kaiama emirate, except for members of the late Emir's family. Here, Hamilton-Browne used a historical justification:

'It is a well established fact that prior to the advent of the European Nations Nikki was regarded as the Head of all that country now composing the Kaiama Emirate together with a large tract which is to the West which is now French Territory. On the advent of the British however Kaiama was taken away from Nikki and constituted a separate

FIRST REFORMS AND A SECOND RISING

entity under an Emir thus conferring upon the Town of Kaiama an importance which it is very doubtful it enjoyed prior to the occupation.

'Murata Sudi, realizing the position of things, by helping us in every possible way obtained for himself the position of Emir over what is now the Kaiama Emirate (1902). He was appointed a first-class chief. He never failed to fulfil the expectations he gave, but on his death a gap was left which was impossible to fill since none of his successors could be compared to him in ability or strength of character.'[51]

The proposal to put a Nikki prince on the throne 'would be merely reverting to following the family which they followed for generations before the British'.[52] As a possible Nikki candidate he suggested one, Alberke.

Hamilton-Browne's latter proposal is breath-taking in its ignorance of the political situation in Kaiama, especially in view of the disturbances that had taken place there. While Okuta, Ilesha and Yashikera might have agreed to follow a Nikki prince, since they were Nikki dependencies at the advent of the British, it would have been highly unlikely that Kaiama, which had been effectively independent of Nikki for well over a century, would have accepted such an arrangement willingly. Earlier, in April 1916, Hamilton-Browne had proposed that, if he could not get further political staff, Kaiama be handed over to Ilorin 'as an outlet for their surplus population. It is not in my opinion of sufficient importance with its miserable population to regard as an Emirate in the true sense. It might be for its ultimate good to become a district of a powerful Emirate'.[53] This proposal, to subject Kaiama to a Fulani-Yoruba emirate, was never pursued, but shows just how insensitive Hamilton-Browne could be to the feelings of the people he was supposed to be administering.

On 20th February 1917 he put forward yet another, but more definite, scheme for the reorganization of Kaiama, this time within the framework of Borgu and Yauri. When he had proposed the amalgamation of Bussa and Yauri, he had not been cognisant, he wrote to the Lieutenant-Governor, of certain facts of the history of Borgu. It was now necessary to go into these, 'even at the expense of criticizing' those earlier recommendations.[54] Strong as the reasons he gave in 1915 for amalgamation of Bussa and Yauri appeared, 'and without hinting for a moment that Sarikin Yauri has failed in one's expectations I am forced to recognize that the feeling of discontent at being placed under Yauri prevailing among the Borgawa is not lessening and is likely to increase in the future. Bussa, though now a mere shadow of its former greatness, clings tenaciously to its old traditions. I have, therefore, reluctantly come to the conclusion that the advantages of the amalgamation are outweighed by later considerations'.[55]

He then proposed that Bussa Emirate be reconstructed, and be divided into six districts consisting of

> Bussa
> Kaiama
> Wawa
> Ilesha
> Okuta
> Yashikera

It should be made an administrative division under a district officer. Kiwotede, the District Head of Bussa, should be made Emir of the enlarged emirate of Bussa.

'He is hard-working and trustworthy. Somewhat tactless and hot tempered but greatly improved of late. If under the supervision of a Political Officer would develop into a reliable Emir. He is the next in succession to the ex-Emir Gani who was undoubtedly the rightful heir and head of the Bariba Tribe.'[56]

The new emirate, which would correspond roughly to the old Borgu Province, less those parts handed over to Sokoto and Yauri, would have a revenue of between £1,850 and £2,000 and an expenditure of between £1,500 and £1,700. He then gave historical justification, quoting locally gathered 'native information'.

'Historically there is no distinction between the Bariba and Borgawa people. They owe their origin to two brothers Kijera, the elder who accompanied by Sabi, the younger and two others younger still, founded Bussa. After residing there sometime Kijera sent out his brothers to found towns of their own. Sabi founded Nikki and the others Kaiama, Ilesha, Kika and Gwen. Apart from any differences of version all who have been questioned agree (a) that the Bariba Tribe was roughly bounded by a line starting from Bussa going northwards to Illo, then westwards to Kandi (or Gwandi) seven days west of Nikki, thence to Zugu onwards to Ilesha and then returned to Bussa via Kaiama and Wawa. (b) That prior to the advent of Europeans

Nikki and Kaiama through Nikki owed allegiance to Bussa. (c) That whenever the succession of the chieftainship of Nikki was in dispute the matter was by ancient custom referred to Bussa whose decision was final. On occasion when the succession was not disputed, Sarkin Bussa was merely informed by messengers from the newly appointed Sarkin Nikki who sent a large number of presents. The latter then sent a return present by his messengers, and it is rather interesting to note that Bussa's messengers did not enter Nikki itself but waited at a village outside where Sarikin Nikki himself came to receive them. Having saluted Bussa's messengers he did not lift his eyes up to look on them until he was bidden to do so. (d) That up to the occupation by the English and French and the consequent severance of the tribe Sarkin Nikki sent a yearly "gaisua" to Bussa. It is stated even once after this a present was sent.

'On the death of Mura-Bane-De, 7th Sarkin Kaiama, Murata-Sudi, realising that he would not be chosen as Sarkin Kaiama by Sarkin Nikki as his elder brother had a prior claim to the title, went to Sarkin Bussa with a present of 100 calabashes of Kolas and asked to be appointed Sarkin Kaiama—Sarkin Bussa agreed and sent his messenger to Kaiama and invested him there. Sarkin Nikki on being informed of Sarkin Bussa's action immediately acquiesced as the action was done by his overlord; nor was there any trouble in Kaiama though the rightful heir had been passed over.'[57]

These facts, he felt, pointed to the overlordship of Bussa over Kaiama and even Nikki in times prior to the advent of the British and French.

The vague overlordship of Bussa over Borgu was now to be used to give it political hegemony over Nigerian Borgu, a course of action that could not be justified by the political situation as it existed on the eve of colonial occupation. Hamilton-Browne attached a map to his proposals in which enough of Bussa was left in the Yauri emirate for expansion of its farmers.

These proposals, Hamilton-Browne argued, were the best, but could only be carried out if a political officer were put in charge of Borgu. If none was available at present, then Yerima Kura, District Head of Kaiama, could be made acting Emir of the Kaiama emirate on the understanding that the appointment was only temporary.[58]

Goldsmith, Acting Lieutenant-Governor of the Northern Provinces, forwarded these proposals to Lugard with the weary comment:

'The Resident Kontagora (Major Hamilton-Browne) is constantly changing his mind and I find some difficulty in keeping in touch with the frequent changes of organization advocated.'[59]

He informed Lugard that there was no district officer available to supervise the enlarged Bussa emirate proposed by Hamilton-Browne. Therefore it seemed unwise to approve the proposals. In his own opinion Kaiama should remain an independent district under Yerima Kura, while Kiwotede should remain District Head of Bussa with no change in status. However, he did not wish to oppose the separation of Bussa from Yauri and its reconstitution as an independent district, provided that it could be done gradually and 'if the Resident still remains of the same opinion as conveyed in his present letter under reference'.

To this Lugard, forgetting his minute of 30th March 1915 (see p. 110), replied: 'Did I ever approve the placing of Boussa under Yelwa? I have never liked it.' He also considered Hamilton-Browne's quotations concerning Borgu history of doubtful accuracy, recalling from his own experience on 'the race to Nikki' in 1894 that the comparative powers of Bussa and Nikki had become an international question. 'It was more or less conceded that they are of equal standing, Boussa being the religious head and Nikki, the secular head of the Bariba.' He ordered that a political officer should be posted to Borgu whether the staff was depleted or not. 'Captain Browne admits that his recommendations', Lugard continued, 'in the first instance are crude and based on crude and imperfect information. They have I understand led to bloodshed and chronic unrest and discontent? This is not creditable. The present proposal seems to stand a better chance of success, but I am doubtful as to the placing of Kaiama under Boussa as you say.'[60]

Hamilton-Browne replied that his information about the pre-colonial situation in Borgu was 'Native information obtained on the spot'.[61]

On 14th April 1917 the Secretary Northern Provinces cabled his approval for the separation of Bussa from Yauri. But Kaiama was not to be placed under Bussa. Five days later he wired that he had no objection to Bussa and Kaiama being called Borgu Division. Thus Bussa's integrity as an Emirate was restored, though with some of its lands still under Yauri's control. The name of Borgu, temporarily erased from the administrative map, was restored. Finally, Kiwotede Kijibrim was installed as emir of the second class. Some of Bussa's grievances were solved, but there remained much more for the British to do before Bussa was to be from their point of view in a satisfactory state.

FIRST REFORMS AND A SECOND RISING

6. The Scape-goat

The administration's concern at the way things had got out of hand in Bussa eventually produced a scapegoat. Hamilton-Browne, who himself escaped censure, turned on Clarke, of whom he had written in 1914: 'He has done excellent work in Yauri Division—I should be very sorry to lose his services in this Province.'[62] Although he had accepted and backed up all Clarke's recommendations with regard to the administrative re-organization of Bussa, in 1917 he wrote a confidential report on him that put all the blame for the Bussa débâcle on him.

'I have been greatly disappointed in his general conduct in 1915 which however I did not discover until I visited Yelwa Division in November 1916. Possessing undoubted ability as well as an exceptional knowledge of the language, which ought to have been a safeguard, he permitted himself to repose a foolish trust in his staff and certain members of the Native Administration which led to abuses and irregularities in the Division nor has he been frank with the Resident as to the feeling of the people towards certain appointments which he has recommended.'[63]

This was endorsed by the Lieutenant-Governor, H. S. Goldsmith, who added 'that Mr. Clarke must gain the confidence formerly reposed in him before his name can be considered for further promotion'.[64]

At the time Hamilton-Browne wrote his confidential report, Clarke was on secondment for war service with the Navy where he now had the rank of Lieutenant-Commander. Clarke, writing from Plymouth where he was serving on H.M.S. *Excellent*, protested that he was being treated unfairly and, alluding to his enemy, Dwyer, suggested that Hamilton-Browne had based his report on information received 'possibly from prejudiced sources'.[65] Clarke asserted that his administration of Yauri had, 'taking it all round', been a success. Though Goldsmith ruled that there was no need to reply to Clarke's letter, and added that Clarke had committed irregularities such as the purchase of a motor-bicycle from Native Authority funds, a Commission of Enquiry was finally held into his administration of Yauri, under the commissionership of G. S. Browne, in 1919 when Clarke returned from his service with the Navy. Unfortunately, though there is a file in the Kaduna archives entitled 'Clarke, Mr. J. C. O.: Commission of Enquiry',[66] it deals merely with the logistics of the Commission. The actual report of the Enquiry and the record of the evidence taken is, alas, lost. The verdict, however, was against Clarke for he was censured by the Governor of Nigeria and forfeited a year's increment of pay.

His subsequent career in the Northern Nigerian administrative service was undistinguished. In 1920, Goldsmith wrote that his work had not been good and that he was 'unpopular with his brother officers and unlikely to be successful if placed in a very responsible position'.[67] In 1923, he left the service a sick man. Perhaps it would have been better all round if he had been granted his earlier wish, expressed when he first applied for a post in Africa, to be placed in command of an armed vessel on Lake Nyasa or any other African lake.[68]

VIII · THE REIGN OF KIJIBRIM

1. Joyce Cary's Borgu

In April 1917 the District Officer of Yauri, Mr. H. W. Cowper, accompanied by Aliu, Sarkin Yauri, and Kijibrim, Sarkin Bussa, went down to Kontagora to discuss the separation of Bussa from Yauri with Hamilton-Browne. There, he indicated to Kijibrim the boundary between Yauri and Bussa, whereby he would lose most of Agwarra to Aliu. On May 8th, Joyce Cary, the future novelist, left Kontagora with Cowper for Yelwa, where he was given the records of Borgu Division.[1] A few days earlier Cary had written to his wife from Kontagora:

'. . . I am going out to start a new Division, a new office, a new everything with two new chiefs . . . the last man made a mess of the place and one morning they all started cutting each other's throats, making such a clean sweep that a new start must be made. The people are not against the white man, so don't be afraid for me darling, they are against bad officials of their own chiefs, who were not properly looked after by an incompetent D.O. H-B who is the best of fellows is making new arrangements all round, and is making things as favourable as possible for me, but I shall have the toughest time yet without a doubt.'[2]

Cary had two headquarters, one at Bussa and one at Kaiama, until it was decided which should be the permanent one. At Bussa, the former Residency, for want of occupation, was in a very dilapidated state, with the thatched roof full of holes. During the rainy season Cary was washed out of it altogether. At Kaiama, the old Residency was in similar condition. Cary later described it in his essay, 'Christmas in Africa'.

'It was falling into ruin, and in one of my two upper rooms most of the floor was a hole. But this too was an advantage. I could see from my bath right down into the office and know at once what I was in for that morning: a visit from old chiefs, anxious to get up a war on the

Fig. 1: Interior of the Residency at Kaiama (from a letter from Joyce Cary to his wife, 17th October 1917) *From* Joyce Cary's Africa *by M.M. Mahood, Methuen, London, 1964.*

French frontier, hunters quarrelling about the correct division of a deer, one of my road gangs complaining of evil spirits who turned the edge of their tools, or a witch murder with about twenty-five witnesses, all convinced of the existence of witches and the expediency of killing them.'[3]

Before settling in at Bussa, Cary had been warned of the magnitude of his task by Cowper at Yelwa. He told him that the province hadn't advanced since 1900 and that Hamilton-Browne was one of those easy-going do-it-tomorrow types who left all his subordinate officers to make bricks without straw, unless the officers demanded straw frequently and urgently.[4]

Once arrived in Borgu, Cowper's gloomy descriptions were soon confirmed for Cary:

'The state of this Province is rotten all through, police, native administration and all, and it won't wake up till we change the Resident. . . .'[5]

Cary had little time to reorganize Borgu. He was there only from May to November, when he was relieved by Diggle. For three of those six

Fig. 2: Joyce Cary on trek with the Emir of Bussa (Kijibrim) *From* Joyce Cary's Africa *by M.M. Mahood, Methuen, London, 1964.*

months, work and especially touring were made difficult by the rains. Nevertheless Hamilton-Browne, when he visited Bussa in December, was able to report 'great progress' and that 'both Yerima Kura at Kaiama and Kiwotede [Kijibrim] at Bussa are shaping well, and thoroughly cooperating with the D.O.'[6] Cary set up Alkali Courts at Bussa, Kaiama and Ilesha, and a Native Court at Yashikera. Kijibrim was put in charge of the Bussa emirate as a whole, as well as metropolitan Bussa; this was in contrast to the system during the last years of the reign of Kitoro Gani, when metropolitan Bussa had been administered by a district head, Turaki. The Lieutenant-Governor, whilst approving the new arrangement, criticized the use of the title of Emir for Sarkin Bussa. 'The Sarikin Bussa is hardly an Emir in the sense that the title is recognized in the Northern Provinces. He should always be referred to as Sarikin Bussa. At present he is not a very important independent chief nor is he a descendant of Mohammed* that I know of.'[7]

Cary himself seems to have done little other than routine work on this tour. By his own admission: 'Such activities as I do perform are little more than vegetable motions. Writing returns and reports, hearing petty cases, taking tax, lecturing chiefs and so on—one could do them in one's sleep.'[8]

Cary gives a deep insight into the loneliness of the political officer in Borgu. And although he was later to take a liberal attitude about Africa, as witnessed by his *The Case for African Freedom*,[9] in 1917 he clearly held the views of most of his colleagues in Northern Nigeria about Africans. His long letter written to his wife from Bussa is perhaps the most revealing document on the personal life of the district officer in the bush:

'I've been four months alone now—considerably longer than I was married, but I haven't been unhappy. I've done really a lot of work of all sorts official and otherwise, and I've found out a good deal about myself. One does in solitude. I often wondered how I would stand

* i.e. a descendant of the Prophet Mohammed.

being alone. There are many men in the country who are not allowed to be alone for long—they break up at once. One man I know had to be rescued by a doctor last February—the doctor did 70 miles in 40 hours and found him going dotty, and he'd only had five weeks of his own company. People at home can't realize it. . . .'

He went on to complain of the lack of 'a white fellow creature' as the real basis of the sense of being alone and commented on how the French tried to solve the problem by the encouragement of mistresses.

'I haven't exchanged a word of rational conversation with a rational being since May, and this is getting to the end of September. When I do talk English I have to pick up the simplest words and repeat my meaning in two or three forms. Today I doubt if I have said more than a score of words altogether—I don't need to talk to Musa [the Political Agent] or the boys—and all those were Hausa words. All this makes it easy for me to understand the queer cases out here of fellows drinking themselves to death, getting homicidal mania, or breaking down nervously into neurotic wrecks, when in the back bush by themselves —though I myself am as fit as a flea, and suffer no ill effects at all. Partly all this is because I know what to guard against—nerves—drink —idleness, etc.—and partly because I have always been able to extract a very high degree of pleasure out of books, and almost companionship.'

Compared to conditions in the Balkans and the Cameroons, where he had been a soldier, he lived in luxury 'but O how I *hate* and *loathe* the sight of the filthy food—meal after meal day after day—greasy soups, watery chicken, milk pudding with bad eggs in it—the only thing that doesn't turn my stomach is the morning porridge. O for a potatoe! [sic] a piece of cold beef! vegetables! cheese! a glass of port!'

He then vented his spleen on the African: '. . . no black man in God's Earth is reliable. Let those blasted "my brother the poor black" put that in his pipe. No black man is morally, mentally or even physically reliable. Not one you can trust. They're charming fellows plenty of them (not my foul cook, who has the face of a devil and is morally and mentally a debased scoundrel) but you cannot trust 'em.'

Of his cook, he continued: 'He tries only when I become violent. And I simply will not lose my temper every time he wants to bake. I hate losing my temper. I never know what I'm going to do, and it makes me feel a wreck after.

'I haven't hit anyone this tour, except some carriers, and then I wasn't angry and I only smacked them with a riding switch and I won't. If a fellow can't manage these people without violence and cruelty he ought to do something else.'[10]

Diggle relieved Cary on November 28th, and just before Christmas made the surprising recommendation that Sabukki and his followers be given an amnesty. It was almost impossible to capture Sabukki and his four followers in 2,000 square miles of bush where every single person was his aider and abettor. Furthermore, he had wrongly supposed that Sabukki was responsible for the rising of November and December 1916. Now he realized it was 'merely the ripples of a more serious rising across the French border'.

'I am therefore submitting a recommendation that His Excellency the Governor-General be asked to grant an amnesty to all those concerned in the original rising. Though Sabukki and his followers were undoubtedly guilty of a very grave and serious offence, yet taking into consideration the fact that for five years previous no political officer had been stationed at Bussa, with the exception of a few months, and that a slave had been appointed in succession to an exceedingly long line of lawful heirs, the rising, the only method of appeal that would appear possible to Sabukki, assumes a rather less heinous aspect. Punishment has already been dealt out in two patrols, and if Sabukki was permitted to return in peace, I feel no ill results would follow, but that it would rather tend to strengthen and popularize the present Native administration.'

He did not know whether there were precedents for such a step in the Protectorate 'but if not I think that is all the more reason to create one. In English history, however, numerous examples of amnesties to rebels can be produced and the result has in most cases justified the experiment and I confidently expect that a similarly successful result would succeed an act of clemency'.[11]

E. C. Duff, who took over as Resident temporarily from Hamilton-Browne, forwarded the recommendation (which Hamilton-Browne, now on leave, had supported) to Kaduna, with the comment that Sabukki's presence in the bush as an outlaw was a latent cause of disaffection and that his pardon would be a most popular event. Duff by implication criticized Hamilton-Browne, with the remark: 'that his crimes were the outcome of harsh and injudicious treatment by the Administration'.[12]

The Acting Lieutenant-Governor, Goldsmith, replied sharply to Diggle's proposal:

'Your application for an amnesty for Sabukki causes me the greatest surprise. Briefly stated the reason given is that because the Govt. has been unsuccessful in effecting his arrest we should give it up or confess our weakness and grant him a pardon. What an example to set to other victims of outlaws who have been the cause of unrest and crimes of violence.'[13]

He refused to forward the request to Lagos, and ordered that every effort be made to capture Sabukki and bring him to trial.

Diggle, when told of the Lieutenant-Governor's reactions, replied that the request for an amnesty was not based on the fact that he could not be arrested but 'on the fact of the Government which by appointing a slave as D.H. of Bussa drove Sabukki to revolt'.[14] He would try his best to take Sabukki but pointed out that he had already tried to use police in plain clothes, dogarai in plain clothes and traders as spies. But Sabukki had 6,000 square miles of bush in Borgu, Dahomey and Sokoto province or Zugurma District of Kontagora Province in which to hide.

The Resident sympathized with Diggle and again forwarded his case to the Lieutenant-Governor. There the request for an amnesty seems to have become bogged down. Meanwhile Sabukki remained at large.

During 1918 Diggle spent a great deal of time on tour. In the first six months he spent 129 days in the bush. The division seems to have been very peaceful, despite Sabukki's still being at large. In May, French recruiting operations in Dahomeyan Borgu brought large numbers of immigrants across the border to settle. But permission to settle was refused them and the Native Authorities of Bussa and Kaiama handed over the refugees to their chiefs across the border.[15]

The Headquarters of Borgu Division were finally established at Kaiama, which Diggle considered nearer the centre of work as well as being a great improvement from the point of view of health. E. C. Duff, the Resident who replaced Hamilton-Browne while he was on leave, toured Bussa; and Kijibrim (who, Diggle reported, had a violent temper and was destitute of tact) petitioned for the restoration of his rule over his lost districts of Agwarra and Kunji. Kijibrim was still without a staff of office, so in August 1918 Duff wrote to Kaduna for a Second-Class Staff to replace the First-Class Staff which had been returned on the deposition of Kitoro Gani. The Secretary of the Northern Provinces replied: 'His Honour is not sure that the Sarkin Bussa deserves a Second

THE REIGN OF KIJIBRIM

Class Staff of Office, but if you think otherwise His Honour will approve the issue.' To this Hamilton-Browne, now back in Kontagora, replied in October: 'I am of the opinion that it would be rather invidious to reduce Sarkin Bussa to 3rd grade and allow Kaiama to remain 2nd grade. Though Bussa is now greatly reduced in importance, the dynasty is regarded by other Emirs as a very ancient one.'[16] While Goldsmith, now the substantive Lieutenant-Governor, did not object to a Second-Class Staff being given to Kijibrim, he felt there was no urgency and that it should be presented to him later 'as a mark of the Government's appreciation of some good administrative work done. The reports, so far, on this chief have not been too good'.[17]

In September 1918 Diggle went on leave and was replaced by Joyce Cary. In 1919 a major event took place as far as Bussa was concerned, though it is only cursorily noted in the annual and quarterly reports for Borgu and Kontagora. Agwarra, which had been handed over to N'Gaski District of the Yauri emirate in the amalgamation of Bussa and Yauri in 1915, was returned to Bussa. Apart from regaining some 144 square miles of its lost lands, it gained 2,725 people, which meant an increase in the Native Authority's revenues. In 1918, the first year after Bussa was separated from Yauri, its revenue had been only £805.[18] The separation was agreed by Cary from Borgu and Cowper from Yauri, and though the tribes and farms of both emirates were inextricably mixed in Agwarra, it was their opinion that the majority wanted to be under Bussa. Under the new arrangement there was to be no *nomajidi* or stranger-farming from one Emirate to the other.[19]

In agreeing to this adjustment of the boundaries between two of the emirates in his province, Hamilton-Browne had made it clear that it was the last he would entertain with regard to Bussa's lost land. In November 1918 he ruled: 'Kunji is to remain under Yauri for racial, historical and administrative reasons. This is final and I do not wish Sarkin Bussa to bring forward any arguments, with all of which I am fully cognisant.'[20]

Cary had an uneventful second tour in Borgu. Much of the time he was supervising the building of roads, bridges and markets, scrimping the funds under headings in his miniscule budget such as 'police uniforms, stationery, miscellaneous and secret services'. In his letters to his wife about his activities as a road-builder and his exasperation with chiefs who were apathetic about his passion for opening up the country to trade, we can see something of Rudbeck, the District Officer in *Mister*

Johnson.[21] In particular he found the Emir of Bussa dilatory in his bridge-building activities once his back was turned. Cary's other main concern, and the one that kept him on tour so much, was district assessment. During his second tour he re-assessed Kaiama and Yashikera districts. The Assessment Reports he had to write on both these districts, when properly done, had to contain detailed descriptions of the history and topography of the area being assessed, its ethnic composition, the occupations and customs of its peoples, the volume of its trade and its agricultural possibilities, all of which would provide a background to assessing the rate of tax the people could be expected to pay. On assessment tour he also had to estimate carefully the number of people in a particular district to make sure they paid tax to their maximum capacity. Under the system of Indirect Rule, whereby most of the administration was carried out, at least theoretically, by the chiefs, this was one of the few areas of direct contact between the political officer and the mass of the people, apart from hearing appeals from the Native Courts. Lugard considered this the main merit of the assessment tours though Cary felt the resulting reports had little scientific value.[22] However, Kaduna was more than pleased with both re-assessments. 'An excellent report,' wrote the Secretary of the Northern Provinces of the Yashikera assessment, 'and one of the best submitted to Headquarters recently. I am sending the report to His Excellency to note the good work done by Mr. Cary.'[23] From the historian's point of view it is only a pity that the painstaking Cary did not carry out a re-assessment of Bussa.

The only real excitement in Cary's last year in Borgu and indeed his last year in Nigeria was his attempt to track down Sabukki. 'I'm trying here to get a noted rebel to surrender to me,' he wrote to his wife. 'I can't catch him in [illegible] and he's been sitting in the bush for three years. One can't find a rebel in thousands of miles of bush with half a dozen police and all the people are his friends. My diplomacy is hardly in the highest style of Lagos and Kaduna. I don't know what the Governor or Chief Justice would say to it. In short, I'm letting it be known by private means that if he surrenders himself I'll give him a short sentence. This is information of high secrecy. A breath of it would ruin your worthy husband, so don't tell on me. I'm sorry for the man who has been unjustly treated. A year or two in jug is all that is required to save the face of the Government, and he'll be happier even in jug than he is now.'[24] That was in January. But Sabukki didn't take the bait. And when Cary left

Borgu and Nigeria for the last time, in December 1919, Sabukki was still at large.

2. A Staff Given, and a Staff Taken Away

With Cary gone from Borgu, there was no political officer available to replace him. Once again Borgu was administered from Yelwa. Indeed, when Cary had arrived for his second tour of Borgu in 1918, he had been instructed soon after to close down the office at Kaiama and actually set off for Kontagora with 135 people: staff, servants, police, prisoners, and bearers carrying all his personal possessions and the office equipment. On arrival at Kontagora, however, he was told that the office was not to be closed after all, and he set off back for Kaiama.[25]

Up till 25th March 1920, Cowper at Yauri was in charge of Borgu; and thereafter, until the posting of Izard to Kaiama on October 26th, Cowper's replacement, Campbell-Irons, had to look after the affairs of Bussa and Kaiama. Even when Izard did arrive, he went down with dysentery for five weeks and so Borgu received little administrative attention during 1920. As far as Bussa was concerned, Cowper, Campbell-Irons and Izard all put in bad reports on the Emir and his Native Authority. The Sarkin Fulani of Bussa District and one of the tax mallams had embezelled part of the taxes and were sent to prison. The Treasurer, or Ma'aji, once great friends with the Emir, had quarrelled with him, and the Emir was doing everything he could to hinder his work. The cash balance in the Treasury was invariably wrong;[26] and Kijibrim was made to repay the sum of £33 which he had borrowed as well as to cover £4 which had become inexplicably lost.[27]

The Emir presided over a Grade 'B' Judicial Court with two members, both princes: Kissoin his earlier rival, and Kikwissoin. He 'was apt to try cases by himself and is not yet conversant with the principles of justice'. Kissoin and Kikwissoin 'mean well, but are both weak'.

'The Waziri is intelligent and hard working but is apt to quarrel with the Emir in a manner unnecessarily undignified. The Emir of Bussa is very fond of sending messengers direct to villages in the various Districts without informing District Heads. The Emir rarely sends information on any subject, unless he is specially asked to do so.'[28] Bussa was now divided into four districts. Kijibrim, as emir, administered the metropolitan district. Wawa District was run by Kantama, still Sarkin Wawa, whom Campbell-Irons described as 'an old man and not over energetic, but he is very popular with his people and should be retained as long as possible'.[29] Aliyara's district head had just died and it was taken over by Kwarra, the popular choice. Despite its role as the trouble-maker of the Emirate, all had been quiet there since the 1916 rising. Agwarra, recently restored, had just been made the fourth district of the Bussa emirate and its administration was only just being established. Its district head was still Sabi Zakara, a slave from Shagunu, who had been its district head under Kitoro Gani as well as Aliu, Sarkin Yauri.

As far as Campbell-Irons was concerned the real problem in the Bussa emirate was Kijibrim: although he wanted to do well, he was 'quite unintelligent and has no knowledge of administration. Does not appear to have any interest in his Emirate beyond Bussa District. Very *unpopular*. He has no personal following and no one will serve him. Bad tempered, hasty.'[30]

Izard, in his annual report for 1920, confirmed Cowper's and Campbell-Irons's assessment of Kijibrim: 'The Emir of Bussa is not intelligent and has no power of administration. He takes but little interest in the Emirate beyond the actual Bussa District.'[31]

Kijibrim's unpopularity with his people was increased by his conversion to Islam around 1920. This angered his subjects, the majority of whom were still devotees of the traditional religion of Bussa. It was particularly resented by the representatives of 'the Owners of the People' such as the Bakarabonde and the Badaburude. There are various accounts of the motives behind Kijibrim's conversion. One is given in such detail that it seems likely to be accurate.

This holds that Kijibrim abducted the daughter of the Chief Imam of Bussa just as she was about to get married, in order that he might marry her himself. The Chief Imam was adamant that she should not marry Kijibrim, who was a 'pagan', even if the Chief. He secured his daughter's release from the palace, some say with the help of the District Officer, though I can find no record of this. Kijibrim realized that one of the reasons the Chief Imam refused him his daughter in marriage was because he was not a Muslim. He therefore decided to become a convert. He embraced Islam with such zeal that he pulled down the Tsafi house and built a mosque in its place. He also threw a number of 'idols' and sacred relics of the Bussa religion into the Niger. This so pleased the Chief Imam, that he gave Kijibrim another of his daughters in marriage.

THE REIGN OF KIJIBRIM

Furthermore, Kijibrim persuaded some of his brothers to be converts, including Wuru Babaki and Sabigoga.

The Chief Imam may have been pleased, but the majority of Kijibrim's subjects, who already disliked him, were now deeply embittered by his desecration of their religion.

When Izard took over Borgu Division he complained of the lack of records in the office which hindered his understanding of current events and past history. He was confronted by the long-standing problem of which islands on the Niger belonged to Bussa for tax purposes, and which to its neighbours. In Shagunu the people had refused to come on to Bussa when called by Kijibrim and would not do customary work on the Emir's farms. 'In each case the position was no doubt complicated by the tactless and high-handed methods of the Emir and in each case the D.O. settled it.'[33] The taxes, with the exception of £55 17s od disputed by the D.O. Yauri, had come in: but Bussa was not much better off than it had been ten years ago, though better than it was in 1918 before the return of Agwarra:

Bussa District	£532	18	0
Wawa District	£688	10	0
Aliyara District	£385	8	6
Agwarra District	£400	0	0
	£2006	16	6d

To this was added £252 8s 6d cattle tax.

The reports for 1921 are made of the same stuff: continual complaints by the District Officer against Kijibrim. These all seem in retrospect petty: the adding of six lashes to a sentence handed out by Sarkin Wawa, for no reason; the use of the dogarai for personal affairs; perpetual quarrels with the Waziri and intrigues with and against the leading men of the emirate. But collectively they exasperated a district officer, trying to administer this huge division and trying to implement the official policy of Indirect Rule. In April 1921 Kijibrim was hauled before Izard and told of his 'many misdeeds'.[34] T. Hoskyns-Abrahall, who joined Izard in February and took over from him in May, reported in exasperation in October: 'There is not a single satisfactory thing in the whole of Bussa.'[35]

Being a district officer in Borgu was difficult. Officially meant to be advising Kijibrim as the Native Authority, he had constantly to intervene in matters that would never have come up before his counterparts in the large emirates of the North. An example of the type of problem handled is the complaint made against the Emir by an old woman who made *kosai* (fried bean-flour cakes); she had a monopoly of the sale of bean-flour cakes which she sold at 20 cowries each:

'The Emir said she was to sell at 5 cowries, and when she refused, confiscated what she had made. He said, I think truthfully, that it was not for his personal benefit that he did this as he never ate the stuff but for the good of the town at large.

'I found on enquiry that 20 cowries, though high, is not an excessive charge, and that 5 cowries at Bussa where the price of food is always high, is absurdly low. These high handed methods not only increase his unpopularity but are, I think, directly responsible for the decrease in the population of Bussa town, which quite apart from this has little enough to recommend it.'[36]

In his personal diary,[37] Hoskyns-Abrahall gave vent to the frustrations he experienced in trying to deal with Kijibrim. On his first visit to Bussa, after a sleepless night because of the mosquitoes, he wrote that it was 'to say the least of it a beastly place'.[38] After his first meeting with Kijibrim he wrote of him with dismay; and by July dismay had become expressed distaste.[39]

By August, however, he was looking at him more sympathetically. When he arrived at Bussa, he 'noted how small a following Sar. Bussa has. Felt a bit sorry for the man for once'.[40] But this did not last long. On a later visit, he found that Kijibrim was using *dogarai* as his personal servants; and he took him to task over the matter. His diary records that he admonished the Emir and inveighs against him and Bussa. In what was clearly a mood of strain he says: 'A few days of Bussa reduces one to a state of concentrated misery so that I could easily burst into tears or torrents of oaths at the slightest provocation'.[41]

Years later, in a letter to the author, Hoskyns-Abrahall wrote: 'I don't think that my handling of Kijibrim was very clever. I was new to the country and new to the work. Also I was so far from my headquarters—much to my delight may I add! In other words I did not realize that Jibrim was in an impossible position. I did not realize that the removal of Gani, which had happened before my time, did not destroy his spiritual power—he lost his staff of office but that which was sacrosanct remained.

THE REIGN OF KIJIBRIM

Jibrim was of very little importance in the eyes of the people and it is not surprising that he was inefficient and unpopular. In the circumstances he could hardly have been otherwise!'[42] In the same letter, Hoskyns-Abrahall (now Sir Chandos) says: 'In spite of all the threatened tears and torrents of oaths, I should end up by saying I was deeply devoted to Borgu and the only time I remember being near to tears was when I finally left her.'

These comments show Hoskyns-Abrahall's modesty and also his ability to detach himself and look at the problems of the Emirate in perspective. At the time, writing in his diary, he compared Borgu to the England of King James I. 'Extraordinary', he wrote in his diary, 'how a few hundred years ago—James I—we were in many ways little more advanced than they are here. There is little to choose between trial by ordeal and trial of a witch by water and the other stunts of James I's time.'[43]

It was this sense of perspective that enabled Hoskyns-Abrahall, to Bussa's great good fortune, to look objectively at the terrible administrative situation in which he found it. He started off by trying to reconstruct the pre-colonial and colonial history of Bussa with the result that, for the first time, Bussa had a political officer who really understood its problems in depth. As a result of this a number of major reforms were to be undertaken in Bussa, which are remembered to this day in Bussa as being largely the work of Hoskyns-Abrahall.[44]

For the time being, however, the administration still lived in the hope that something could be salvaged from Kijibrim. On 15th February 1922 the Governor of Nigeria, Sir Hugh Clifford, visited Kontagora, where the Emirs of the Province were assembled to greet him. On this occasion it was decided at last to present Kijibrim with his staff of office, even though he had not shown any signs of improvement since the administration had taken the decision in 1917 to withhold giving him his staff until he had shown he had earned it. It was however agreed 'to experiment with the presentation of the outward and visible sign of authority in the hope that the desired result, which the withholding of it failed to accomplish, might be achieved'.[45] On the occasion, Bussa was the last of the emirs to be presented, following after the new Emir of Kaiama, Haliru, who had succeeded in 1921 on the death of Yerima Kuru. However, while Kaiama was given a Third-Class Staff of Office, Kijibrim, after some confusion, was granted a Second-Class Staff.[46]

Kijibrim was not to hold it for long. In July he was ordered to return it, which he did 'to the accompaniment of the periodic letter of repentance and promise of reformation'.⁴⁷

Soon after being presented with his staff by the Governor, Kijibrim had to be warned that, if there were any further irregularities in the Treasury, it must be placed directly under the District Officer at Kaiama. Again in June the Emir was found to have borrowed £1 2s 6d from the Treasury. There were difficulties in retrieving from Bussa the personal possessions of Turaki, who was released from jail after serving six years of his sentence, but was not allowed to settle in Bussa itself.

The prisoners at Bussa complained they got no food. By October, things seemed to have improved rather too much, for Captain Smith, the A.D.O., reported that the prisoners were allowed music, their favourite musician being a dogari.⁴⁸ The Emir was again reported for using workers illicitly.

The one big project in which the Emir could have shown leadership, the re-siting of Bussa in a position where it would be more strategic for trade, though mooted in 1920, did not get off the ground till 1922. While he personally agreed to the move of Bussa, the Bakarabonde and other representatives of the owners of the land did not want the move. Old Bussa was the site of the burial of the kings of Bussa, and they could not therefore vacate. As far as they were concerned the Emir could move, but they would stay.⁴⁹ Many of the townspeople were stubborn about the move just because it was the unpopular Emir who was trying to get them to leave their old homes. Furthermore, the Emir frequently used labour specified for the new town for work on his farm. His chief preoccupation with the new town was his own house. The D.O.'s visits to Bussa to do with the new town are one long record of frustration with the Emir, whom A. C. G. Hastings, Resident of Kontagora Province in 1922, described later 'as a bit of a thorn in the flesh to all of us. . . .'⁵⁰

3. Kissoin's Attempted Assassination of Kijibrim

On the 18th March 1923 Kissoin, elder half-brother of Kijibrim and one of his two councillors, visited Kagogi. He was a tall, heavily built man with a thick beard, always morose and often scowling. He inspired fear in most of those who met him. In the afternoon, around 4.00 p.m., he sought to quench his thirst with beer—of which he was (like his other brother, Kitoro Gani) somewhat overfond. At the beer-seller's hut he was told that the last calabash had already been sold to a Kagogi man called Kongiri, who was related to Kissoin's wife. At that moment Kongiri arrived and Kissoin ordered him:

'They say that this is your beer—well then, give me some to drink.'

'No, I won't', Kongiri replied. 'If I give you any, you will get up and start beating me about as you did before.'

Kongiri left immediately, for several months previously Kissoin had found his wife, who was Kongiri's relative, spending the evening with Kongiri's own wife. A sullen and quick-tempered man, Kissoin had called out Kongori from his own hut and beaten him; Kongiri could do little about it, since Kissoin was a prince, but he did resolve at the time never to give beer to his in-law again.

When Kongiri left the beer-seller's, Kissoin did not immediately follow him, since it appeared he thought he would return. When it became clear he was not returning, Kissoin left the beer-seller's and went to Kongiri's house. He caught up with Kongiri just outside his house and coming from the other direction. He stopped him and asked him what it was he had said to him in the beer-seller's. Kongiri did not answer, so Kissoin hit him hard in the face with the flat of his hand. Kongiri threw up his arms and fell backwards on the ground. Kissoin then walked away in the direction of a group of Kongiri's neighbours, who were sitting watching what was happening.

One of them, Yoru, fell on his knees and begged Kissoin: 'Be patient with the man, Sir.' But then Kongiri, still prostrate, called out:

'Now that you have knocked me down, you may as well come and make an end of me.'

Kissoin now lost his temper and turned back and struck Kongiri three heavy blows on the head with his first and kicked him in the ribs. Kongiri gave a groan and then lay still. Kissoin turned to the onlookers and told them angrily: 'Get away with you, all of you, and leave him here.' He then walked away.

None of the onlookers had dared lift a finger to help Kongiri, for Kissoin, apart from being a strong man, was also a prince. As Woru, one of the onlookers, later told the Provincial Court of Ilorin, 'We are poor men, and he [Kissoin] is a man of importance, and therefore we could not seize him, but sent to the village headman.'[51] Meanwhile they just stared at Kongiri, frightened to do anything.

Sule, the village headman of Kagogi, successor to the Sarkin Kagogi jailed with Turaki, arrived on the scene. He did not inspect the corpse closely for no Sarkin Kagogi was allowed to come close to a corpse, let alone touch it. Sule then called together the elders of Kagogi to decide what to do. Kissoin was nowhere to be found so they sent to inform Kijibrim, Sarkin Bussa, what had happened. They had tried to revive Kongiri with medicines, in case he had just passed out, but to no avail. They then covered the corpse with a cloth and kept vigil over it, and only buried it the next morning.

The Court later asked Sule why he had not attempted to arrest Kissoin. To this he replied: 'Kissoin is the Emir of Bussa's cousin, and so a bigger man than I. Kissoin was no longer in the village, so I considered the best thing that I could do was to tell the Emir what had happened.'

Late that night the messenger from Kagogi arrived in Bussa and told Kijibrim what had happened. He summoned four drummers, a retainer and a scribe and set off in search of Kissoin. A little north of Ganikassai, where Kijibrim had been joined by his half-brother, Sabigoga, the party came to a narrow and rocky dry watercourse. As Kijibrim, in the rear of the party, was descending the ravine, he felt and heard something strike the raised part of his saddle, which was of the Hausa style, made of wood, and like the seat of a child's rocking-horse. As he turned round to see what it was, another arrow flew by, just touching his gown. A voice, which he recognized as that of Kissoin, cried out from the bush: 'Sarkin Bussa, you are out to catch me, but I won't die alone. We will die together.' Kijibrim set spur to his horse and crashed into Sabigoga's mount, shouting 'I have been shot.' Sabigoga got clear to the side of the road, and heard Kissoin cry from the bush: 'It is I, Baba dan Mayaki*—stop, Sarki, we will die together.'

Kijibrim replied, 'No, you alone' and started to gallop off. Sabigoga then called to Kijibrim 'I'll spear him.' But Kijibrim shouted back 'No, don't.' At this point Kissoin jumped out from the undergrowth and made as if to seize Kijibrim's horse but the latter was already well on his way.

Sabigoga then told the drummers to drum Sarkin Bussa's call and then Kissoin's call—every prince of Bussa has his own drum call—hoping that he would come out again. But there was no sign of him so the party pushed on to Kagogi where they learnt that Kijibrim had crossed the Niger by canoe to Warra. At Kagogi they saw the saddle, with the arrow firmly embedded in the wood. It was poisoned, and had it hit Kijibrim he would certainly have died.

* a title borne by Kissoin.

The next morning Sabigoga and the drummers took the road back to Bussa. At Ganikassai they met Kijibrim. Sabigoga remained at Ganikassai, but Kijibrim returned to Bussa with the rest of the party after sending out further search-parties for Kissoin. He entered Bussa accompanied by his drummers. When they reached the palace, he called them around him. They stacked their spears and bows and arrows round a nearby tree, and gathered at the feet of his horse on which he was still mounted. Momman, a dogari, was sent into the palace to check whether, by chance, Kissoin was inside. He rushed out almost immediately shouting: 'Look out, here's Kissoin.' Everybody fell down in fright and out came Kissoin armed with a bow and arrow. He was only about fifteen feet from Kijibrim and prepared to shoot him, but as he drew the bow the string snapped. Kijibrim then galloped round to the back of the palace, ordering the large number of his subjects who had now gathered outside the palace to catch Kissoin. From the back of the house he heard shouts that Kissoin had got hold of another bow and arrow. Since it was clear to him the people had not caught Kissoin, Kijibrim started off towards Ganikassai, but he was again followed by Kissoin who had now also got hold of a spear from the pile on the tree in front of the palace. Kissoin chased after Sarkin Bussa, to the apparent amusement of the people.[52] Sarkin Bussa, being mounted, made good his escape. Kissoin, who according to witnesses looked mad, walked away and sat down on the far side of the dry marsh to the west of Bussa. Two dogarai set off somewhat half-heartedly to catch him, but Kissoin had disappeared.

Early on March 21st two messengers arrived at Kaiama with news of Kissoin's murder of Kongiri and his attempted assassination of Sarkin Bussa. Hoskyns-Abrahall, who had taken over the division only the day before from Captain Smith, sent off three police to arrest him. On the 28th he got news from Smith, who presumably had passed through Bussa on his way to his next posting, that Kissoin was still at large and after Kijibrim's blood.[53]

In mid April Kissoin was still at large. The Political Agent, Audu, learnt from Sabukki who, though still an outlaw, seems not to have been molested by the authorities, that Kissoin was in Dahomey. Sabukki promised to send one of his 'boys' to find out exactly where he was. Further reports came that he was in Babana.[54] In June rumours reached Hoskyns-Abrahall that Kissoin was somewhere in the Nikki region with a swollen stomach. At the end of the year he was still a fugitive from justice.

In his annual report for Borgu for 1923, Hoskyns-Abrahall commented that, despite his crime, Kissoin had been a useful Councillor: 'as he was not afraid of the Emir, and was quite ready to disagree with his decisions in judicial cases: he therefore had, in a way, a healthy influence on the deliberation of the council, which has now deteriorated into a one-man show. To describe him as a "harmless nonentity" as has been done in the past is quite incorrect. He has, however, been much addicted to the consumption of native beer, and this weakness was the direct cause of the unfortunate occurrences of last March. The Emir now naturally lays the blame for everything that has ever been wrong in the Emirate on the shoulders of Kissoin, but such must be accepted for what it is worth.'[55]

Hoskyns-Abrahall did not start full investigation of the murder until December 1923, when he also took evidence concerning the attempted assassination of Kijibrim. Kissoin was eventually tracked down in Dahomey and extradition proceedings based on the evidence taken by Hoskyns-Abrahall were initiated with the French authorities. He was handed over to the Provincial Authorities of Ilorin some time in mid 1924 and brought to trial for murder at the end of the year. On December 16th he was sentenced to death by the Resident of Ilorin, the Hon. H. B Hermon-Hodge, who gave no recommendation to mercy when submitting his verdict to the Lieutenant-Governor for confirmation:

'Except that accused is an extra hot-headed member of a naturally quick-tempered community, I can find no extenuating circumstances attending the crime. . . . Indeed I consider the crime to have been peculiarly savage and cold-blooded. . . .

'He was a man of influence and standing; had considerably more comprehension of the difference between right and wrong than the average Bussawa; and both the facts disclosed and his demeanour at the trial, and his general antecedents, show him in the light of a bully and a bandit.'[56]

The Lieutenant-Governor, too, could find no extenuating circumstances, and recommended the death sentence to the Chief Justice in Lagos on January 5th. On January 27th Governor Clifford gave the order for his execution. The Resident decided against a public execution, and Kissoin was hanged at Ilorin jail at 7.30 a.m. on 31st January 1925.

Kissoin did not 'take' his brother and former rival for the throne of Bussa with him. But he may at least have had the satisfaction before he was hanged of knowing that Kijibrim had been deposed and replaced by Kitoro Gani.[57]

4. The Deposition of Kijibrim

Even apart from the public humiliation of his brother's attempted assassination of him, 1923 was a bad year for Kijibrim. In January, Sabi Zakara, the District Head of Agwarra, when brought to trial for fraud and peculation, tried to implicate Kijibrim in his misdeeds. Sabi Zakara had collected tax at 5/- per head from 228 people in Agwarra district who were not in fact on the assessment roll. Most of them were boys and girls, or old people, not normally subject to tax. Sabi Zakara did not deny the charge but said that when in 1921 Agwarra District was counted for tax purposes he went to Kaiama to give the District Officer the totals. Kijibrim, on learning of this, grew angry with him and asked why he had included everyone who was eligible. To placate him, Sabi Zakara gave him 13/- and a gown worth 35/-. Kijibrim, Sabi Zakara alleged, told him not to do such a thing again. He also told him to collect money from young boys and girls not on the assessment roll so that he, Kijibrim, could have the money to cover the shortages in the Native Treasury which he had been ordered to make good. Sabi Zakara then came to Bussa to hand over the taxes, and Kijibrim visited him in his house late at night to collect the money, which Sabi Zakara alleged was £25 all in 2/- pieces.

Sabi Zakara's only witness was his wife, so that while Captain Smith, the A.D.O. at Bussa, was quite convinced that Kijibrim had received the money, he did not have enough evidence to try him.[58] Smith gave Sabi Zakara a modified sentence of six months in all, on the grounds that he believed Kijibrim to be involved, and wrote in his Touring Diary: 'Personally I have not the slightest doubt that Bussa got the £25. He hasn't been able to eat or move since I left for K'gora and since my arrival has hardly been able to speak.'[59]

In even more serious trouble with the administration at this time was Bussa's old enemy, Aliu, Sarkin Yauri. Since 1917, of course, he had had nothing to do with the administration of Bussa. Nevertheless, it was a source of satisfaction there when in April Aliu was, in the words of P. G. Harris, the Resident of Sokoto, 'none too soon, deposed for embezzlement of Tax and general mismanagement. . . .'[60] Aliu's administration of Yauri had first been the object of a serious enquiry in 1918, though Dwyer, when Acting Resident of Kontagora, as we have seen, had been very critical of Aliu. In April 1918 E. C. Duff, Acting as Resident of

Kontagora, reported on the complaints made by the Gungawa river people against Aliu. On his four-day visit to Yauri Duff found not only that the Gungawa had been threatening to emigrate because of the Emir's administration, but also that he was universally disliked by the *sarakuna* and *talakawa* of the emirate. Duff, who described Aliu as inordinately vain and extravagant in his personal habits, listed the complaints against him: outstanding personal debts amounting to £149; claims for materials and labour supplied for various public works amounting to £97; and appeals against unjust or excessive fines amounting to £45.[61]

Despite the gravity of the situation in Yauri, Aliu continued as emir. It was not until 1922, when Diggle was District Officer of Yauri, that he really exceeded himself. Despite warnings against his poor administration early in the year, in the third quarter he was found to have borrowed jangali tax, neglected his official duties to look after his personal farms, and imprisoned an innocent dogari to cover up for the Sarkin Dogarai who had let a prisoner escape.[62] Aliu was censured for this by the Resident. But in October, when Diggle was on tour of N'Gaski District, he discovered deficiencies in the tax directly attributable to Aliu. Proceedings were then initiated for his deposition and in April 1923 he was deported to Jabo, his home town. Thereafter, in the words of Resident Harris, his activities were 'diverted from upsetting the peace to the more useful occupation of repairing motor roads as a headman of the Sokoto Native Administration works staff'.[63]

1923 was to be a bad year for Kijibrim as well. The touring diaries, handing-over notes and annual reports are a catalogue of irritation with him on the part of the administration. He reinstated a dogari who had been imprisoned for allowing a prisoner to escape and for beating a mallam. He was not getting on with the new town of Bussa, and was using the labour for it on his own farm. He was accused of keeping the money for food for the prisoners in Bussa jail for himself. He was heavily in debt and there were allegations that he was 'eating' court fines. When Smith handed over to Hoskyns-Abrahall in March 1923, he wrote: 'Bussa is much the same and always will be under the present regime. A new Emir might do some good but there isn't a decent candidate in the whole district.'[64]

In May there were further shortages in the Native Treasury, which the Emir was meant to supervise. Ibrahim, the Ma'aji of Bussa, was dismissed for borrowing money from it. The Emir was also quarrelling with the District Head of Aliyara. Hoskyns-Abrahall attributed the reluctance of people to move to the new site to their 'obviously very pronounced dislike of the Emir'.[65]

So exasperated had Hoskyns-Abrahall become with Kijibrim by the end of 1923 that he wrote one of the most stinging criticisms of any Borgu chief to be found in the archives:

'After 28 months experience of Sarkin Bussa and his counsellors I have come regretfully to the conclusion that under the present regime Bussa Emirate will never be anything but backward, unsatisfactory, dissatisfied, and ridden with peculation, bribery and corruption. The shortages of cash in the Native Treasury, on the subject of which the Emir has been so often warned, continued during the present year. Furthermore Bussa was the only district which brought in Jangali short of receipts which had been issued. All moneys paid in on behalf of Jangali were kept in the Emir's house, so it is not unnatural to conclude that the leakages took place there. The Emir's indignant protestations of innocence and honesty could only impress one to whom his character was unknown.

'Leman of Bussa died during the year and this gave Sarkin Bussa an opportunity of adding to his universal unpopularity by choosing a favourite of his, the District Mallam of Bussa, as successor. The legitimate claims of the popular candidate were turned down by the Emir, and feeling ran and still runs high among the Mohammedans of Bussa at this rough-shod riding over their wishes on a matter which touches them nearly. Though I spoke strongly to the Emir on this particular subject, he refused, as always, advice which is not supported by a definite order, with the result in this case that a number of people who had intended to come and live in the new town, now refuse to do so.'

He then went on to consider alternatives:

'Mention must be made of Kissanti, cousin of the Emir, son of the Kikwassoin Zakurdi (brother of Dan Toro) who next to Sabukki (ineligible as being a refugee from justice) would, in the event of the Bussa sarauta* becoming vacant, be the most popular claimant. He is much liked by the talakawa and is consequently and naturally much disliked by the Emir and Waziri: for this latter reason he has never held a paid post in the Native Administration. . . . Among the many

---

* throne: however, *sarautan Sarkin Bussa* would be translated as the office of the King of Bussa.

dan sarki* who would have some claim to the sarauta, Sabuki and Kissanti are the only two who would meet with popular approval.'[66]

Hoskyns-Abrahall's consideration of an alternative to Kijibrim was to be heard sympathetically by the Resident of Ilorin, to which Borgu Division was transferred on 1st December 1923. The old Kontagora Province was dismembered and shared between Sokoto, Niger and Ilorin provinces. Both Captain Lonsdale, the Resident, and the Hon. Hermon-Hodge, Acting Resident during parts of 1924, were determined to show that Borgu would benefit by its inclusion in Ilorin Province. Indeed in August Hermon-Hodge went to Kaiama to see the Emir to assure him that, contrary to his fears, 'the incorporation of Borgu in Ilorin Province entailed no interference with the status quo either politically or territorially, but would carry with it, if not more certainly not less interest on the part of the Resident in their welfare than before. (In this connection I do not think I should be far wrong in saying that the visits in *one year* twice by the Resident, three times by the Commissioner of Police, once by the Senior Sanitary Officer, and twice by the Superintendent of Education compare favourably with the attention this much neglected division received during the whole of its previous association with Kontagora Province.)'[67]

Hermon-Hodge also went to Bussa to effect the deposition of 'the obstructive, discredited and useless Emir of Bussa'. From this act, he hoped, would date the renaissance of Bussa.

The first direct intimation of his impending dismissal was given to Kijibrim by Hoskyns-Abrahall on August 21st. Hoskyns-Abrahall went over all his failings with him and told him that he was not to be surprised if he were kicked out.[68]

On October 11th C. H. Alexander, the Acting Secretary of the Northern Provinces, forwarded the Resident of Ilorin's request for the deposition of Kijibrim to Lagos for approval.[69] After cataloguing all the defects of Kijibrim, he added that it was clear from the attitude of the people of Bussa that 'they viewed him with intense dislike.' Hermon-Hodge had further said that, if anything were to be made of the Bussa Native Authority, the removal of the Emir was essential. 'A recommendation to that effect', Alexander continued, 'would have been made some little time ago, had it not been for the fact that it was difficult to find a successor.' He then wrote a long paragraph to justify the surprising recommendation that Kitoro Gani be reinstated as Emir of Bussa. This

* sons of the chief.

was accepted, as we shall see, with remarkable enthusiasm in Lagos and Kijibrim was duly hauled up by Hoskyns-Abrahall and told his services were no longer required. 'Took it very well,' Hoskyns-Abrahall noted tersely in his Political Diary.[70]

Unlike Kitoro Gani in 1915, Kijibrim was not sent into exile but was allowed to live in Bussa where he died in November, 1944.

IX · THE RESTORATION OF KITORO GANI

1. Return from Exile

On 6th November 1924 at 4.30 p.m. Kitoro Gani returned to Bussa from Ilorin after nearly a decade in exile. He was installed Emir of Bussa that same afternoon. According to Hoskyns-Abrahall his return caused universal rejoicing in Bussa.[1]

The decision to restore Kitoro Gani was not made only because there was no other suitable candidate, but because the administration of Ilorin Province genuinely felt that his deposition in 1915 had been unfair and that Bussa had suffered deeply under Kontagora Province.

'It is noticeable', wrote Hermon-Hodge, 'throughout the records of events in the Emirate that it is admitted on all hands that Gani was and is the rightful Emir. Even in 1917 Major H. B. admitted that he is undoubtedly the rightful heir to the Emirate and religious head of the Bariba tribe. In spite of his long separation, the people regard him with affection and would rally round him. His residence at Ilorin has brought him into contact with civilization and the developments which result from an advanced and intelligent N.A. His experience should deter him from repetition of such faults as he may have committed in the past. The charge of insobriety at any rate does not now hold.'[2] The Lieutenant-Governor further argued that the 'restoration of Gani will correct what appears to have been an act of injustice committed principally with a view to the introduction of an artificial organization of the present Borgu Division'.[3]

Lagos also indulged in self-recrimination about the way Bussa had been administered over the past decade.

'It appears from these papers', S. M. Grier, Secretary for Native Affairs minuted to Governor Clifford, 'that a serious mistake was made in 1915, when the Baribas were placed under an alien chief. There was at the time open trouble resulting in a patrol, and I remember at that

THE RESTORATION OF KITORO GANI

time (I was acting for Capt. Ross) I had to proceed to Kishi to meet D.O. Borgu (Lt.-Com. Clarke) who was operating with the patrol to hand over a number of Baribas who had crossed the border and taken refuge in Kishi. I came away from Kishi with the impression that the "trouble" had been caused by our mistaken policy and with considerable sympathy for the Baribas.

'If as H.H. states, Gani is the rightful Chief and religious head of the Baribas, and if further the main reason for his removal was a desire to amalgamate for purposes of "administrative convenience" 3 small Emirates previously independent of one another, the reinstatement of Gani, in my opinion, is a tardy act of justice.'[4]

To these observations Clifford minuted in reply:

'On the face of it, judging purely from the facts as they are related in this file, this supplies an example of one of the most inept pieces of mismanagement of native affairs that I remember to have encountered in Nigeria. The sacrifice of native institutions, desires, tribal sentiments, traditions and customs to the mere administrative convenience of Government and its Officers can hardly ever have been carried out anywhere with more cynical indifference and ineptitude.'[5]

Clifford then gave his approval to Kitoro Gani's restoration, though the Attorney-General, Donald Kingdon, felt it might be a good idea to see how Kitoro Gani behaved himself before removing his name from the schedule of deposed chiefs. But the Lieutenant-Governor of the Northern Provinces did not agree with this.

Kitoro Gani thus regained his throne with the goodwill not only of his people, but of the administration from the Governor down to the District Officer, all of whom felt he had suffered unjustly at the hands of the British administration itself. The man directly responsible for his restoration was Hoskyns-Abrahall, perhaps the most brilliant, and certainly the most sympathetic British administrator to have served in Bussa. His research into the past of Bussa was responsible not only for Kitoro Gani's return from exile, but also, as we shall see, for the restoration of some of Bussa's lost lands.

Kitoro Gani, who had now become a nominal Muslim and taken the name Mohammedu, showed himself duly grateful to the administration and sent a letter in Arabic to the Governor on December 8th:

'I begin this letter with the name of Allah. Thanks be to Allah who teaches man to write with pen and ink to establish the truth that cannot be altered. This letter is from Emir of Bussa Gani to His

Excellency the Governor Sir Hugh Clifford, with greetings and salutations without limit.

'I am exceedingly pleased for the inestimable freedom Your Excellency has so kindly given me to return to my country; and I am still rejoicing. After this I pray heartily that Allah may assist and increase Your Excellency's power as you have hitherto helped me to uplift the welfare of my people at Bussa.'[6]

2. The Pardoning of Sabukki

With the restoration of Kitoro Gani an uncharacteristic note of euphoria begins to infect the official reports on Borgu. Only in the political diaries is there any intimation that things might not be so rosy as they seemed. From the British administration's point of view, Borgu had never been better looked after. There were now, though not for long, two officers in the division, one at Kaiama, the Headquarters, and one at Bussa. In Bussa the restored Emir settled down to work with surprising efficiency. He appears to have kept himself well informed of affairs in Bussa during his nine years in exile. His judicial work was particularly careful.[7] The District Head of Aliyara was a capable chief, and was no longer troubled by his own emir inciting his people against him. The new District Head of Agwarra, Babaki, a younger brother of Kitoro Gani, was settling down to work well. In Wawa, the third district, old Kantama had tight control of his subjects, but the fact that he held Kitoro Gani in great respect, even awe, meant that his authoritarian tendencies would be kept in check. The Assistant District Officer at Bussa, Theodore Hoskyns-Abrahall, was the best Borgu had had up to that time.

As early as December 1924, Walter Nash, the District Officer in charge of Borgu Division, was reporting from Kaiama that there were already signs that the change of emir was a salutary one and that the administration of Bussa would now emerge from the chaotic and altogether unsatisfactory state into which it had fallen under Kijibrim.[8] Kitoro Gani, the drunken and inefficient chief of yester-year, was now telling Nash that he was fully aware of the appalling state into which the emirate had fallen in his absence and was making suggestions for improvement.[9] People were now settling into the new town as a result of the restored Emir's popularity. Kitoro Gani had even selected two of his sons to go to the school at Birnin Kebbi—at that time, a quarter of a century after

Britain had established her rule in Bussa, only one Bussa boy was attending school.

The only note of caution was sounded by Hermon-Hodge, the Acting Resident, who warned, on reading the annual report:

'While agreeing that Gani is popular, anxious to do well and in a *strong position*, I do not think we can assume he is "strong and able" personally till he has proved this to be the case—Please therefore keep in touch with him as much as your duties in Kaiama will permit.'[10]

The euphoria seemed complete when on May 12th the Governor approved the pardoning of Sabukki and his return to Bussa. Although he had been guilty of armed insurrection in 1915, there seemed to have been 'a good deal of provocation' in the fact that his brother Kitoro Gani had been deposed and Bussa placed under Aliu, Sarkin Yauri, who had slaves as his district heads in Bussa. No definite proof had been established that Sabukki and his followers were guilty of murder or of conspiracy to murder. *Prima facie*, the only charge seemed to have been armed insurrection.[11]

Sabukki's return was discussed between Hoskyns-Abrahall and Kitoro Gani on July 11th when the former visited Bussa from Kaiama. On the 14th, Sabukki, Layan Gaba and other erstwhile outlaws were called in by Hoskyns-Abrahall and told that the Government would take no further action against them. They said they would settle in Bussa during the dry season, that is after September. Sabukki, who was next in line of succession to the throne of Bussa, made it clear that he would acknowledge his brother's authority. Indeed, on his return, he seems to have made no trouble at all, for his name rarely crops up in the official reports or the political diaries after 1925.

A further sign of the times was the fact that in Shagunu, deserted after the suppression of the rebellion, and now in ruins, people were returning and had been persuaded by the Emir to rebuild their town. Hoskyns-Abrahall's Annual Report for 1925 is worth quoting *in extenso* since it shows just how confident the British administration were that the return of Kitoro Gani heralded a new dawn in Bussa, and that this meant that at last the British administration could practise real Indirect Rule there:

'While last year was described as one of considerable achievement, this as regards Bussa Emirate has been one of consolidation. Largely as a result of changes at Bussa it has been possible to make our rule

more indirect than previously, as regards both emirates. It was not many years ago that the chiefs were looked upon as merely mouthpieces of ourselves with no responsibilities beyond but the time has come that they should be given rope and encouraged to take the initiative. The tendency among District Heads to look upon the Divisional Officer as the ruler of Borgu and the Emirs as his assistants has been discouraged, and letters, for instance, from District Heads on administrative matters, addressed direct to ourselves discontinued. With no Political Officer stationed at Bussa this presents some difficulty (especially as regards Aliyara District), but the principle can and I think should be maintained, even if occasional difficulties and mistakes arise. That it is encouraging to chiefs to feel we have confidence in them is obvious, nor is anything more likely to inspire them with confidence in their own abilities. I believe that in the long run this policy will result in simpler and more effective administration. . . .'
On the reinstatement of Kitoro Gani, he continued:

'Nothing has occurred to cause any regret whatever for this; on the contrary there is an atmosphere of satisfaction and well-being which had been painfully absent in my previous experiences of the capital. The popularity which the Emir enjoys at the hands of the talakawa and the respect not unmixed with fear which office-holders and brothers—of whom there are in all about ninety—show towards him, have effectively destroyed the quarrels and intrigues for which his brother's reign was notorious. The delay in the carrying out of instructions, the question whether they would ever be carried out, are troubles of the past, and while problems still exist, notably relations with Yelwa and land disputes, the administration of the Emirate itself is now on a sound basis.

'The office-holders are for the most part satisfactory. The Waziri is efficient and extremely energetic, considering his seventy odd years, but it would be unwise to place unlimited confidence in him: after the 1915–16 inter-regnum he, though a dan mache,* made a bid for the sarota, an act which has not been forgotten against him, and rightly so. Within his limitations he is however most useful to the Divisional

---

* *dan mache:* literally 'son of a woman' and can imply that a man is a bastard, i.e. his father is unknown. In this context it means that the Waziri was a member of the royal family but through the female line and was therefore not eligible for the throne.

Officer and is moreover an interesting and intelligent man. Treasurer Jibrim, a young Nupe Mallam . . . is really excellent—he combines honesty, industry and brains.'

The pardoning of Sabukki and his fellow rebels, Hoskyns-Abrahall enthused, 'was the natural sequel to the reinstatement of the Emir, and has written finis to the story of 1915'.[12]

This, as it proved, was a much too optimistic report. Certainly the story of 1915 was not ended: the loss of land to Yauri was still bitter to Kitoro Gani and the people of Bussa; more important, perhaps, from the administration's point of view, Kitoro Gani was not the reformed character they chose to see. Indications of this are apparent in the political officers' diaries.

When Kitoro Gani visited Ilorin in April he had an open row with the Emir of Kaiama whom he accused of trying to take precedence over him, and of refusing to accept his salutation. The old jealousy of the position of Kaiama, who earned more than he did, £250 a year as against his £200, still burned. So much so, that Kitoro Gani was 'almost beside himself with rage all the time he was at Ilorin and was most offensive to everyone'.[13] Worse still, Kitoro Gani was reported as having started to drink heavily again whilst in Ilorin. Nash tried to assuage Kitoro Gani's hurt feelings by telling Sarkin Kaiama that the Emir of Bussa was unquestionably the senior of the two, with which he apparently agreed. Kitoro Gani later acknowledged that he had behaved wildly about the whole matter, but said that he had been greatly provoked by the Ilorin rabble.[14]

By May, Kitoro Gani had started a quarrel with his half-brother, Babaki, the District Head of Agwarra, and Nash had to report there was no love lost between them. Kitoro Gani also had to be warned about exacting tribute in kind from the Kamberri. Furthermore, he believed there was a conspiracy against him led by Kijibrim, the Waziri and Mai Ndagi, Kijibrim's unpopular choice as Liman whom Kitoro Gani had replaced by the people's choice, Audu. While Nash was able to settle Kitoro Gani's fears of conspiracy by threatening Kijibrim with exile, the conflict with Agwarra continued.[15]

Small matters these may have been, but in the context of what was to happen over the next decade they were pointers that all was not as well as it seemed in Bussa. Meanwhile, administrative reparations to Bussa were to be completed the next year with the return of much of the land lost to Yauri.

3. The Return of Rofia

In July 1926 H. R. Palmer, the Lieutenant-Governor of the Northern Provinces, read Hoskyns-Abrahall's *History of Bussa* and instructed the Secretary of the Northern Provinces to inform the Resident of Ilorin that as far as the sections on British rule were concerned he considered it 'the most damning account of Political incompetence in the past he has read, and I am to say that His Honour would be glad to know whether you consider it would be possible to give back to Boussa any part of the lost territory or whether it would be best now to let matters rest'.[16] Hermon-Hodge forwarded Palmer's request to the District Officer of Borgu, Walter Nash, saying: 'I am not anxious to raise extravagant or prehistoric claims, but I consider this is a golden opportunity of making amends for comparatively recent injustices.'[17]

Actually, Hoskyns-Abrahall was not the first to raise the question of the restoration of Bussa's lost lands. In 1923, immediately before the dismemberment of Kontagora Province, Captain Lonsdale, the Resident of Ilorin, had suggested that Kunji be given back to Bussa, rather than go with Yauri to Sokoto Province. But unfortunately he was unable to back up his request with the historical data which Hoskyns-Abrahall was later to produce in favour of its return. Now Walter Nash and Hoskyns-Abrahall marshalled every possible historical fact in support of returning not only Kunji and Rofia to Bussa, but also Illo and Kaoje. This task, wrote Nash, 'has been rendered somewhat difficult by the fact that, apart from some diaries and reports relating to the years 1902–1905, which arrived from Kontagora early this year, there is not a single record in this office with a date earlier than 1912—due I assume to the amalgamation of Borgu Province with Kontagora in 1907 and later to the transfer to Yelwa of the Hq. of Borgu division in 1912'.[18]

Not deterred by this lack of documentation, Nash argued at length that Illo should be returned, its earlier loss having caused 'dismay and heartburning . . . not only to Sarkin Bussa who was deprived of one of his most populous districts but also to the people of Bussa who were thus separated from their kinsfolk'.[19] He referred to the tributary relationship of Illo to Bussa in pre-colonial times, and the fact that Sarkin Illo always received his turban from Bussa and was installed by a representative from Sarkin Bussa.

With regard to Kaoje, however, Nash admitted that Bussa never

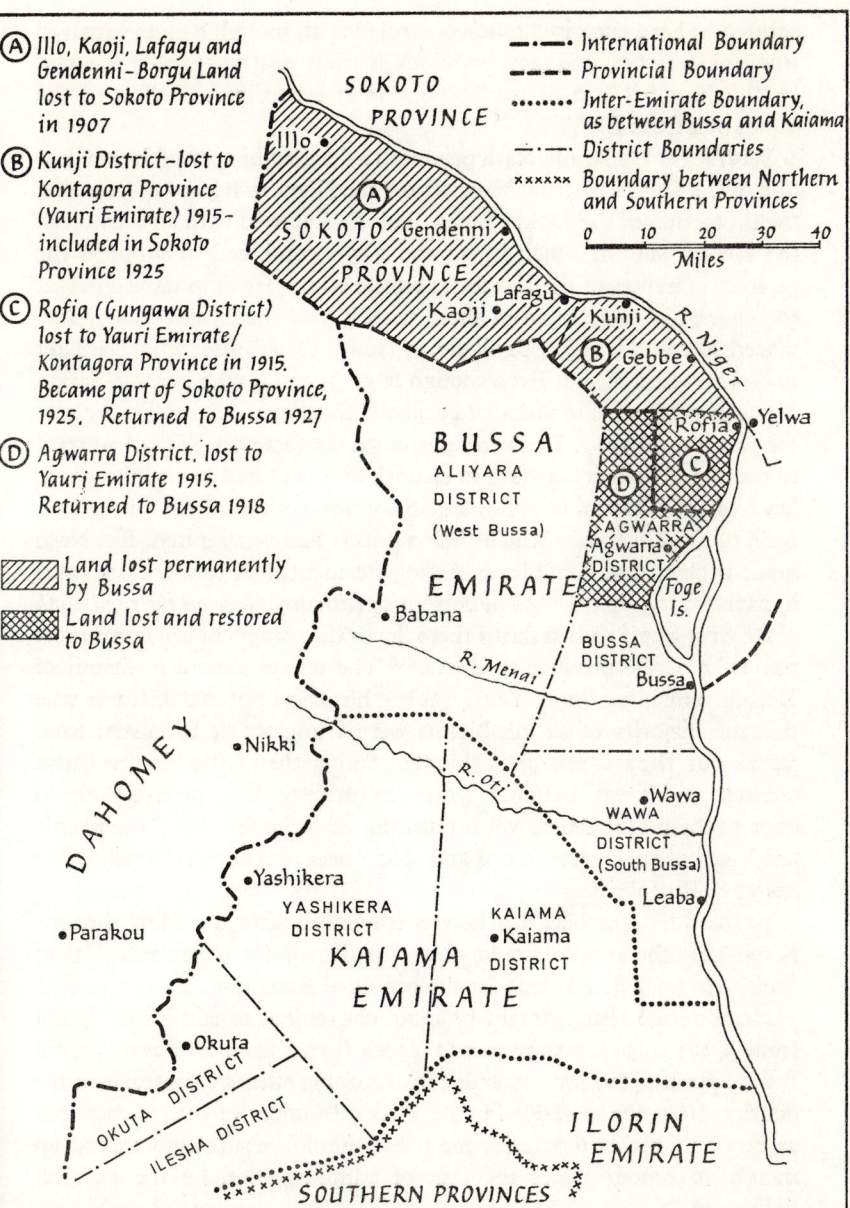

Map 8: Bussa's Lost Lands, 1915–1927

seemed to have exercised much control over it, though its loss deprived Bussa of its richest and most populous districts 'and was greatly resented by the Emir; it had of course none of the sentimental effect of the separation from Illo'.[20]

With regard to Kunji, Nash produced a detailed history of the emigration of the Kamberri from Yauri across the Niger to Bussa land, seeking the protection of the Sarkin Bussa. This he followed with an account of the Gebbe wars in which Bussa and Yauri combined to suppress the piratical activities of the Kamberri on the Niger. He emphasized that at the successful conclusion of these wars it was Bussa, not Yauri, who placed an administrator, Barjibelo, in Gebbe to look after what was later to be known as Kunji. Even though later Abershi, who became Sarkin Yauri in 1888, tried to dislodge Barjibelo, the latter in fact ruled the area for Bussa until 1912. He even referred to the fact that Yelwa had tried to use the British occupation to claim Kunji, and had ousted the Bussa headman of Kalkami in order to gain control of all the areas on the west bank of the Niger into which their subjects had immigrated. But Nash made it clear that Kemble, as Acting Resident, had told Sarkin Yauri in March 1903 that '*he had nothing to do with any place on the right bank of the river* but if he had farms there, he or the owners of the farms must pay 10% of the produce to Bussa.'[21] The one argument in favour of Kunji's remaining under Yauri was not historical but racial. It was true that the majority of its inhabitants were Gungawa or Kamberri from Yauri, but 'the fact remained that the country they settled in was Bussa territory and it was, I submit, a great injustice to the people of Bussa to deprive them of it. Moreover it must not be forgotten that these people left Yauri of their own accord and solely because they preferred to live under S. Bussa'.[22]

Nash added, further, that he was convinced after travelling through Kunji that the people would prefer to live under Bussa rather than Yauri. He felt this was true for the people of Rofia too.

He admitted that it might be more convenient to administer Kunji from Yauri since it was nearer to Yelwa than Bussa. However, Sarkin Bussa appeared to have succeeded in exercising effective control over the district. 'It made it easier for the Political Officer of course, but it is a question whether territories and tribes should be ruthlessly carved up merely to render easier the task of administration by the Political Officer.'[23]

With regard to Rofia, Nash argued, there was no doubt that it was

THE RESTORATION OF KITORO GANI

Bussa land on to which Kamberri from Rofia Island, in the Niger, had immigrated. The island itself had once belonged to Yauri, but was ceded to Dan Toro, King of Bussa, by Gallo, King of Yauri, because he could not control it. However, under British occupation, when Yauri had reclaimed it, Kemble had given it back to Yauri. (See p. 56.) One of the reasons the Kamberri from Rofia crossed to the Bussa mainland was their reluctance to remain under Yauri. In 1915, under the reorganization of Bussa, it had been given to Yauri. In 1918, when the question of restoring Bussa's land was raised, whilst what became Agwarra was returned, Hamilton-Browne had ruled that a strip of land ten miles wide along the southern boundary of Kunji be given to Yauri 'for reasonable expansion'. This, argued Nash, was a tacit admission that the strip of land belonged to Bussa.

Whilst Nash considered that Illo 'was perhaps the most ill-advised and unjust of all the transfers, yet the people have almost forgotten it in the further and later calamaties that have befallen them. I very much doubt, moreover, if, after the lapse of time, Sarkin Illo, and his following would elect to leave the pretentious Gwandu Emirate and return to their more humble Bussa brethren.' While Kitoro Gani had not asked about the return of Illo since his restoration, he had raised the question of the restoration of Rofia and Kunji on several occasions. Nash therefore only suggested the return of the latter two areas, which apart from giving Bussa a larger taxable population would restore 'the complete confidence and good will of the people'.

Hermon-Hodge, however, went further, and advocated to Kaduna that the question of the return of Illo and Kaoje be put to the District Officer of Gwandu, who happened to be Diggle who was 'fully conversant with Bussa history, and I believe an advocate of Bussa claims'. He even suggested a rough plebiscite might be taken. Pressing his point, Hermon-Hodge argued further in another letter to Kaduna: 'I do indeed feel that some reparation should be made to Bussa for the sufferings and sacrifices which have reduced a proud and comparatively populous race to a soured and sporadic handful.'[24]

G. W. Webster, the Resident of Sokoto Province, under which Yauri was now administered, would not contemplate the return of Kunji and the Rofia hinterland. 'The history of these areas, as recorded in the files here, does not agree with that given by Mr. Hoskyns-Abrahall.'[25] He considered that whatever Bussa's claims, which he felt were never strong in recent times, Kunji had become in fact a Yauri colony. He did not, however, defend 'the excision of Rofia, which only became a Yauri colony in our time, though Yauri had farmed there earlier, still I think it must remain. The inclusion of Agwarra in Yauri had no basis but, fortunately, this was put right long ago'.[26] A few days later, however, after discussions with the Resident of Ilorin, he agreed that Rofia should be negotiable. But Illo and Kunji were not.[27]

Diggle now put a spoke in the wheel. At this time he was D.O. in Gwandu and on September 23rd he wrote to the Resident, Sokoto, agreeing with the restoration of Rofia in theory but doubting whether it would be advisable politically. There were now thousands of Yauri subjects on the west bank, working land more fertile than that on the east bank. If they were forbidden to farm on the west bank unless they disowned their allegiance to Yauri they would be placed in a cleft stick. In spite of Nash's statement that they would prefer to be under Bussa, he believed they would prefer not to be.

'In passing,' he added, 'I would like to enquire from what source Mr. Nash obtained this information: if from the Bussawa it is obviously not worth the paper it is written on; while if from the Gungawa he must have gone behind the back of the District Officer Yelwa to obtain this information.'[28]

This was very much a *volte-face* on the part of Diggle, who as A.D.O. Borgu in 1918 had put up a strong case that Kunji be returned to Bussa. Kunji, he had argued then, had never followed Yauri, but was independent in the first place and then followed Bussa.[29] He even showed that the District Head of Kunji, deposed in 1916 after the amalgamation of Bussa with Yauri, had been a Bussa resident. So too had the village head of Gebbe, in Kunji. The village head of Kalkami was a son of Barjibelo; the village head of Kawara, deposed by Sarkin Yauri on the amalgamation, had been appointed with reference to Bussa; while the Fulani village head of Ilalope had been appointed by Sarkin Bussa. He then listed minor villages in Kunji, all of whom had been appointed after reference by Barjebelo to Sarkin Bussa, to whom they had all sent presents.

Webster, the Senior Resident of Sokoto, however, while he agreed with Diggle, now a Yauri nationalist, that the transfer would be politically disturbing, wrote:

'We acted wrongly and have now got to suffer in prestige.

'It is most unfortunate that owing to blunders in the past, and an apparent inability to grasp the very first principles of our policy of

THE RESTORATION OF KITORO GANI

indirect administration we should have been placed today in this difficulty. But we have been so placed and we must now find the best way out. It is a matter of equity not expediency.'[30]

Nash, on reading Diggle's report, wrote angrily, and understandably so, that he could not let Diggle's remarks 'pass in silence particularly as the District Officer Yelwa [Beck] is a personal friend as well as a colleague of mine. I most deeply resent the gross insinuation made by Mr. Diggle which I need hardly say, has not the slightest foundation; and I am surprised that one Political Officer should have thought fit to write in such a manner about a brother officer. I hope you will see your way clear to forwarding a copy of this statement to Resident Sokoto, as I do not think it would be wise to allow such a charge to remain on the files unanswered.'[31] Hermon-Hodge had feared such a reaction when he forwarded Diggle's report with the caution:

'There is much in what Mr. Diggle puts up: and it is a pity he has introduced personal rancour into the matter. Mr. Webster, S[enior] Resident Sokoto, however, has dealt with that aspect of Mr. Diggle's memo in a manner very much to the point, and I do not propose to dwell further on it. You might also endeavour to forget it and go into the question with the political officer from across the water strictly on the merits of the case.'[32]

Both Hermon-Hodge and Webster in Sokoto were worried about the partisan nature of Diggle's remarks and indeed the tendency to local nationalism on the part of political officers. Webster had reprimanded Diggle, informing him that Nash had got his information on a visit to the District Officer, Yelwa.

'Anyway there is no question of going behind any one's back, one takes information as it comes; this is a Nigerian service, not a Divisional or Provincial one.'[33]

Abandoning local nationalism, Molyneux, now District Officer, Yelwa, and Nash, the District Officer, Borgu, met to make a joint report on the future of Kunji and the Rofia hinterland. While they both agreed that the latter should be restored to Bussa, they were divided over the future of Kunji. Nash argued from the historical fact of Bussa's administration of Kunji from 1882 to 1915, emphasizing that the fact that Yauri subjects had settled on the land did not give them ownership or the Sarkin Yauri claim to it. On the other hand Molyneux emphasized the fact that the inhabitants of Kunji were natives of the Yauri emirate. He was also against the alteration of the divisional and provincial boundaries where it could be avoided, and did not feel there was sufficient justification in this case.[34]

The two officers therefore submitted the question of Kunji to their respective Residents for arbitration. Hermon-Hodge not unnaturally took Bussa's side, and, playing on the administration's feelings of guilt, suggested that the restoration of Kunji would supply the necessary redress for the injustices all were agreed had been done to Bussa. He further felt it 'eminently unfair that Yauri, who had to call upon Bussa to administer the independent Kunji when it was too much of a handful for this latter to tackle herself, should profit by the tranquillity established by the British to claim Kunji as her own'.[35]

C. M. Woodhouse, now Resident at Sokoto, felt otherwise. He dismissed the historical arguments: 'oral tradition throughout Nigeria is notoriously warped by local partisanship. If any general conclusion at all can be drawn from the account it would seem to be that both the Yauri and Bussa claims to the District are of comparatively recent origin and are supported by the authority which each rival claimant exercised at various times.'

Given the nebulous nature of the historical claims, he recommended that Hermon-Hodge accept the hard political facts of the present-day political situation. Kunji had for many years now been an integral part of Yauri and it was ruled by a district head who was exceedingly well reported on by all political officers. The District Head, being a relative of Sarkin Yauri, would not accept a position under Sarkin Bussa and there was no village head in Kunji suitable to replace him. He therefore felt that the best solution was to maintain the *status quo*.[36]

The two Residents, having reached a stalemate over Kunji, referred the matter to Palmer, the Lieutenant-Governor, for a decision. He recommended to Lagos that Rofia be restored to Bussa but that Kunji remain where it was.

'I have agreed to the restoration of Rofia to Bussa,' he minuted to the Resident Ilorin, 'and I trust, if this is ratified by His Excellency, the Bussa Emirate will accept this as a final decision in this matter. Though I admit the strength of the arguments with regard to Kunji that matter is, I think, too much of a *fait accompli* to reopen.'[37]

The Governor was clearly very confused by all the arguments and counter-arguments and the Chief Secretary wrote to the Secretary of the Northern Provinces:

'In conclusion His Excellency is quite at a loss to know how to reconcile these conflicting statements or to understand the disregard of the work that has been expended on the preparation of maps and descriptions of boundaries consequent on the reorganization of the NPs [Northern Provinces] which was approved last year. If no other factors had to be considered, the transfer of Rofia to Bussa would naturally be approved without demur. But as things are, His Excellency feels bound to ask whether, in His Honour's opinion, the importance of the transfer is such as to justify the re-opening of the general question of Provincial Reorganization.

'Whatever . . . may be the decision about the enlargement of the Bussa Emirate, His Excellency would be extremely reluctant to contemplate any further alterations, however small.'[38]

Palmer instructed his Secretary to reply that these claims were not connected with the general scheme for reorganization of the Northern provinces, but were separate issues and the result of considerable ill feeling which unfortunate changes, brought about under the old Kontagora Province, had caused. 'In His Honour's opinion it is a necessary act of justice—which, if not approved, would entail unfortunate consequences.'[39]

On 11th July 1927 Rofia, an area of some 100 square miles, with a population of some 3,000, was finally transferred to Bussa, although the transfer was nearly prevented by concern in Lagos that it would upset the maps.[40] Lagos, in finally giving approval, made it clear that no more claims of this nature would be entertained.[41]

The transfer of Rofia marked the final act of reparation by the British for the injustices they admitted they had done to Bussa. Kitoro Gani had to be satisfied with the return of Rofia alone. But in Bussa, to this day, the continued administrative separation from Kunji, Kaoje and Illo is still a burning issue and one for which the people have not forgiven the British.

X · THE SECOND DEPOSITION OF KITORO GANI

1. Disenchantment

The British administration's euphoria about affairs in Bussa continued right through to the end of 1926. Hermon-Hodge praised his subalterns, Walter Nash and Theodore Hoskyns-Abrahall, and enthused in his annual report that they 'have infused vitality into Borgu, helped it to gain self respect, and restore its place, so to speak, to the comity of Nations'. Nash, for his part, wrote: 'I think it may fairly be said that the people of Bussa Emirate are experiencing such peace and prosperity as they have not enjoyed at any rate for the past 14 years.'[1] Kitoro Gani remained from the administration's point of view almost a model emir: very popular, with his emirate well under control. At the same time he was willing to accept and act on advice.[2] Administration had become as indirect as it was possible to make it in a 'pagan' division; both Kitoro Gani and the Emir of Kaiama had a good grasp of the system and did their best to see that it was adhered to. Kitoro Gani, however, was a little the victim of his own background, occasionally trying to administer his emirate in the way he had done before 1912, when he had slaves as kofas. The only major problem was his jealousy of his brother Babaki, District Head of Agwarra. But then all the other princes were jealous of Babaki, who was one of the youngest among them.[3] While Nash felt that there was no doubt that Babaki was 'too Prussian in his treatment of the Kamberri', he wrote in his Political Diary that there appeared to be a conspiracy, to which the Emir was party, to get him removed. He therefore warned Kitoro Gani that Babaki was 'the best D.H. that has been in Agwarra and that it would be difficult—if not impossible to replace him'.[4]

By 1927, the tone of the annual reports and the Political Diary began to change. The problems which Kitoro Gani, who had first come to the throne nearly a quarter of a century ago, was experiencing in fitting into the administrative patterns of the 1920s were beginning to become apparent. In September, a few days after he had taken over Borgu Division, Captain P. E. Lewis set off from Kaiama to Bussa by bicycle to greet the emir in the best spirit of Indirect Rule. 'My reason for doing this', he wrote in his diary, 'was that I thought it at least politic, in view of the present feeling between the two Emirs, to know and make myself known to Sar. Bussa at the earliest possible moment—quite apart from the fact that it seems more courteous and seeing that Bussa has only been toured during the last 3 months I did not feel a visit from me was necessary until I had been to Gwanara, Ilesha and Okuta which would have meant 6 weeks before I met Sar. Bussa.'[5] Within less than two months, as a result of his visit and reports he had received from Bussa, he was writing to Kitoro Gani that he considered 'all the work in Bussa far from satisfactory—Court work, road work and tax work need a lot of gingering up. In comparison with similar work in Kaiama, it is really bad.'[6] On his second visit to Bussa he concluded that the strained relations between Kitoro Gani and Babaki were chiefly the former's fault.[7] By December he had concluded: 'Bussa quite impossible.'[8] These reservations about Kitoro Gani were not confined to the Diary. When Rofia was returned, it was reported that Kitoro Gani wanted to make it a separate district to give his son, the Dan Galadima, a position as district head. When this was refused, and the administration insisted that Rofia be placed under the efficient Babaki, District Head of Agwarra, he suggested that a second court member be appointed in Agwarra with his headquarters in Bunsuru. This court member should be his son. After a lot of persuasion he accepted the advice of Captain Lewis that the appointment of his son to such a position would lead to endless trouble.

The annual report commented on the lack of cooperation between the Emir and the leading officials of the Native Authority, who all performed their duties 'entirely satisfactorily'; this, the annual report recorded, was the only obstacle to progress. Responsibility was attributed to the Emir, who could not forget the days when he gave kofas, as slaves, direct orders. Furthermore, he was badly advised by members of his household staff who had followed him into exile. The Resident warned the District Officer about Kitoro Gani: 'He is not moving with the times, I fear. He hides stubbornness and native cunning behind a charming personality. It is annoying for you to have to be always criticising him or even undoing what has done but "jacta est alea." '[9]

Strained relations between the Emir and the district heads of Agwarra and Aliyara, and his tendency to bypass them and deal directly with the peasantry, were again the subject of comment in 1928.[10] The only district head who seemed to have no problem with the Emir was Kantama, Sarkin Wawa, 'an ill-mannered and prejudiced old man' in the eyes of the administration, but one who gave no trouble.[11] A disquieting new feature in the 1928 report was shortages in the Bussa Treasury, due to the laxity of the Treasurer, and 'borrowing' by the Emir. H. C. Gill, the District Officer, observed ominously that 'there are signs that the Emir is brooding less on what might have been and turning more to what is and may be.'[12] When N. P. M. Jones, who replaced Gill for a short time from September to the end of November, checked the Bussa Treasury in November he, too, found it short. He wrote in his diary that it appeared that a lot of borrowing had been going on.[13] The people supposed to be concerned with the borrowing were: the Emir—£9; Bawa, the Government Messenger—15/-; the Waziri—£5; the Ma'aji—£3; and the Assistant Ma'aji—£2. Bawa was thought to have borrowed £4 in all. The fact that the Treasury was only £3 0s 0d down was due to loans supplied by the clerk at the Niger Company store across the Niger at Warra, as Gill had found out on his check in August.

Kitoro Gani's long-standing jealousy of the position of the Emir of Kaiama manifested itself again, though covertly. When the Emir of Kaiama was returning home from a visit to Bussa to meet the Governor in April 1928, Sarkin Wawa, whom Lewis described as an 'impossible old man', refused to escort him out of the town with the other Bussa district heads. He also closed the wells in Wawa just before the Emir and his entourage passed through on the pretext that he wanted to make sure there would be enough water for the District Officer.[14] In June, Lewis's successor, Gill, reported that the Emir of Kaiama had complained of the 'habit in Bussa villages—particularly Wawa—of holding up Kaiama letters to the D.O. to "get the Emir of Kaiama into trouble" '.[15]

By 1929 Walter Nash, again in Borgu and once so enthusiastic about Kitoro Gani, was beginning to show considerable concern at the way things were going in Bussa:

'The smooth running of Kaiama Emirate always offers a sharp contrast to the state of affairs in Bussa Emirate and the reason is not far to seek—i.e. the mentality of the respective Emirs. Whereas the Emir of Kaiama is all out for progress, the Emir of Bussa would prefer things to remain as they were in the good old days before the advent of the British, when Emirs of Bussa, with the Divine Right of Kings, were allowed to do precisely as they liked, with no one to question them and no one to say them "yea" or "nay". In other words, he is a die-hard of the old school. It is unfortunate for Bussa that the headquarters of the Division is at Kaiama, for with only one Political Officer in the Division it is inevitable that most of his time should be spent in the Kaiama Emirate, whereas if more time could be spent in Bussa and the Emir "nursed" on his duties, it is not inconceivable that he could be induced to see things more from our angle and to administer his Emirate more in accordance with our ideas on the subject of administration.'[16]

The Lieutenant-Governor was, however, not over-concerned by this report. In a minute to the Resident of Ilorin he wrote: 'I think that we have room in this country for a limited number of Emirs of the type of the Emir of Bussa for the danger is, I think, rather in the direction of progress being too rapid than being too slow.'[17]

Whatever his defects from the administration's point of view, Kitoro Gani remained popular with his people. His main objective seemed to be to avoid trouble. The Kamberri, for instance, much preferred his dilatory methods to the much more autocratic methods of Babaki. Much of the Emir's energies seem to have been expended in quarrels with his district heads and other Native Authority officials. He interfered little in the daily lives of his subjects, rarely leaving Bussa. Gill, despite all his reservations about the Emir's administration, felt that as far as the temperament of the people was concerned they were fortunate in having him as emir.[18]

Gill's successor, Captain L. C. Schlotel, had a different view. He felt that Bussa needed all the direct supervision possible, even though with usually only one political officer in Borgu this was impossible. Finally, by 1932 resigned acceptance of Bussa's tranquil but inefficient administration gave way to a concern more characteristic of the reports on Kitoro Gani's rule immediately prior to the first deposition: the taxes were not coming in on time.[19]

2. Trouble in the Bussa Treasury

In October 1932, D. F. Heath, the District Officer of Borgu, instructed his assistant district officer, B. A. Roberts, to go on tour of Bussa and chase up the tax which was late coming in. 'I do not wish you to distrain forcibly for tax without prior instructions from me. You must make the Emir and District Head do all the "dirty work". (Under no circumstances of course must you handle any tax yourself—neither must your government staff.)'[20]

Late payment of tax was not the only thing Roberts found wrong on his tour of Bussa. The Native Treasury was filthy and full of junk. The Bussa prison was in a foul condition. 'A foetid stench pervades the place.' The Emir and the Waziri, his senior counsellor, were quarrelling: the Emir had accused the Waziri of plotting with the District Head of Agwarra against him. In conversation with Roberts, the Emir not only said that Sarkin Agwarra had given the Waziri a horse and *alkyabba* (gown) but that the Waziri went to salute him rather more often than was necessary. But 'it was the matter of the virgins that gets old Bussa every time, especially as the Waziri's inevitable reply consists of mumbling something about the will of Allah.' Apparently the Emir and the Waziri were in close competition for the young girls of the town.

There seems to have been a love-hate relationship between the two old men, for Sarkin Bussa did not want to get rid of him; he merely wanted to make sure he could be kept under control. So Roberts agreed that the Waziri's activities should be confined to Bussa, and Kitoro Gani's son Gunu should become the Wakil Waziri, doing most of his work.

In the districts, matters were in a bad state. Apart from the jealousy existing between the Emir and Babaki, District Head of Agwarra, the latter had become unpopular and 'all the able bodied during the last 3 years have gone to bush and left him alone with the aged, blind, etc.'[21] because of his strong-arm methods. Aliyara, the richest of the districts, only looked good on paper, but was according to the Emir as badly administered as Wawa, whose chief, Kantama, had been threatened with deposition the year before for inefficiency. Roberts took the Emir on tour of Aliyara to collect the tax: it was his first visit to the district for twenty years. Roberts took a great dislike to Sarkin Aliyara who weighed sixteen stone and needed two men to get him up on his pony, which had to be blindfolded during the proceedings. 'I find [Aliyara] to be a big, fat, lazy, insolent hog—with so far no saving grace whatsoever.'[22] Roberts felt, however, that his tour of Aliyara with Kitoro Gani had done a lot of good. But Heath cautioned him: 'Be careful not to fall too much under the well-known charm of the Emir.'[23]

Despite the bad reports on Sarkin Wawa the year before, he began to show surprising energy and actually toured his district collecting tax without the presence of Roberts.[24] When Roberts did visit Kantama he warmed to him—'Old Wawa is at heart rather a dear, with a sense of humour.'[25]

By January, however, the Bussa tax was still not complete. Heath once again instructed Roberts to go on tour of Bussa to bring in the tax.

'You should set your face against all "wasas"* and jollifications in the afternoon and evening and forbid the Emir to hold them, giving the non-completion of the tax as the reason. Nag, nag and nag until the tax is complete and don't give the Emir five minutes peace. Let non-completion of tax be the reason for refusing every possible request. Everything must be subordinated to this main consideration of tax completion.'[26]

Roberts arrived at Bussa on January 9th to find Kitoro Gani was away at Shagunu collecting tax. On January 10th he checked the Ma'aji Jibrim's books for December and found them in order. On the 13th he gave Kitoro Gani, who had returned from Shagunu, a lecture on his general slackness which he repeated again two days later. On the 17th he rode out to Kagogi and gave the people 'a lecture on foresight and economics—without tears—which they had the grace to applaud'.[27] On the 19th, in response to two queries by Heath as to the Bussa tax returns, he made investigations through Gunu, the Wakil Waziri, and one Mallam Umaru. On the 20th they came in with some startling revelations, including rumours that over the past four years the Ma'aji and Alkali of Bussa had been manipulating the funds of the Native Treasury. Roberts took these rumours to Kitoro Gani, who denied ever hearing them. He did, however, admit that he rarely went to the Treasury to open the cash tank and check the funds. Even though officially he was in charge of the Treasury as head of the Native Administration and held the key to the cash tank, he usually gave it to the Ma'aji when he asked for it. It so happened that the counting of the Agwarra tax had just been completed so Roberts thought it would be a good opportunity for him to show the Emir how his monthly check should be done. The result was that they found that the Treasury was £117 12s 5d short. The Ma'aji and the Alkali were immediately arrested and jailed by the Emir.

For some time, it transpired at the trial of Jibrim the Ma'aji before the Provincial Court on February 17th, he had been lending out money from the Native Treasury. One of his chief creditors was the Alkali; the other,

* wasa = drumming and dancing.

he alleged, was the Emir himself. These shortages had not been discovered before, since the Ma'aji always had plenty of warning of the arrival of the District Officer from Kaiama, five days' trek away. The Emir, Jibrim told the Court,[28] would summon him when he heard the District Officer was coming, and tell him to make sure the money was correctly balanced. When Roberts first checked the Treasury on January 13th, the Emir advanced Jibrim tax money which was then coming in fast, so that Roberts found the cash to be in order. At that time there had in fact been a shortage of over £100. The Emir, Jibrim alleged, had been able to get together only £51 from the tax money, but suggested they might be able to make up the balance with a loan from the clerk of the Niger Company canteen at Warra, an arrangement that dated at least from 1928. (See above, p. 204.) Accordingly Jibrim wrote to the clerk asking him to send £71. However, there was talk at the time of closing down the Niger Company canteen, so he decided not to send the letter after all, and tried to borrow the money from another source. He approached an old friend of his, Momman, a trader from Bida, who obliged him with £49 which was sufficient with the £51 from the Emir to cover the deficiencies when Roberts checked the Treasury on the 13th. Jibrim then gave the £49 back to Momman who went on his way northwards, while the £51 was given back to the Emir, who paid it into the Treasury shortly afterwards. The sum was properly entered into the cash book so that when Roberts did his surprise check on January 17th the Treasury was still short. The method 'I have described as used for this occasion' Jibrim told the Court 'has been used by us on many occasions before, when a District Officer was coming and always with the help and knowledge of the Emir. If the Emir had not helped me thus I could never have managed to get the money together. I know no-one who could have produced the large sums that have been required from time to time. I cannot get money from the earth.'

In contemporary terms, the loss of £117 12s 5d may seem small. But it was more than half the Emir's annual salary, and a twentieth of the total annual revenue of the Bussa emirate. It was three times the annual salary of the Ma'aji himself.

On the evening of his arrest, the Ma'aji had been brought before the Emir and his Council had asked what had happened to the money. He provided a list of loans he had made from the Treasury funds, but it did not total up to the amount missing. The Waziri alleged that, when asked what had happened to the balance, the Ma'aji Jibrim admitted he had stolen it. In court, the Ma'aji Jibrim accounted for the deficiency in detail. Below is a summary extracted from the Court Record, implicating most of the Bussa Native Authority officials, great and small.

Mallam Aliyu, the Government messenger	£6. 0. 0
Bawa, the Government messenger	3. 6. 0
Gunu, the son of the Emir	8. 0
Mallam Bagidi, the Assistant Treasurer	15. 0
Mallam Umuru, the Emir's scribe	5. 0
The Alkali of Bussa	8. 0. 0
(This amount is made up of many small amounts.)	
There was also a loan given by permission of the District Officer to the Alkali of	5. 0. 0
The Alkali of Bussa, deficiency on Court Fees and Fines	6. 13. 1
The Emir of Bussa:	
(a) Loan to pay a trader pressing for payment of a mantle: Feb. 1932	4. 0. 0
(b) taken by the Emir in cash: June 1932	3. 0. 0
(c) loan to pay for a horse: August 1932	7. 0. 0
(d) payments to various of the Emir's creditors: August 1932	2. 0. 0
(e) balance owing on a horse, paid to the seller on the Emir's orders, Sept. 1932	3. 0. 0
(f) payment for an outstanding debt on a sword: November 1932	5. 0. 0
(g) cash taken by the Emir	18. 2. 0
(h) sundry small loans to the Emir of which he had no account	
Mallam Lafia, Tax Collector and son of the Emir, shortage on the Jangali tax: December 1931	£35. 0. 0
Mallam Lafia, further shortage on taxes	5. 0. 0
Emir of Bussa, a further £3. 0. 0d omitted in the first list supplied by the Ma'aji	3. 0. 0
Ma'aji Jibrim himself £2 odd in loans to himself	2. 0. 0
Total	£117. 9. 1d

The Emir was deeply implicated by the Ma'aji, who had with reluctance admitted to taking some £2 0s 0d himself. According to the Ma'aji, the shortages all started because of the Emir in 1931:

'Mallam Lafia, a son of the Emir, was then doing the work of collecting Jangali tax. He brought me an account of money he had collected and some money. On counting the money I found that it was £35 short of the account. I asked him where the balance was. The District Officer was then in Bussa and it had been reported to him that this Jangali had been collected and paid in to the Treasury. I therefore told Mallam Lafia that I must report the shortage to the District Officer. He asked me to have patience and that he would raise the balance. I therefore entered in the cash book the amount which should have been brought in on the understanding that the money which was short would be brought to me, and I did not report any shortage to the District Officer. I think that this was in December 1930. Mallam Lafia promised me that the money would be forthcoming within twenty days. I thought that perhaps in his collection he had taken cattle in lieu of cash in the hope that he might sell them for more than the amount they had been taken for and that he would thus get a profit. I therefore thought that the money would be easily forthcoming. Money was not difficult to get then as it is now. About three months after this we heard that the District Officer was on his way to Bussa again and I went to Mallam Lafia and asked him what he was going to do about it as the money in the Treasury was certain to be checked and it was this £35 short. He produced £25 that day and all day I waited for the balance of £10. In the evening I was called by the Emir to his house. The matter of the money was discussed and in the end the Emir sent me the £10 to make up the deficiency. The District Officer counted the money and went away. The Emir then gave me instructions to give back both his £10 and the £25 to Mallam Lafia so that it could be returned to the people who had put up the money. This I did. The Emir told me that he himself would be responsible for his son's debt of £35 and that he would repay the money out of his salary in easy instalments. This was in March 1931. In, I think, to the best of my recollection, the month of May 1931 when the salary time came round the Emir paid the first instalment of £10 out of his salary. The actual amount he drew from me on that pay day was not more than five shillings. The rest he had had in small amounts during the month. Ever since he came back from exile in Ilorin many years ago he has had his salary in loans long before the month was finished. In the following month after this payment of £10 he took it back again as he said creditors were worrying him. Not only that but he took another £5 later to make good a further shortage in his son's tax money. The total that he owed the Treasury on account of Mallam Lafia was then £40.'

The Court asked Jibrim whether the Emir himself had ever made a monthly check on the cash in the Bussa Treasury. He insisted that he had never once done so. All that happened was that when the Emir was required to send in the return of how much was in the Treasury, he asked the Ma'aji to tell him how much there was supposed to be. They then made out a return to say the Emir had counted it and found it to be correct. Once in fact, he agreed, the Emir, at the instigation of the Waziri, had been to the Treasury to count the money, but even though he found a deficiency he sent in a return that it was correct.

Mallam Jibrim was asked why he did not deduct the advances taken by the Emir from his salary each month. 'I have always protested, at the time of paying out monthly salaries,' he told the Court. 'He has always told me that I have no power to refuse his order to give him money.' The Court then asked him why he never complained to the District Officer. 'That is the mistake I have made, but the Emir has always told me that the matter of the Treasury was only between him and myself. Only we two have known the real affairs of the Treasury.'

'Why have you not complained to the members of the Bussa Council?' the Court continued.

'The Council have no power,' Jibrim answered. 'They could not have helped me even if I had complained.'

The Court, after extracting from Jibrim an admission that he was fully aware of 'the fraudulence of his actions' in loaning money to various Native Authority officials after entering in the cash book that he had received moneys they should have paid into the Treasury, found him guilty of stealing the £117 12s 5d. He was sentenced to two years imprisonment with forced labour and his property was to be sold by public auction or private sale to recover as much as possible of the amount he had 'stolen'. The Court ordered that goods only up to the value of £117 12s 5d should be sold. If part of his property was in corn and foodstuffs, sufficient to feed his wives and children for three months should be set aside.

Heath, the District Officer who presided over the trial, and who had given Jibrim the maximum sentence within his powers, wrote in the report on the case:

> 'Had there been no Emir, head of the Native Administration, covering up and encouraging the thefts, I do not consider, that my powers of two years would have been sufficient to ensure adequate punishment for the long drawn out and carefully concealed peculations. As the facts stand, however, I consider two years adequate punishment.

'The whole Native Administration at Bussa is corrupt and slack, due to the laziness and easy going nature of the Emir. An example is therefore necessary, and any punishment of less than two years would not have this exemplary effect.'

No case was brought against the Emir, but he was confined to his house, and the Native Treasury was taken over by Roberts. Bussa was now under *direct* British rule. It was cardinal to the British system of Indirect Rule that the Emir, as Native Authority, run his own Treasury. The experiment with the return of Kitoro Gani seemed to have failed.

The only person brought to trial as a result of the Ma'aji Jibrim's revelations was the Alkali Abdu. He was accused of stealing £6 13s 1d which he had received for and on account of the Bussa Native Administration. He was also accused of stealing and receiving the sum of £8 0s 0d knowing it to have been stolen. The former sum was in respect of court fines which he failed to pay into the Treasury and which the Ma'aji Jibrim had written in the cash book as having been received. The latter sum represented sundry advances of which the Ma'aji kept a record. In July of 1932 the Ma'aji had become concerned about the outstanding court moneys and went to see the Alkali about their repayment. The Alkali asked him to go and make out a statement of exactly what he did owe, adding that he could not pay anyway, which was hardly surprising since he earned only £3 a month. The Ma'aji made out a statement of account for £14 13s 1d which the Alkali signed in Arabic: 'Abdu Kali Bussa'. The Ma'aji carefully put away the paper, whose contents were written in English. 'Alkali, that which he owes to the Ma'aji of Bussa because of advances and fees and fines £14.13.1d 27/7/32. I have totalled them and they come to fourteen pounds thirteen shillings and one penny. This owing for three years. After that he has bought a gown for £1. 10s 0d. He owes 8/- of that, also a roll of clothes, worth 6/-.'

When the Ma'aji learned he was in trouble, and just before his arrest, he told his servant Labaran to burn all the slips of paper showing outstanding debts and I.O.U.s from the Alkali. Only the I.O.U. presented in court remained.

The Alkali, in his turn, denied that the signature on the paper was his. But witnesses literate in Arabic were brought to testify that it was. 'All of us Arabic writers in Bussa know each other's handwriting.' The Scribe of the Court of the Emir of Bussa told the Alkali in court: 'We all write differently, and that is verily your signature.'

The Court brought witnesses to prove that the Alkali was heavily in

THE SECOND DEPOSITION OF KITORO GANI

debt, certainly beyond the level manageable for a man receiving a monthly salary of £3 os od. But the Alkali continued to deny the charges against him.

The Court found him guilty of stealing the £6 13s 1d since it was the Alkali's 'clear duty' to pay these sums in to the Treasury, 'and his failure to do so proves at least the temporary intent to use the money at his will.' However, the Court took a more charitable view of the £8 os od, that the sum was taken in small amounts as advances against his salary. 'The Court is therefore not satisfied that there was any mens rea or fraudulent intent in the taking or converting or receiving.' The Alkali was jailed for one year with hard labour, and his personal property to the value of £6 13s 1d was to be sold by public auction or private sale and the proceeds credited to the Bussa Native Administration.

3. More Trouble in the Bussa Treasury

That Kitoro Gani was privy to the fact that there were deficiencies in the Bussa Treasury nobody in the Administration doubted. He did, after all, officially hold one of the keys to the cash tank. Consideration was given to his deposition for his laxity in supervision of a treasury for which he was responsible: 'But the prestige the Emir enjoys among his people, based as it is on his traditional temporal and spiritual claims to the chieftainship, and his popularity and long period of office—19 years, make it impossible that a successor would be accorded respect during the life time of the Emir were he deposed.'[29] The one viable alternative to Kitoro Gani, Babaki, the District Head of Agwarra, had been told by Heath that he need have no further ambitions in the direction of the emirship, because of his methods of tax collection in the 1932–3 season.[30]

Since the administration felt they were stuck with Kitoro Gani, they sent another A.D.O., E. R. Rowse, 'on tour' from Kaiama, to relieve Roberts at Bussa, who had also been officially 'on tour'. Rowse arrived in Bussa on 5th April 1933 and was instructed to keep control of the Bussa Native Treasury and to supervise the activities of the Emir and other Native Authority officials much more closely than was usually compatible with the policy of Indirect Rule.[31] The Emir himself was still confined to his house. The Native Court, which had been run on an *ad hoc* basis by the Waziri and Liman until this arrangement was overruled on March 25th, was closed. As far as Bussa Metropolitan District was concerned, this was being run by Gunu, son of the Emir, who during the Emir's confinement was acting as Wakil Sarki. The sentence of 2 years on the Ma'aji Jibrim had been confirmed and a warrant for the Kaduna prison had arrived. The Alkali's sentence had not yet been confirmed. He had a cough for which he had been given some mixture. A new treasurer, a young boy just out of Middle School, had been found and had taken up work at Bussa under Roberts's supervision, with the title of joint Ma'aji.[32]

There had been some difficulty in recruiting a treasurer from Bussa. The decision to take a boy straight from Middle School was very much a last resort. But Bio was a Borgu man from Okuta and would not have personal difficulties in settling down in Bussa. Heath, the A.D.O. in charge of Borgu Division, agreed with Nash, the Acting Resident of Ilorin, that 'Bio sounds the very man for this work as assistant. . . .' But, he cautioned, '. . . it has in the past proved dangerous to give a boy straight from school responsibility for and custody of large sums of money. The temptation seems to me too great and not fair on a boy who may become of very great use if allowed to settle down. I personally therefore should not be in favour of giving him the position of Ma'aji straight away.'[33] He reiterated his warnings a week later: 'I respectfully submit that my objections to a young boy straight from school having such large responsibility have foundation in examples from the past.' He then advocated the arrangement he had earlier proposed that Sabi, the District Scribe of Agwarra, aged 30, who could read and write in the Roman script, and had a record of honesty as far as tax collection was concerned, be made Ma'aji with Bio doing the accounting.[34] Somewhat tetchily Nash replied: 'I was and am fully alive to the dangers to which you allude. You had however reported the situation as somewhat desperate. I therefore explored every avenue to help you. The opportunity of availing ourselves of the Borgu-bred Head Boy of the Middle School, a youth of reliability and character rather than genius (which often degenerates into cunning) was too good to be missed.

'The situation', he felt, was 'further safeguarded by the fact that he will be under tutelage of the Political Officer—not the Emir—for some time to come, that is until Indirect Rule is put on its feet again.'

Nash then suggested that Sabi and Bio be made joint Ma'ajis, for Bio, having given up the opportunity of Higher College, should not lose by it if he gave satisfaction.[35] In the event, Sabi was left in Agwarra, and Mallam Lafiya, the incumbent Assistant Ma'aji of Bussa, was made joint

Ma'aji with Mallam Bio under the supervision of Roberts, who complained to his successor that Bio's 'practical experience is *NIL*.'[36]

In April, after receiving stern warnings about his future conduct from the administration, Kitoro Gani was reinstated and the Native Court started work again. Despite Bio's lack of experience, he and Lafiya both proved 'willing and are picking up the work quite well'.[37] Indeed by the end of the year a familiar cautious note of optimism crept into the annual report: Major B. Glasson, who took over charge of Borgu Division from Heath in May, wrote that there had been progress in the Bussa emirate, and cited as evidence the fact that though in the past it had been impossible to collect the taxes within a specified time, all the taxes, with the exception of a small proportion of Jangali, had come in by October 31st.[38] Even though the Emir was fast showing signs of decay, under 'constant supervision' he had 'shown himself willing but would quickly relapse if left alone'.[39]

Bio was soon made full Ma'aji of Bussa, and there were early indications that all might not be well with his conduct of the emirate's financial affairs. On January 16th Glasson, accompanied by Heath, set off by car along the Kaiama–Bussa road, which was motorable in the dry season, to make a surprise check on the Bussa Treasury. Unfortunately for Mallam Bio, cars travelled faster than the 'bush telegraph' and when they arrived they found he had crossed to Warra to see the Niger Company clerk to change £52 into smaller money. He had no witness to the transaction and had made no entry in the cash book. He had already been warned about this practice on several occasions. The Waziri was sent across the Niger to Warra to check whether the story was true and returned confirming it.

The taxes from the Bussa emirate all came in by the end of the financial year, that is 31st March 1934, though as usual metropolitan Bussa's was the last in. This was 'entirely due to the lack of Personality and energy on Sarkin Bussa's part'.[40] On April 12th Glasson made another surprise check on the Bussa Treasury and only with difficulty was he able to balance the accounts. 'The situation in the Borgu Division is hopeless', he wrote, 'with one officer on it.' Nevertheless, Glasson, when he handed over to Heath in November 1934, was 'by no means despondent over Bussa'. The report by the Government Auditor,* F. E. L. Carter, on

---

* It was only in 1934 that Native Treasury accounts became susceptible of audit by the Government Audit as distinct from internal audit by the District Officer, as had been the practice hitherto.

the Bussa emirate showed that steady progress had been made and was by no means discouraging. Provided a second political officer who could tour the division was always available, 'much useful work in developing the Emirate can be done.'[41] Heath, however, was pessimistic about the Bussa Treasury in his Annual Report for 1934:

'While Mallam Bio was not overbright, he had a steady and good character and he progressed rapidly under my constant personal supervision, but it is correct to say that after a year of what was most rigid training, his figures had to be checked very carefully.

'With the withdrawal of the second official car from Bussa things rapidly deteriorated. The Ma'aji could not have the constant supervision necessary. This year's accounts are far from good and the method of routine drummed into him with such persistence has been let go. He has foolishly been living beyond his means and has got into debt. I sincerely hope it will be possible to pull him together again—if not he will have to go, as with other things as they are at Bussa it is absolutely essential to have a really trustworthy man there.'[42]

Concerning Kitoro Gani, Heath was even more pessimistic in his confidential report on him for 1934: 'Complaisant but hopelessly inefficient and will do nothing unless driven. Has once again been privy to Treasury defalcations.'[44]

On January 4th R. E. Beevor, the Assistant District Officer at Kaiama, visited Bussa and found a shortage of £10 14s 0d in the Treasury. On the 8th he made a surprise check but this time found no shortage. On the night of the 12th–13th January he made yet another surprise check and found the following deficiencies:

Shortage in strong room bags (being net shortages obtained by offsetting excesses £3.18.0d against shortages £11.2.6)	£7.4.6
shortage in safe	£45.5.0
giving with the sum debited	£10.0.0
	£62.9.6

Bio, the Ma'aji, was arrested and Beevor took over the duties of treasurer. It was clear that the Emir, who held one of the keys of the safe/cash tank, knew that there had been on several occasions one or two shortages of cash and did not report the matter to the administrative officer. Similarly, though the Emir stated that the Ma'aji had been living beyond his salary, he had said nothing to the administrative officer. Trouble had begun after July 1934 when the Kaiama-Bussa road became unmotorable because of the rains and the only way a political officer could get to Bussa was by a five-day ride on horseback. This gave Mallam Bio, as it had his predecessor, Jibrim, plenty of time to square his accounts. The deficiency was only discovered because a political officer was able to make a surprise check and complete audit after all the taxes had come in so that unregistered tax money was not available to cover the deficiency on an overnight basis.

After a prolonged audit, the total deficiency was discovered to be £91 7s od. The losses had been occurring for a considerable period of time and 'had been covered up by a most ingenious falsification of the books and juggling with the incoming tax'.[45] Mallam Bio was sent for trial before the High Court where he was given one year for each of three counts or one year for three counts. Unfortunately the record of the case cannot be traced in the archives. But from the various reports connected with the deposition of the Emir, and from information recorded at Bussa, it is clear that the Emir and Waziri were deeply implicated. The Waziri had failed to report shortages of which he was aware, while three district scribes (mallams) ignored repeated warnings by allowing the Ma'aji to take tax money from them without insisting on the issue of receipts. £9 was recovered from the Waziri and the three district scribes for their part in the losses.[46]

Major Glasson, the District Officer in charge of Borgu at the time of the embezzlement, was called on for an explanation as to why he had not kept a regular check on the books. In defence he replied that from March to September 1934 he had been left single-handed in a division of 11,000 square miles:

> 'Supervision of a Division of this size is very difficult. The place is so backward that all clerical work has to be done by the D.O. The Mallams cannot be trusted to do the simplest things and every little detail has to be carefully watched.'

He also wished to draw attention to the fact that he had vigorously protested at being left single-handed during the rains in a division the size of Borgu with its difficult communications:

> 'But more particularly with Bussa Emirate in it, the Emir of which is notoriously disloyal and his staff corrupt. I did, however, realize that

the Administrative Staff of the Province did not admit of a second officer being available.'

Whenever he summoned Bio, the Ma'aji, to Kaiama, he invariably left something behind. 'It was useless to send back to the Emir of Bussa for anything as he ignored all correspondence.'

He had been unable to visit Bussa in August and September because of very heavy rains. He deeply regretted his omission to see that the Daily Abstract and Vote Service Ledger were kept up to date. 'I can only plead that I was considerably worried over the many districts for which I was responsible, each with a Native Court, which I felt were being neglected. I venture to hope that H.H. will appreciate that I had no easy task to perform in this Division. I endeavoured, however, to perform my duties to the best of my ability.'[47]

While the Chief Commissioner of the Northern Provinces considered 'that Major Glasson's omission to see the proper books were kept in Native Treasury, was inexcusable, he agrees with Res. Ilorin, Mr. Daniel, that the major responsibility for the loss rests on the Emir of Bussa. The latter's checks had been perfunctory and of no real value. It is obvious that the Native Treasurer's mishandling of funds *could not have been possible without his connivance as a key holder*, and indeed on one occasion it seems the Emir actually opened the strong room to enable the Native Treasurer to make up his safe balance by taking money from strong room bags.'[48]

The wheels were now fully in motion for the second deposition of Kitoro Gani.

4. The Second Deposition

The administration could now no longer put off the decision it had been considering ever since the Ma'aji Jibrim was jailed for defrauding the Bussa Treasury in 1933. Even so, in proposing the deposition of Kitoro Gani, the Chief Commissioner did consider the possibility of retaining him as emir under the close supervision of an administrative officer stationed permanently at Bussa. But even then, he felt, no real authority could be entrusted to him. In any case, shortage of staff due to the financial stringencies of the depression made the posting of an administrative officer to Bussa impossible. 'But,' concluded his Secretary, 'in spite of all these considerations, H.H's opinion is that the continuance of an ineffective and unjust administration cannot be justified, and Gani, having failed to respond to all efforts made to assist him, ought to be removed.'[49]

The catalogue of Kitoro Gani's 'crimes' was simply too large. Apart from his failure to supervise his treasury, the cornerstone of British Native Administration in Northern Nigeria, he had apparently 'connived at the fraudulent methods of the Treasurer'.[50] In his court he showed favour to parties in whom he was interested and he adjourned many of the cases brought against his own dependants indefinitely. With the administrative officers he adopted a policy of obstruction. Administrative orders which he should have passed on to his district heads were never sent. As soon as an administrative officer left Bussa, the Emir reversed judicial decisions which had been given in the former's presence.

'Generally he is surrounded by hangers-on whose intrigues he is always ready to assist, takes no interest in the admin. of his Emirate and his efforts are directed to doing as little as possible and evading all his responsibilities.

'The Emir belongs to the older generation and owing to the geographical remoteness of his Emirate and shortage of staff, he has not always received the supervision and guidance required to enable him to keep abreast of modern requirements.'[51]

To replace Kitoro Gani, the Resident proposed his younger brother Babaki, District Head of Agwarra. In recommending him, the Resident said that he had been consistently well reported on during his eleven years as district head, which means he can hardly have read the files very closely. The only other candidates were the Emir's son, Lafia, village head of Rofia, who was 'too weak and like his father to be considered', and Mallam Lafiya, the Assistant Ma'aji, who was 'too closely implicated' in the loss of money from the Treasury.

Babaki, apart from his administrative experience as district head of Agwarra, was a man of substance. The Resident's only fear was that the Bakarabonde might refuse to initiate another Bussa king during the life-time of Kitoro Gani. But the Bakarabonde had indicated he would install Babaki. 'Succession in Bussa has always been from an elder to a younger brother where possible, and Babaki would be the most acceptable to the people of the only three possible candidates.'[52] The Governor gave his approval to the deposition of Kitoro Gani on 25th June 1935. However, even though the administration had decided on his successor, the Chief Commissioner proposed that the District Officer in charge of Borgu be appointed as the Native Authority of Bussa, temporarily, 'to give the Bussa people an opportunity of electing Gani's successor with due deliberation—as well as to avoid any appearance of imposing Babaki on the people without their consent'.[53]

Lagos approved this arrangement since they felt that the earlier proposal for the immediate imposition of Babaki had 'rather savoured of a coup d'état'.[54] The Governor, however, felt that if it were announced that the District Officer would now be the Native Authority, without any intimation that his appointment was only an interim arrangement to enable the people to choose Kitoro Gani's successor, Kitoro Gani might rapidly gain supporters.[55] But he was assured that the District Officer would see there was no delay in the 'selection committee's deliberations'.[56]

The Resident was not quite sure how Kitoro Gani would take his deposition, and felt it best to serve the deportation order on him in the presence of a force of Government Police. The Resident, accompanied by the District Officer and 20 Touring Police, arrived in Kaiama to prepare for Kitoro Gani's deposition. He was summoned to Kaiama, just as he had been when first installed in 1903, and arrived there at 11.30 a.m. on Wednesday August 21st with a small following.

At 3 o'clock in the afternoon, Kitoro Gani was called to the District Office for an interview with the Resident, F. de F. Daniel. According to the Resident 'he showed no surprise and had probably expected such action.'[57] The District Officer, R. E. Beevor, wrote in his diary that Kitoro Gani accepted his sentence with considerable fortitude.[58] He was informed that there were three courses open to him. He could return to Bussa and arrange his affairs and then go down river near to Jebba. He could send his servants back to Bussa to pack up his loads and wait in Kaiama till they had finished. Or else he could make use of the Resident's lorry which was returning to Ilorin the next day. Clearly he would be humiliated if he returned to Bussa deprived of the *sarauta*. Equally it would be humiliating for him to remain in the capital of his rival in his reduced circumstances.

Kitoro Gani's immediate decision was to go down to Ilorin and thence to Igbetti in Oyo Province, where, he hoped, the Alafin of Oyo would give him permission to reside in Oyo. He was then told he would be paid his salary up to the end of August, and thereafter he would receive a pension of £72 a year, which seemed to satisfy him.

THE SECOND DEPOSITION OF KITORO GANI

The next morning, Kitoro Gani again came to the District Office to see the Resident. He told him that he had changed his mind about his place of exile. He wanted to reside in Auna, his mother's birthplace which was just across the Niger from Bussa. The Resident informed him that this was not possible, so he told the Resident that he wished to throw himself on the mercy of the Etsu Nupe (the Emir of Bida), and ask him for asylum at Mokwa in the Bida emirate. This request was granted by the Etsu Nupe and Kitoro Gani went into quiet exile there.

Before Kitoro Gani left Kaiama, he was given permission by the Resident to take the state umbrella which was a personal gift of the Emir of Ilorin. He was also told that he could keep a small silver ring inscribed 'Mohammedu Gani, Sarkin Bussa', which he had purchased personally. He handed over the famous 'Mungo Park' ring to the District Officer for safekeeping until his successor was elected.*

The Resident left for Bussa on August 26th taking the police escort with him in case of any trouble there, even though he did not anticipate it. On arrival he found that the news of Kitoro Gani's deposition had preceded him, but apparently caused little interest. The Resident's impression was that it was a foregone conclusion among the people. The Resident then called together the traditional kingmakers and instructed them to choose Kitoro Gani's successor.

It was not, however, until August 29th and after several discussions between the Resident and the kingmakers, that Babaki, Sarkin Agwarra, was finally chosen. Babaki was informed that his name would be put forward to the Governor for approval. Meanwhile, he would act as Wakilin Sarkin Bussa.

Although there were a great number of aspirants, only Babaki seemed to command general support, and even when his selection was announced to a general meeting of the townspeople the Resident's impression was that they showed little interest in his appointment, indeed appeared to be indifferent to it.[59] Beevor recorded that the announcement of his

---

* The so-called Mungo Park ring was given to the reigning king of Bussa not by Mungo Park, but by the Lander brothers. Since it was a medal for Indian Chiefs struck in 1814, it could not have been a gift of Mungo Park, who met his death in 1805/1806. The Landers, however, do record presenting a medal to the reigning King of Bussa. This was since made into a ring and forms part of the Bussa regalia. The Emir Jibrim can be seen wearing it, plate 6. (See: K. Lupton 'The Death of Mungo Park on the Niger' *Nigeria Magazine*, no 72, March 1962, pp. 58–70).

appointment was 'received with a marked lack of enthusiasm by all present'.⁶⁰ Only one disgruntled older brother, however, refused to salute the new Emir. For seven days Babaki went into seclusion, as tradition required, and came out on September 6th ready to enter the palace. Beevor, who was present at Bussa at the time of his ritual assumption of office, wrote:

'He appeared mounted and in full regalia. His women and loads of money went into the house first. He followed by a large crowd to the accompaniment of drumming etc. appeared in the main palace and stayed there for an hour. All the notables made their obeisance. Then the Emir entered his house. But was prevented by the young Women of the house of Kisra. He was stopped thus at the door of the house for ten minutes, then having, in accordance with custom, paid a forfeit to the women was permitted to enter.'⁶¹

After a full night of dancing and drinking by townspeople, the new Emir was ritually shaved before his District Heads, who then, together with the other notables of Bussa, made obeisance to him. Beevor recorded in his diary:

'The Emir takes up his seat on a native bed under a tree in the main place and the dance goes on. I hear that the Emir has given away four horses, four cows and eighteen gowns this day and many lesser items. However he is reported to be a rich man.'⁶²

Babaki was gazetted Sarkin Bussa on September 19th under an order dated September 17th. On 25th January 1937 he asked to be known as Mohamman Sani, his Muslim name. He reigned until 1968. Kitoro Gani himself lived quietly in exile until 3rd February 1939, when he died. He and his half-brother spanned the whole period of colonial rule. Mohamman Sani had been born before the occupation of Bussa by the British, and lived to see Bussa part of an independent Nigeria. He proved a very different ruler from his half-brother, ruling efficiently, understanding the principles of Native Administration as laid down by the British. The annual reports for Bussa took on a new tone, and though the emirate was impoverished, Mohamman Sani administered it to the considerable satisfaction of the British and, later, of the Nigerian-dominated Northern Government, which in 1955 rewarded him for his loyalty and efficiency by raising him to the position of emir of all Nigerian Borgu. Where Kitoro Gani had refused to accept the new order of things, and had been deposed twice on this account—a unique record for an emir in colonial Northern Nigeria—Mohamman Sani proved a wise and adaptable ruler, who came to be much loved by his people. To him, above all, is due Bussa's successful integration into the modern world of Nigeria, in which Kitoro Gani had refused to interest himself.

EPILOGUE

The accession of Babaki to the throne of Bussa as Mohamman Sani may largely have solved the administrative problems that had beset the British from the appointment of Kitoro Sani as emir in 1903. But the poverty of Bussa still remained an obstacle to any real progress in the emirate. While Indirect Rule operated successfully under the firm and intelligent rule of Mohamman Gani, while law and order were maintained, the people of Bussa saw little material benefit from the British hegemony. In 1935, shortly before the deposition of Kitoro Gani, Heath had made an eloquent plea for a positive policy of development in Borgu, which had the strong support of his Resident. 'To describe present-day Borgu,' Heath had written in 1934, 'one could quite easily copy one of Lord Lugard's early reports and give an accurate picture.'[1] He proposed the reduction of the incidence of taxation from 10/- to 7/- per adult male, to halt the emigration from Borgu. He asked for an increase of the Native Authority's share of the taxation from 50 per cent to 60 per cent. He also suggested that the Reserve Funds be used for development projects. An all-season road should be built from Bussa to Ilorin. A canoe ferry should connect Bussa with the Yelwa-Jebba road, thus giving it direct access to the Molendo gold-fields and the Western Sokoto region. These should be paid for by the Government of the Northern Provinces, while Native Authority funds would pay for feeder roads.

The problem of emigration was acute. In 1931, Borgu was the most sparsely populated division in Nigeria. By 1934, it had lost a further 3,3000 people, which meant a corresponding decrease in its revenues. There was a steady movement southward. Between 1931 and 1934 Bussa had lost 435 people, Wawa 204. Only Agwarra had increased its population—by 382 people. These had come in from Yauri, confirming the southward drift. On top of this, the tsetse fly had been seen in Bussa town for the first time in history, and was spreading in Borgu Division. A major factor encouraging migration was the lower incidence of taxation in the neighbouring divisions: Gwandu 7/7d, Yauri 9/9d and Kontagora

7/11d. It was difficult to calculate the rate of taxation for Dahomey, but Borgawa could live there undetected for taxation purposes for up to six years, since assessment took place only at census time and many years elapsed between censuses. The world depression had deprived Borgu of revenues from its main export crop, the shea-nut. In French Dahomey compulsory crop cultivation and road construction had brought comparative prosperity. 'The better dress of the natives there and the wide use of European cloth is outstanding. The peasant's greatly exaggerated, and material prosperity undoubtedly draws much that is best from our side of the border.'

The road running from the Dahomeyan coast northwards parallel to the border had contributed to the decline in trade on the old Western Borgu caravan route. The younger generation of Borgawa were leaving for the towns on the railway to the east of Borgu; or for Kishi, Ilorin, Shaki and Ibadan. 'What', Heath asked, 'has been done for Borgu in the past 35 years? Three years ago one dispensary was opened at Kaiama. Only recently has it been possible to motor to Kaiama itself. Medical attention and motor transport are easily obtained to the south. These may seem small points, but they count with the natives rapidly becoming sophisticated, and give a fillip to general prosperity.'

The Borgu towns could not grow for lack of water. Suggestions for the locking and barraging of the Niger, he realized, could not be entertained in the present financial circumstances, but if the Government was not even to increase the Native Authorities' share of taxation from 50 per cent to 60 per cent the only way to avoid bankruptcy would be to cut out development heads in their budgets.

'The problem of Borgu', Heath concluded, 'has never been seriously tackled and, if we except the Great North Road proposal, nothing has been done to improve the possibilities of this vast tract of fertile country since Lord Lugard tried to open a trade route between Kaiama and Jebba.

'My object in writing this monograph has been to get a settled policy of progress laid down, independent of the apathy of the individual District Officers or of the irregular and wasteful action "done out of sheer desperation by despondent local officials".'

Heath's proposals met with general approval in Kaduna and Lagos but nothing was done at the time because of the bad financial situation of Nigeria. In 1936, however, a few wells were sunk in Kaiama, which freed the town from guinea-worm. The Southern provinces undertook the improvement of their section of the Kaiama road which meant that it was motorable as far as the Oli river. The emirs of both Kaiama and Bussa were reported as being anxious for development, but were unable to do anything about it for lack of funds. Nevertheless, there was money to enable both Bussa and Kaiama to celebrate King George VI's Coronation in 1937 with fireworks, provided by 'the generosity of Lord Trenchard and the United Africa Company'.[2] In 1937, the tax share of the Bussa and Kaiama Native Authorities was increased from 50 per cent to 60 per cent, but this only enabled them to restore salaries which had hitherto been cut back and undertake 'a cautious extension of activities'.[3] In 1938 a new elementary school, the first of its grade, was built in Bussa, and one was under construction in Kaiama. In April 1939 F. de F. Daniel, Resident of Ilorin, concerned about the lack of development in Borgu, asked whether it might not receive some assistance from the Colonial Development Fund. It had, after all, never received any assistance from the Central Government.[4] But the outbreak of war put a halt to any development in the division. By 1946 the old theme—'Frustration has been the keynote of the year—no men, no materials, no inspiration' —was the summing-up for the year in the Ilorin Province Annual Report.[5] Two years later, in 1948, over a decade after Heath had submitted his proposals for the development of Borgu, the Resident of Ilorin reported that the Bussa road to the south was still motorable only in the dry season. 'Lack of communications, sparsity of population and limited funds are a severe handicap to progress,' he complained, but added optimistically: 'the people are happy and not oppressed.'[6]

In 1949 the District Officer for Borgu proposed a five-year development plan for the Bussa Native Authority for a total of £32,200, of which the Northern Region Government would be asked to put up £12,500. The plan was approved, but reduced to £16,160 of which the Northern Region put up only £1,090. It is worth looking at the two plans to see how pathetically small were the amounts allocated for development in this huge division.[7]

The annual reports for the next decade give little indication of development, certainly none that was of any significance. In 1954, the aged Haliru, Emir of Kaiama, retired after over thirty years as emir and native administration in Borgu was reorganized along the lines suggested fifteen years before by Resident Daniel. The emirate of Kaiama was suppressed, and Kaiama was made one of the nine constituent districts of the new emirate of Borgu: Bussa, Wawa, Aliyara, Agwarra, Kaiama, Okuta,

Bussa Native Authority 5 Year Development Plan
1949–1954

Put forward by D. O. Borgu

1 Section	2 Govt.	3 N.A.	4 Total	5 Percentage of total sectional expenditure (col. 4) to total funds allocated
AGRICULTURE	—	—	—	—
EDUCATION	500	500	1,000	5·1
FORESTRY	—	—	—	—
MEDICAL	600	600	1,200	6·1
VETERINARY	—	—	—	—
COMMUNICATIONS	5,000	5,000	10,000	50·7
PUBLIC BUILDINGS	—	200	200	1·0
URBAN DEV.	—	—	—	—
RURAL DEV.	1,100	3,300	4,400	22·4
PUBLIC UTILIT.	—	—	—	—
MISC. EQPT.	—	650	650	3·3
TOTALS	7,200	10,250	17,450	
UNALLOCATED	—	2,250	2,250	11·4
	7,200	12,500	19,700	100%

Total Reserve Funds, 1st April 1949	£14,700
Less, Special Reserve (one-third Estimated Ordinary Reserve 1949–50)	2,200
Total Development Funds	£12,500

Actually approved by Northern Provinces Govt.

Section	Govt.	N.A.	Total	Percentage of total sectional expenditure to total funds
AGRICULTURE	—	—	—	—
EDUCATION	300	450	750	4·7
FORESTRY	—	—	—	—
MEDICAL	790	890	1,680	10·4
VETERINARY	—	—	—	—
COMMUNICATIONS	—	5,000	5,000	30·9
PUBLIC BUILDINGS	—	950	950	5·9
URBAN DEVELOPMENT	—	—	—	—
RURAL DEVELOPMENT	—	3,300	3,300	20·4
PUBLIC UTILIT.	—	—	—	—
MISC. EQPT.	—	650	650	4·0
TOTALS	1,090	11,240	12,330	76·3
UNALLOCATED	2,400	1,430	3,830	23·7
	3,490	12,670	16,160	100%

Total Reserve Funds, 1st April, 1949	£14,770
Less, Special Reserve (one-third Estimated Ordinary Revenue, 1949–50)	2,100
Total Development Funds	£12,670

Ilesha, Yashikera and Gwanara. The nine Borgu districts were united under Mohamman Sani, now designated Emir of Borgu.

This new organization of Borgu saved money, in that only one Native Administration had to be supported from taxes, instead of two, though,

EPILOGUE

in recognition of the Nikki connection, Yashikera, Okuta, Ilesha and Gwanara were constituted as a Sub-Native Authority to be known as West Borgu. The new Native Authorities were partially democratized. The Borgu Native Authority, under the Emir of Borgu as president, had fifteen elected members, as against three titled members and five nominated members.[8]

The Western Borgu Sub-Native Authority had ten elected members and four nominated members to represent the cattle-owning population. Significantly, none of the district heads sat on these two councils by right, so that Kaiama's ruling house was disenfranchised. For Bussa, this reorganization was of course a triumph; for the Western Borgu districts of the Nikki connection it meant an end to the much-resented domination of Kaiama. For Kaiama itself, the new order was a bitter pill, since the emirate became directly subordinate to Bussa, whose suzerainty at the end of the nineteenth century had been purely nominal. M. J. Campbell, the District Officer, who put forward the scheme for reorganization, is to this day remembered in Kaiama, because of the abolition of the emirate.[9]

The elevation of Mohamman Sani to emir of Borgu may have added to the prestige of Bussa, but it changed little. Economically, Borgu remained one of the most backward areas of Nigeria, with few development funds allocated to it.

Change at last came in the wake of an investigation commissioned by the Federal Government of Nigeria in 1960–61 as to the relative merits of hydro-electric power and gas- or oil-generated power. It was decided to choose the former, harnessing the rivers Niger and Benue to this end. The site chosen for the first dam on the Niger was at Kainji, some 50 miles downstream from Bussa town which was to be flooded as a consequence of its construction. The Government's decision was to revolutionize the economic life of the old Bussa emirate. In the first place, nearly 50,000 people living on the banks of, or near to, the Niger had to be resettled to make way for the huge lake that would be created by the dam. In the second place, roads connecting Kainji with the main North-South road were built, to bring in the materials for the construction of the dam and the resettlement scheme, and Kainji was designated as the new site of Bussa. Thirdly, the dam represented a vast injection of capital into the area. True, it was a once-and-for-all injection into a project which would not provide many jobs after its completion, but it did draw public attention to Bussa, now a fine modern architect-designed town.

Bussa may still be poor in comparison with many other areas of Nigeria. But the construction of the dam was one of two events which brought Bussa firmly into the modern world. The second was the accession to the Borgu throne in 1969 of Musa Mohammed Kigera III, the first Western-educated ruler of the emirate. And while Bussawa still regret the loss of Illo, Kaoje and Kunji, they are, as was once remarked of Kitoro Gani, 'brooding less on what might have been and turning more to what is and may be.' Their present emir is a former junior minister in the Northern Nigerian Government, and commissioner in the Kwara State Government of which Borgu forms part. His brother, the Ciroma, is a state commissioner. Borgu has a secondary school, and numerous primary schools. There are now Borgawa at university.

Apart from the rapid material progress made since Independence in Borgu, and more particularly in what was the Bussa emirate, the prestige of the emirate itself has also recently been restored. On 26th November 1971, Musa Muhammadu Kigera III, Emir of Borgu, was raised by the Government of the Kwara State to the status of a first-class chief, just as his uncle, Kitoro Gani, had been during his first reign under the British. Though under the present military regime emirs have much less power than before, the present Emir lives in a fine concrete architect-designed palace in the centre of a bustling modern town which is a far cry from the collection of mud huts that so disappointed Mrs. Larymore in 1906. Bussa is no longer the backwater that it became under colonial rule.

APPENDIX I · ADMINISTRATORS OF NORTHERN NIGERIA, 1900-1935

1900-01	F. D. Lugard—High Commissioner
1901	William Wallace—A[ctin]g. High Commissioner
1902	F. D. Lugard—High Commissioner
1902	Thomas L. N. Morland—Ag. High Commissioner
1903	F. D. Lugard—High Commissioner
1903	William Wallace—Ag. High Commissioner
1904-05	F. D. Lugard—High Commissioner
1906	William Wallace—Ag. High Commissioner
1907	E. P. C. Girouard—High Commissioner
1907	William Wallace—Ag. High Commissioner
1908	E. P. C. Girouard—Governor
1908	William Wallace—Ag. Governor
1909	E. P. C. Girouard—Governor
1909	H. H. J. Bell—Governor
1909	William Wallace—Ag. Governor
1910-11	H. H. J. Bell—Governor
1911	C. L. Temple—Ag. Governor
1912	H. H. J. Bell—Governor
1912	F. D. Lugard—Governor, Northern Provinces (C. L. Temple—Deputy Governor)
1913-14	F. D. Lugard—Governor, Northern Provinces C. L. Temple—Acting Governor (H. S. Goldsmith—Acting Deputy Governor)
1915	C. L. Temple—Lt.-Governor
1915	H. S. Goldsmith—Ag. Lt.-Governor
1916	C. L. Temple—Lt.-Governor
1917-19	H. S. Goldsmith—Lt.-Governor
1919	W. F. Gowers—Ag. Lt.-Governor
1919	F. B. Gall—Ag. Lt.-Governor
1920	H. S. Goldsmith—Lt.-Governor

1920	W. F. Gowers—Ag. Lt.-Governor
1920	E. J. Arnett—Ag. Lt.-Governor
1921	W. F. Gowers—Lt.-Governor
1921	E. J. Arnett—Ag. Lt.-Governor
1921	H. R. Palmer—Ag. Lt.-Governor
1922–3	W. F. Gowers—Lt.-Governor
1923	E. J. Arnett—Ag. Lt.-Governor
1924	W. F. Gowers—Lt.-Governor
1924	H. R. Palmer—Ag. Lt.-Governor
1925	H. R. Palmer—Lt.-Governor
1925	J. M. Fremantle—Ag. Lt.-Governor
1926–7	H. R. Palmer—Lt.-Governor
1927	C. W. Alexander—Ag. Lt.-Governor
1928–9	H. R. Palmer—Lt.-Governor
1929	C. W. Alexander—Ag. Lt.-Governor
1929	P. Lansdale—Ag. Lt.-Governor
1930	C. W. Alexander—Lt.-Governor
1930	C. S. Browne—Ag. Lt.-Governor
1931	C. W. Alexander—Lt.-Governor
1931	G. J. Lethem—Ag. Lt.-Governor
1932	Vacant—Lt.-Governor
1932	G. J. Lethem—Ag. Lt.-Governor
1932	G. S. Browne—Ag. Lt.-Governor
1933	G. S. Browne—Chief Commissioner
1933	G. J. Lethem—Ag. Chief Commissioner
1934–5	G. S. Browne—Chief Commissioner

APPENDIX II · RESIDENTS OF BORGU AND KONTAGORA PROVINCES

Borgu

February 1902–May 1903—Mr. H. Kemble (Acting)
May 1903–October 1903—Capt. P. W. Anderson
October 1903–January 1904—Lt. A. C. C. Stevens (Acting)
January 1904–July 1904(?)—Mr. H. Kemble (Acting)*
July 1904(?)–November 1904—Capt. P. W. Anderson*
November 1904–(?)March 1905—Mr. H. Kemble*
(?)March 1905–April 1905—Capt. P. W. Anderson*
April 1905–August 1905—Mr. H. Kemble (Acting)
August 1905–January 1906—Mr. F. Dwyer (Acting)
January 1906–December 1906—Capt. H. D. Larymore
December 1906–March 1907—Major J. M. Fremantle

Kontagora Province

January 1906–April 1907—Major W. S. Sharpe
May 1907–December 1907—Mr. F. Dwyer (Acting)
January 1908–March 1909—Major W. S. Sharpe
April 1909—Mr. H. Kemble (Acting)
May 1909–July 1909—Mr. R. M. McAllister (Acting)
August 1909—Mr. T. C. Newton (Acting)
August 1909–October 1909—Mr. N. M. Gepp (Acting)
November 1909–September 1910—Major H. D. Larymore, C.M.G.
November 1910–December 1910—Mr. C. E. Boyd (Acting)

* It is unclear from the records for the period January 1904 to April 1905 who was actually in charge of Borgu Province. Anderson was frequently ill, and various lists appearing in reports do not make clear when he was effectively in charge, or when either Kemble or Capt. C. A. M. Howard acted for him.
Extracted from E. C. Duff, *Gazetteer of Kontagora Province*, London, 1920.

December 1910–August 1911—Mr. E. G. M. Dupigny (Acting)
August 1911–December 1912—Major J. E. C. Blakeney
December 1912–June 1913—Major W. Hamilton-Browne, D.S.O.,
(Acting)
June 1913–June 1914—Major J. E. C. Blakeney
June 1914–August 1915—Major W. Hamilton-Browne
August 1915—Mr. A. Campbell-Irons (Acting)
September 1915–January 1916—Mr. F. Dwyer (Acting)
February 1916–November 1917—Major W. Hamilton-Browne
December 1917–September 1918—Mr. E. C. Duff
August 1918–January 1920—Major W. Hamilton-Browne
January 1920–June 1921—Mr. K. V. Elphinstone

APPENDIX III · OFFICERS IN CHARGE OF BORGU DIVISION, 1917–1935

May 1917	Joyce Cary
November 1917	P. R. Diggle
September 1918	Joyce Cary
December 1918–October 1920	Borgu administered from Yauri
October 1920	G. W. Izard
May 1921	T. Hoskyns-Abrahall
August 1922	J. P. Smith
March 1923	T. Hoskyns-Abrahall
May 1924	W. Nash
June 1925	T. Hoskyns-Abrahall
February 1926	W. Nash
April 1927	G. R. Osborn
August 1927	P. E. Lewis
June 1928	H. C. Gill
September 1928	H. C. Gill
	W. Nash
July 1929	H. C. Gill
February 1931	N. P. M. Jones
September 1931	G. R. Osborne
January 1932	L. C. Schlotel
September 1932	B. A. Roberts
October 1932	D. F. Heath
May 1933	B. Glasson
November 1934	D. F. Heath
July 1935	R. E. Beevor

APPENDIX IV · KINGS OF BUSSA

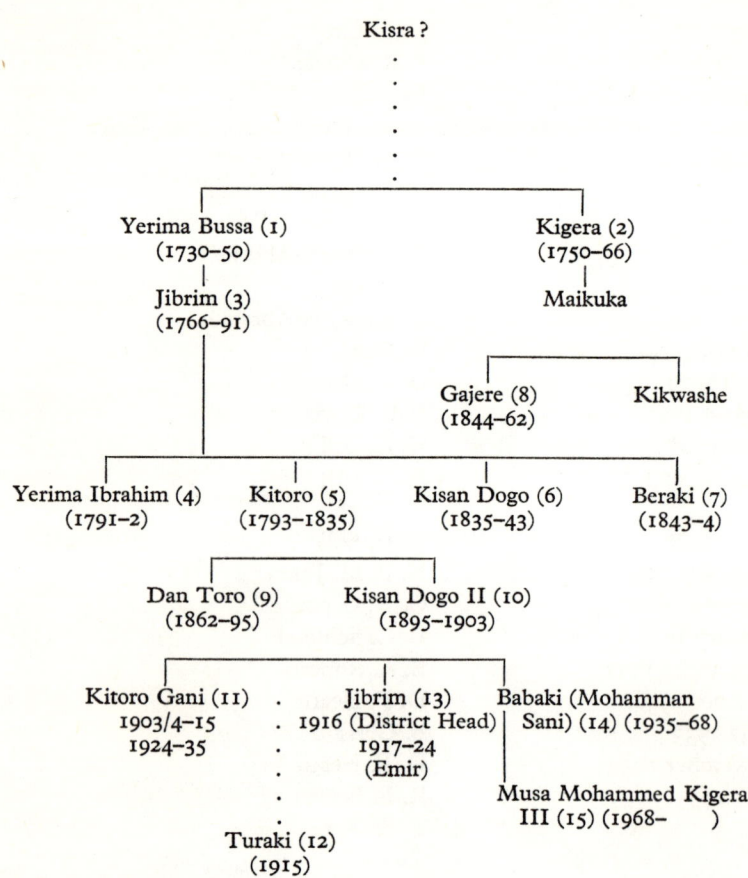

[a British-imposed slave District Head who did not rule as Emir]

APPENDIX IV

The dates for the pre-colonial rulers of Bussa are taken from S. J. Hogben and A. H. M. Kirk-Greene, *The Emirates of Northern Nigeria*, London, 1966, p. 584.

The dates in Hogben and Kirk-Greene for Kitoro Gani are 1902–14. His accession here is put as 1903(4) depending on whether Lt. Stevens's installation in December 1903 or Lugard's approval in 1904 is accepted as the *official* date of his accession. Hogben and Kirk-Greene also give the date of Kitoro Gani's deposal as 1914, when in fact it should be 1915. They also give Jibrim's date of accession as 1917, which is correct as far as his recognition as Emir is concerned, but not in so far as he became District Head in 1916. They give Turaki's date as 1916 as Emir: he was never Emir, only District Head in 1915.

APPENDIX V · 'YAWURI AND BOUSSA: PETITION BY PEOPLES OF'*

Translation

The people of Yawuri and Bussa salute the Governor. We are suffering from hunger, but it is the hunger of fear not of the flesh. We are afraid of the Resident who is at Yelwa now and his interpreter Abba. They are fining us heavily, and we have done nothing. If we come to salute Abba he brings trouble upon us. If we meet the Resident on the road, he tells Abba to beat us if we do not salute him and he fines us. Once the Resident started from Yelwa to go to Bussa, on the way to Bussa he took fines amounting to £50 and on the way back he took £30. We ask the Governor to remove the Resident of Yelwa and Abba. This Resident at Yelwa has four wives, one the Sarikin Yawuri gave him and she had a child by him, one the Sar. Yamma gave him, one Abba took from the Sarikin 'Ngaski and gave him, and one is the wife of Yusufu Sar. Anamimai who died, Abba took her and gave him [sic]. These women are all kept at Abba's house and we have to give the rice and fish every Saturday. They have taken the food from our farms. We ask the Governor how we are to pay the tax under these circumstances. We pray for the removal of the Resident and Abba. How can Abba with a salary of £3 a month afford to maintain a large household like his and horses as well?

The death of Sar. Kunji was caused by the Resident and Abba because the Resident was always threatening to turn him out of his rank, and Sar. Kunji told him he could not turn him out because he had done no wrong. Two days after the Resident left for Kontagora Sar. Kunji died.

The white man and Abba wanted the rank of Sar. Kunji but not with the knowledge of the white man of Bussa. When the white man was there he asked the Sar. Kunji who was the chief man. They replied that Agara was the chief man, and the white man fined Agara £5. Agara said that he was attached to the Sar. Bussa not to the Sar. Yawuri. Because he said

* NAK/SNP/20/1/p67/1913

APPENDIX V

this the white man fined him £5. The white man took away all the land of Bussa and gave the Sarikin Yawuri. We do not understand this. We wish the Governor to listen to what we say because this matter is in the heart of the Sarikin Bussa and he has not had an opportunity to speak till now. Once the white man at Yelwa took away the Stave from the Sarikin Wawa, he said 'I turn you out of your rank and if you come to Laba I will fine you heavily.' The people of Laba were grieved at this, because the Sarikin Wawa was fined. We wish the Governor to send a truthful god-fearing man to ask us about this. He will hear more than what we have written.

With reference to the planting of cotton seed, Abba and Sarikin Yamma took away the cotton from us. We people of Yawuri cultivated our crop but they said that the cotton seed was the Governor's. They took it from us and sold it to a clerk who was buying cotton. We received not a farthing. They would not let even one of us go to the clerk. Owing to this we sent one of our number to the Resident Kontagora to obtain redress. The Resident Kontagora drove away our messenger. We beg the Governor for God's sake to look into this. We think that the Residents of Kontagora and Yelwa are men of the same stamp, not sympathetic with the talakawa.

The people of Yawuri and Bussa are not at ease. When the big white man 'Giwa' (Major Sharpe) and 'Laramir' (Captain Larymore) were here, we were happy, now we are not happy. We beseech the Governor to give us peace that we may cultivate our lands: we ask only to be allowed to rest in peace. Sarikin Yamma and Abba are in treacherous league against the Resident. When the Governor called the people to Kano for the Durbar Sarikin Yawuri returned ill. After three or four days the Resident took away his stave of office and the Court Warrant and gave them to Alie Sarkin Yamma. He said to him 'Administer the district as you think fit, but do not go to the Sarikin Yawuri because now he is ill he is useless.' The monthly salary of Sarikin Yawuri the Resident took (viz. £15) and gave to Sarikin Yamma. Now Abba and Sarikin Yamma are the only councillors summoned by the Resident. If anything happens we are told to go to Abba and the Sarikin Yamma. How shall a man walk if his head be on the ground and his feet in the air, (i.e. if the Resident will not help us it is not much good going to Abba.) We know that even if the Sarikin Yawuri were to die the Sarikin Yamma would never succeed him. For, about four months ago the Resident said that he would give the Sarikin Yamma the rank, but not without the consent of the Resident Kontagora.

We talakawa of Yawuri, if Sarikin Yamma succeeds Sarikin Yawuri, know not whither we shall go. We shall scatter in all directions. We pray God to send us a new Resident who will allow everyone to exercise the authority to which he is entitled, who will prevent the Sarikin Yamma obtaining the rank of Sarikin Yawuri. Sarikin Yawuri cannot send a messenger one mile in his country, only the Sarikin Yamma can do this. Sarikin Yamma can send 20 messengers if he likes. We beg the Governor to forgive us if we have done any wrong, formerly the horse was eating the grass but now the grass is eating the horse. Now the stave and the Court Warrant have been taken from the Sarikin Yawuri for two months. The Resident does not consult the Sarikin Yawuri. Everything that Abba and the Sarikin Yamma say to him he agrees to. We ask for another Resident not because we are disloyal but because we wish peace.

When Sarikin Yamma was given the rank of Tukura he had 2 men, now he has more than 50 adherents. He disregards the people of Yawuri. If the Sarikin Yamma puts on a black gown today, he will wear a white one to-morrow. If we talakawa bring a complaint to the Resident Yelwa we cannot obtain an audience of the Resident under 7 days and then only with the consent of Abba and the Sarikin Yamma. When we come to the Resident he drives us away and sends us to the Sarikin Yamma and Abba for them to listen to our complaint. They do not help us. Sarikin Yamma does not obey the Sarikin Yawuri as District Headmen obey their Chief. We wish Sarikin Yamma to be sent back to Jega whence he came for he is a native of Jega. We beg you not to make him Sarikin Yawuri. Sarikin Yamma sent 3 saddlecloths, one he gave to Magaji the interpreter at Kontagora, one he sold to Waziri-n-Sakaba Alhaji, one he gave Ubandawaki in order that they might help him to obtain a rank. He also gave Magaji a wife. We talakawa of Yawuri are of opinion that the Sarikin Yamma should not have even the rank he now holds much less that of Sarikin Yawuri. Sarikin Yamma sent a woman to Magaji the interpreter for him to give the white man at Kontagora. The Sarikin Yamma was not born in this country. He was a stranger from Jega. The Native Court which was established at Telu was abolished by the Resident Yelwa. Sarikin Yamma caused the Sarikin 'Ngaski to be turned out because he was his enemy. The Sarikin Yamma can get anything he likes in this country, because the Resident Yelwa always agrees to his proposals. The Sarikin Yamma is frying cakes without butter, for everything done by him here is lies and the white man does not know it. The complaint made on behalf of Sarikin 'Ngaski against Sarikin Yamma and

APPENDIX V

Abba was true but the Resident Yelwa believed Sarikin Yamma and not Sarikin 'Ngaski. He deprived Sarikin 'Ngaski of his rank. The people say if they do not restore Sarikin 'Ngaski they will all go away. The Resident Yelwa is a son-in-law of the Sarikin Yamma, of course he will agree with Sarikin Yamma's views. We ask the Governor to enquire into this matter. The Sarikin 'Ngaski wishes to appeal to the Governor. He complained against the Sarikin Yamma, Abba and the Alkali. He appealed to the Residents of Kontagora and Yelwa and sent to Zungeru. Witnesses were not called before the Resident Kontagora and Sarikin 'Ngaski was made to appear a liar. People are imprisoned here not for the wrong they have done but from spite. Abba tells the Resident Yelwa that whatever Sarikin 'Ngaski says is lies.

The Sarikin 'Ngaski asked for permission to call witnesses but the Residents of Kontagora and Yelwa refused permission. We know that the two Residents understand Hausa but they did not allow us to come before them. If true justice had been administered at Kontagora we should not have come here. As the two Residents understand Hausa why should Magaji intervene? We ask that we may call witnesses in the matter of the Sarikin 'Ngaski, and of Abba, and that you will give us a fair hearing. The enquiry into Abba's conduct at Kontagora was all lies as we were not allowed to appear before the Resident Kontagora. The Sarikin 'Ngaski was unjustly dealt by but we do not think the white man knew it. The monthly salary of Sarikin 'Ngaski was not paid him. The Sarikin 'Ngaski did us no harm, he did not fine us for no reason. He did exactly what the Resident Yelwa told him to do. What wrong then did he do?

Confidential

To the Resident Kontagora:

With reference to the attached anonymous letter in which I presume I am the Resident referred to, I have the honour to inform you that it is simply a tissue of lies from beginning to end. No fines have ever been inflicted by me in 'Ngaski or in any other part of my Division. The part about women is absolutely untrue and I have never had any dealings with any of the sarakuna except on purely business matters. The question of the retirement of Sar. Kunji was under consideration at the time of his death, only his advanced age prevented me from advising him to resign.

Agwarra (Agara) has certainly never been fined by me. No Hausa land has been given to Yauri. Sar. Wawa's stave was taken away by the Emir and the question of his resignation is under consideration. Sar. Wawa has nothing to do with Leaba which is not in his District—neither Sar. Yamma nor Abba has sold any cotton belonging to other people—neither his stave nor court warrant have ever been taken from Sarikin Yauri—Sar. Yamma is Sar. Yauri's righthand man, his adviser and friend.

In January 1913 Dr. Black reported that the Emir of Yauri was dying and that even if he lasted a few months he would never work again. With the concurrence of Major Hamilton-Browne D.S.O. Sar. Yamma was appointed Acting Emir and drew half pay, viz. £15 p.a., towards meeting the expenses of the sarauta. Regarding the succession there are, as you are aware, confidential papers at Kontagora recommending Sarikin Yamma for the Emirship of Yauri on the decease of the present holder, and it will be a very suitable and popular appointment—So far as it is consistent with my office as Resident at the Court of the Emir of Yauri I am at all times accessible to complainants. The complaint against Sar. Yamma, Alkalin 'Ngaski, Abba and others made in Department and purporting to come from ex Sar. 'Ngaski was not written by him or with his knowledge. At the inquiry he admitted he knew nothing about the letters and that he had no definite complaint against these people. The letter was written at the dictation of Yahaiya assisted, I strongly suspect, by Clerk Agbebi, P. A. Musa etc. who no doubt, thought they would have an opportunity to inform ex Sar. 'Ngaski of the contents. This plot was frustrated by allowing no previous communication between them. Witnesses were called but ex Sar. 'Ngaski had no idea of the charges preferred in the letter purporting to come from him, and consequently he was unable to examine them. You are aware of the intrigue now being carried on by Clerk Agbebi and various members of the staff, and you will no doubt realize that this is simply an attempt to take away our most useful men and increase the influence and power of the ring of 'barrack politicians' who are working against indirect administration and trying to transfer authority from the sarakuna to the 'educated' native from the south and his followers. I am trying to trace the letter to its source and if I am successful criminal proceedings for defamation of character will be taken.

J. C. O. Clarke
3.1.14.

A NOTE ON SOURCES

There is very little published material relating directly to the history of Bussa under British administration. This study is primarily based on records held in the Nigerian National Archives in Kaduna. While material relating to Bussa is widely scattered in these archives, the historian of colonial rule is fortunate that a large number of files from the District Office at Bussa, particularly those covering the period before the rebellion, have been deposited in Kaduna. These files are catalogued under the code BORGDIST. Despite laments by early Political Officers that most of the records had been eaten by white ants, the Borgu collection as far as the early history of Northern Nigeria under British rule is concerned is one of, if not the richest.

The Borgu District Records are supplemented by records from Ilorin Province for the period after 1923, when Borgu came under Ilorin. Unfortunately the Kontagora Province records covering the period 1907–23 do not seem to have been preserved as such. However, correspondence between the Resident, Kontagora Province, and the Political Officer in charge of Borgu on the one hand, and between the Resident Kontagora and the Government of Northern Nigeria (later Northern Provinces of Nigeria) on the other, has survived in sufficient detail to form a coherent picture of the respective roles of Political Officer, Resident and Governor in the administration of Borgu. Apart from the archives of the Provincial Office at Ilorin, catalogued under the code ILORPROF, use was made of the Provincial Archives of Sokoto Province, particularly with respect to Bussa's relations with Yauri, which after the break-up of Kontagora Province became part of Sokoto Province.

There is a great deal of material relating directly to Borgu in the archives of the Secretary to the Northern Provinces, catalogued under the code word SNP. However, this groups together a vast amount of material and sometimes searching for a vital file became very much like looking

243

for the proverbial needle in the haystack. However the majority of files relating to Borgu are to be found in the SNP 6, 7, 8 9 and 10p series.

Over and above archival materials in Kaduna, files from the office of the Chief Secretary to the Government of Nigeria, held in the Nigerian National Archives in Ibadan, were consulted. These concerned matters relating to Bussa that were of sufficient importance to be brought to the attention of the Lagos government, including such questions as capital sentences and deposition of chiefs. In addition a number of relevant annual reports covering the post-amalgamation period are held in Ibadan.

For the rebellion itself, I consulted the Senegalese National Archives in Dakar where there are large holdings of the former Government-General of French West Africa relating to the rebellion in French-occupied Borgu, as well as a certain amount concerning the impact of the Bussa rebellion on French administration in Dahomey. Because of the heavy centralization of administration on Dakar, the holdings relating to the rebellions in both French and British Borgu are very detailed, especially since they concerned possible and actual military action in which only Dakar had the initiative.

For the rebellion in French Borgu I was also able to obtain from the Archives Nationales de France, Section Outre-Mer, a copy of the report made by Inspector-General Phérivong on the rebellion in French Borgu through the courtesy of Madame Marie-Antoinette Menier.

I was able to consult the Joyce Cary Papers held in the Bodleian Library, Oxford, through kind permission of Mrs. D. Davin. I was also able to consult the Hoskyns-Abrahall papers in the Rhodes House Library and I am grateful to Sir Chandos Hoskyns-Abrahall for permission to quote from his Personal Diary.

While one cannot be certain at having tracked down every relevant file, I am conscious of only three important ones which I was unable to trace. The first is that of the Commission of Enquiry by Mr. G. S. Browne into Lt.-Commander J. C. O. Clarke's Administration of Yauri. This file, which was 'lost' from the District Office, Bussa, Mr. K. Lupton tells me, when he was District Officer there in the late 1950s, might have shed valuable extra sidelights on the complex history of the events leading up to the rebellion. All efforts to trace it in Kaduna failed, and Mr. Lupton tells me that it was known to be missing there when he was at Bussa. The second major file I was unable to track down in Kaduna was the record of the trial of Kissoin for murder. This is listed in Kaduna

A NOTE ON SOURCES

under SNP/O/P.C/279/1924, but it is recorded as having been sent to the Chief Justice in Lagos. In the Ibadan archives it appears under C.S.O./26/1179/Vol. XI, in the list of Murder Case files, where it should be no. XIII but is not available. There is a pencil note saying it is with the SNA, (Secretary, Native Affairs). Fortunately, though the transcript of the trial is not available, the transcripts of evidence on which the trial is based are very full (see footnote 57 to Chapter VIII). Finally, all attempts to track down the transcript of the trial of the Ma'aji (Native Authority Treasurer) Bio for embezzlement in 1935 have failed. It is thus not absolutely clear how the Emir of Bussa, Kitoro Gani, was implicated in the embezzlement, which is a great pity since this was a crucial factor in his second deposition.

As far as oral sources are concerned, apart from several visits to Borgu on which the Emir of Borgu, H.H. Muhammadu Kigera III and the Ciroma of Borgu, were particularly helpful, I have relied on field assistants. Mr. Sola Agbelusi, who had worked in Borgu for the Nigerian Institute for Economic and Social Research as a field assistant, and had travelled widely round Borgu, spent two months collecting information for me in the principal Borgu towns and villages. After I had completed my archival research, Mallam Suleiman Haliru Idris, grandson of the retired Emir of Kaiama, Haliru, made two extended trips to Borgu to check on questions that could only be answered satisfactorily by someone who was a native speaker of the Borgu languages. He has been particularly helpful over the section relating to the pre-colonial history of Borgu. In this respect, I have been particularly fortunate in being able to have my first chapter checked by Mallam Musa Baba Idris, who is just completing a doctoral thesis on the pre-colonial history of Borgu. His own work, when published, will add a broad new dimension to our understanding of the complexities of the political and social structure of Borgu.

Apart from archival sources I have relied on a few books and articles which are listed below. Special mention must be made of Jacques Lombard's *Structures de type 'féodal' en Afrique noire: Etude des dynamismes internes et des relations sociales chez les Baribas du Dahomey*, Paris, 1965, which is a major study of Nikki with valuable material on Bussa.

MADI ADAMU, 'A Hausa Government in Decline: Yauri in the Nineteenth Century', unpublished M.A. thesis, Ahmadu Bello University, Zaria, 1968.

R. A. ADELEYE, *Power and Diplomacy in Northern Nigeria: the Sokoto Caliphate and its Enemies*, London, 1971.
PIERRE ALEXANDRE, 'Chiefs, *Commandants* and Clerks: Their Relationship from Conquest to Decolonization in French West Africa' in Michael Crowder and Obaro Ikime, eds., *West African Chiefs: Their Changing Status under Colonial Rule and Independence*, Ife and New York, 1970, pp. 2–13.
JOYCE CARY, *The Case for African Freedom*, second edition, Austin, Texas, 1964.
HUGH CLAPPERTON, *Journal of a Second Expedition into the Interior of Africa from the Bight of Benin to Soccattoo in which is added the Journal of Richard Lander from Kano to the Sea-Coast partly by a More Eastern Route*, London, 1829.
Colonial Annual Reports for Northern Nigeria, London, 1901–1906.
R. CORNEVIN, *Histoire du Dahomey*, Paris, 1963.
MICHAEL CROWDER, *The Story of Nigeria*, revised edition, London, 1966.
MICHAEL CROWDER, *West Africa under Colonial Rule*, London, 1968.
MICHAEL CROWDER and OBARO IKIME, Introduction to *West African Chiefs under Colonial Rule: Their Changing Status under Colonial Rule and Independence*, Ife and New York, 1970.
MICHAEL CROWDER, 'West Africa and the 1914–18 War', *Bulletin de l'IFAN*, T. XXX, sér. B, 1, 1968, pp. 227–247.
J. E. FLINT, *Sir George Goldie and the Making of Nigeria*, London, 1960.
A. F. FREMANTLE, ed., *Two African Journals and other Papers of the late John Morton Fremantle, C.M.G., M.B.E.* Printed for private circulation, 1938.
A. C. G. HASTINGS, *The Voyage of the Dayspring Being the Journal of the late Sir John Hawley Glover, R.N., G.C.M.G., together with some account of the Expedition up the Niger River in 1857*, London, 1926.
A. C. G. HASTINGS, *Nigerian Days*, London, 1925.
H. HERMON-HODGE, *A Gazetteer of Ilorin Province*, London, 1929, reprinted 1972.
SIR E. HERTSLET, *The Map of Africa by Treaty*, third edition. 3 vols. Reprinted, London, 1967.
S. J. HOGBEN and A. H. M. KIRK-GREENE, *Emirates of Northern Nigeria*, London, 1966.
ROBIN HORTON, 'Stateless Societies in the History of West Africa' in J. F. A. Ajayi & Michael Crowder, eds., *History of West Africa*, Vol. I, London, 1972, pp. 78–119.

A NOTE ON SOURCES

RICHARD and JOHN LANDER, *Journals of an Expedition to Explore the Course and Termination of the Niger* etc., London, 1832.

R. C. C. LAW, 'The Oyo Kingdom and its Northern Neighbours', *Kano Studies*, N.S.I, 1973.

CAPITAINE LENFANT, *Le Niger*, Paris, 1901.

CONSTANCE LARYMORE, *A Resident's Wife in Nigeria*, London, 1908.

JACQUES LOMBARD, *Structures de type 'féodal' en Afrique noire*, Paris, 1965.

JACQUES LOMBARD, 'Un système politique traditionel de type féodal: les Baribas du Nord Dahomey. Aperçu sur l'organisation sociale et le pouvoir central', *Bulletin de l'IFAN*, T. XIX, sér. B. 3-4, 1957.

LORD LUGARD, *Political Memoranda*, London, 1919.

K. LUPTON, 'The Death of Mungo Park at Bussa', *Nigeria Magazine*, 72, 1962, pp. 58-70.

M. M. MAHOOD, *Joyce Cary's Africa*, London, 1964.

DR. PAUL CONSTANTIN MEYER, *Account of the Origin of the States of the Western Sudan* trans. Major E. Agar, R.E., Colonial Office, Africa West, No. 541, London, 1898.

CAPTAIN A. F. MOCKLER-FERRYMAN, *Up the Niger*, London, 1892.

MARGERY PERHAM, *Lugard: the Years of Adventure 1858-1898*, London, 1956.

MARGERY PERHAM, *Lugard: the Years of Authority 1899-1945*, London, 1961.

MARGERY PERHAM and MARY BULL, eds., *The Diaries of Lord Lugard*, Vol. IV, London, 1963.

COMMANDANT G. J. TOUTÉE, *Dahomé-Niger-Touareg*, Paris, 1897.

SIR JAMES WILLCOCKS, *From Kabul to Kumasi: Twenty-four Years of Soldiering and Sport*, London, 1904.

NOTES

Prologue

1. See for instance Sir Alan Burns, *A History of Nigeria*, London, 1958, 5th edition, and my own *The Story of Nigeria*, revised edition, London 1966. There is, however, a brief reference to it in S. J. Hogben and A. H. M. Kirk-Greene, *The Emirates of Northern Nigeria*, London, 1966.
2. The probable date is June 14th. (See pp. 113–14)
3. N[ational] A[rchives] K[aduna]/S[ecretary] N[orthern] P[rovinces]/15/ACC. No. 52 Borgu Monthly Reports 1903. January–April.
4. Bodleian Library, Oxford, Joyce Cary Papers. Box 267, Cary to his wife, Bussa 19.10.1917.
5. N[ational] A[rchives] I[badan]/C[hief] S[ecretary's] O[ffice]/26/2/File No. 13556 Minute of 20/10/1924.

I · Pre-Colonial Borgu

1. Capitaine Lenfant, *Le Niger*, Paris, 1901, p. 135.
2. Constance Larymore, *A Resident' Wife in Nigeria*, London, 1908, pp. 160–161.
3. Hugh Clapperton, *Journal of a Second Expedition into the Interior of Africa from the Bight of Benin to Soccattoo to which is added the Journal of Richard Lander from Kano to the Sea-Coast, Partly by a More Eastern Route*, London, 1829, p. 90.
4. *ibid.*, p. 98.
5. NAK/BORGDIST/6 Borgu Provincial Record Book, 1905.
6. Bussa changed its sites several times. See Dr. Paul Constantin Meyer, *Account of the Origin of the States of the Western Sudan*, translated by Major E. Agar R.E. Colonial Office, Africa West No. 541. See also note 17.
7. R. C. C. Law, 'The Oyo Kingdom and its Northern Neighbours', *Kano Studies*, No. 5, 1973, provides convincing evidence that Nupe was never subject to Oyo as is usually claimed.
8. Captain A. F. Mockler-Ferryman, *Up the Niger*, London, 1892, p. 145.
9. Lander, 1829, p. 317. See note 3.
10. Communication from Mr. K. Lupton, a former District Officer of Borgu and a student of its nineteenth-century history.
11. Clapperton, 1829, p. 68.
12. NAK/BORGDIST/DOB/AR/19/1924; NAI/CSO/26/12687/II/1924; NAK/BORGDIST/DOB/AR/29/1934; and NAI/CSO/26/2/12687/XII/1939.

NOTES

13. Jacques Lombard, *Structures de type 'féodal' en Afrique noire: Etude des dynamismes internes et des relations sociales chez les Baribas du Dahomey*, Paris, 1965.
14. *ibid.*, pp. 44–45.
15. *ibid.*, p. 35.
16. H. Hermon-Hodge, *A Gazetteer of Ilorin Province*, London, 1929.
17. See K. Lupton, 'The Death of Mungo Park at Bussa'. *Nigeria Magazine*, No. 72 March 1962, pp. 58–70. Musa Baba Idris, who is completing a doctoral dissertation on the Bariba States was informed by Mallam Issa, Sarkin Agwarra, that at one time each new ruler of Bussa had to found his own capital.
18. This is borne out by interviews conducted by my informant Mr. Sola Agbelusi in 1968 in villages about to be flooded by the Kainji dam. Mallam Madi Adamu writes in his study of neighbouring Yauri that '. . . conditions under which the traditions were passed on to the administrative officers were not always good. Most of the interviews were group discussions conducted in the open air; the administrative officers used to sit in one place and then gather some old people round them and start asking questions. My experience of this system of recording oral traditions shows that wrong versions could be recorded by the officers without their knowing that they were wrong: it is rare that an informant in such a group will hear something wrongly put by another informant and raise objection.' He also suggests that it was the policy of the British not to record anything that would arouse the hostility of people or a section of people. He says this is why Hoskyns-Abrahall's *History of Bussa* file 104/1925 was returned for rewriting. *Nowhere in Yauri did he find established public institutions for preserving orally the history of the people of the locality*. This holds true for Bussa. Madi Adamu *A Hausa Government in Decline: Yauri in the Nineteenth Century* unpublished M.A. thesis, Ahmadu Bello University, 1968.
19. Clapperton, 1829, p. 94.
20. NAK/BORGDIST/DOB/ASR/10 'Kaiama District Assessment Report: Joyce Cary A.D.O.'
21. Clapperton, 1929, p. 68.
22. Robin Hallett ed., *The Niger Journal of Richard and John Lander*, London, 1965, Chapter 6.
23. NAK/BORGDIST/DOB/ASR/10 'Kaiama District Assessment Report: Joyce Cary A.D.O.'
24. Personal communication from Mr. K. Lupton.
25. Alhaji Musa Muhammadu Kigera III, Emir of Borgu, *History of Bussa*, typescript, 1968.
26. The other version is that the followers of the Prophet enlarged the stream so that Kisra would not return. See E. C. Duff, *Gazetteer of the Kontagora Province* (revised by Major W. Hamilton-Browne), London, 1920, pp. 23–24 'Bussa History' (authorities Mr. Harry Kemble, Police Officer, and Mr. A. J. L. Cary, A.D.O.).
27. *ibid.* The September 1912 Quarterly Report insists that Kitoro Gani, 'after much hesitation' accompanied Assistant Resident Boyd down the Niger or a canoe. NAK/BORGDIST/DOB/AR/3. However, it seems clear that the 1908 date is correct, since on 16th June 1911 Kitoro Gani left for Kontagora for the festivities connected with the Coronation of King George V which meant crossing the Niger. NAK/BORGDIST/DOB/QHR/5 Bussa and Kaiama Reports, 2nd Quarter, 1911.

28. Emir of Borgu, *History of Bussa*.
29. NAK/ILORPROF/3353A Borgu Province Report for July 1902, Ag. Resident H. Kemble to Lugard, High Commissioner.
30. Traditions collected in Kaiama by M. Suleiman Haliru Idris, July–August, 1971.
31. The chains have been removed to new Bussa and are in the safe keeping of the Emir of Borgu.
32. D. F. Heath, 'Bussa Regalia', *Man*, May 1937, Nos. 90–91, pp. 77–78.
33. R. Cornevin, *Histoire du Dahomey*, Paris, 1963, p. 162.
34. T. Hoskyns-Abrahall, *History of Bussa* NAK/SNP/13 × 14/K.C. Series/K.6.
35. NAK/BORGDIST/6 Borgu Provincial Record Book.
36. Clapperton, 1829, p. 88.
37. *ibid.*, p. 117.
38. Hallett ed., *Niger Journal*, p. 106.
39. Clapperton, 1829, p. 83.
40. J. C. Anene, *International Boundaries of Nigeria*, London, 1970, p. 192, citing P.R.O. Confidential No. 7297. Enclosure in no. 24, C.O. to F.O. 15. 4.1898.
41. NAK/SNP/15/1/3 Nikki—Treaty with the Royal Niger Company, 1894.
42. Jacques Lombard, 'Un système politique traditionel de type féodal: les Baribas du Nord Dahomey. Aperçu sur l'organisation sociale et le pouvoir central', *Bulletin de l'IFAN*, T. XIX. sér B. nos. 3–4, 1957, p. 481.
43. Hallett ed., *Niger Journal*, p. 106.
44. NAK/ILORPROF/2849 D. F. Heath, A.D.O. Borgu, Monograph on Tsofon Bussa.
45. Anene, *The International Boundaries of Nigeria*, pp. 204–5.
46. Interview with Alhaji Musa Muhammadu Kigera III, Emir of Borgu. Also information collected in Borgu by my research assistant, M. Haliru Suleiman Idris.
47. Hallett ed., *Niger Journal*, p. 106.
48. Clapperton, 1829, p. 117.
49. See Law, *op. cit.*
50. Hallett ed., *Niger Journal*, p. 120.
51. Margery Perham and Mary Bull eds., *The Diaries of Lord Lugard*, IV, London, 1963, p. 144. Musa Baba Idris confirms from his own research that all the Borgu states respected the nominal seniority of Bussa by referring to Bussa as the *father*.
52. Traditions vary as to the exact circumstances of the migration of Boroboko from Nikki. One tradition says he was a brother of the King of Nikki whose throne, on his death, was seized by the Kisra immigrants. This is the version recorded by Muhammad Tukur Omar of the Ministry of Establishments and Training at Kaduna, in 1970(?) The version recorded by Joyce Cary in 1919 (NAK/BORGDIST/DOB/ASR/10) has Boroboko a relation of the Kisra-descended King of Nikki. What does seem important for our purposes is that Kaiama acknowledges its Nikki origin and, even in Muhammad Tukur Omar's version, the nominal suzerainty of Nikki is acknowledged. It will be recalled that in Kemble's version, recorded from three Kaiama elders in 1902, the Nikki relationship is accepted.
53. Law, *op. cit.*
54. This tradition is related by W. Hamilton-Browne, Resident of Kontagora Province, in a letter to the Lt. Governor Northern Provinces, 20th Feb. 1917, NAK/SNP/9/3405/1923.

55. Lugard, *Diaries*, IV, p. 152.
It is very difficult to sort out the traditions with regard to Kaiama's relationship with Nikki and Bussa. Modern recordings of the traditions of the foundation of Kaiama and its relationship with Nikki and Bussa seem to have been coloured by both the division of Borgu by the Anglo-French boundary of 1898 and the decision to subordinate Kaiama to Bussa in 1955. The people of Kaiama are particularly sensitive about this, and Kaiama traditions today emphasize (*a*) that Kaiama was an ancient foundation; (*b*) that Kaiama never acknowledged the precedence of either Bussa or Nikki; (*c*) that Yashikera, Ilesha and Okuta were Kaiama rather than Nikki foundations. The importance of the latter assertion relates to the decision not only to make Kaiama subordinate to Bussa, but to separate from it its three districts of Yashikera, Okuta and Ilesha on the grounds that in pre-colonial times they were tributaries of Nikki.
56. In 1903, 1935.
57. One Kaiama version holds that Yashikera was founded by a son of Mora Dazide, the father of Sabi Agba, thus making it a Kaiama foundation. Tradition recorded in July–August 1971 by Haliru Idris Suleiman. But this is difficult to reconcile with the fact that rulers of Yashikera considered themselves as members of the Nikki ruling house during the period of colonial rule and accordingly presented the Nikki throne. See note 56 above.
58. Clapperton, 1829, p. 90.
59. NAK/SNP/13 × 14/K.C. Series/K.2099.
'Anthropological and Historical Report on the Yaurawa' by A. B. Mathews, 1926. See also his report on Bussa of the same year in NAK/ILORPROF/5/2907 in which he writes: 'Among Kishira's *talakawa* [people] came an Arab, one JEREBANA, who founded Yauri: which is why Sarkin Yauri is Sarkin Bussa's grandson.'
60 Adamu, 'A Hausa Government'.
61. *ibid.*, p. 187 and p. 166 n. 7. See also R. A. Adeleye, *Power and Diplomacy in Northern Nigeria: The Sokoto Caliphate and its Enemies*, London, 1971, p. 73.
62. Clapperton, 1829, p. 74.
Hallett ed., *Niger Journal*, p. 112: 'The Borgoo people will not suffer them to carry any weapon of defence.' See also A. C. G. Hastings, *Voyage of the Dayspring*, London, 1926 p. 155. Commander R. H. Glover reported in his journal for 12.12.1857? that the Fulani in Borgu were kept in great subjection and allowed 'to carry a stick and a bow but only three arrows in their quiver and no sword'.
63. Lombard, *Structures de type féodal*, p. 37.
64. Hallett ed., *Niger Journal*, p. 120.
65. Adamu, 'A Hausa Government', pp. 297–300.
66. *ibid.*
67. For a full discussion of this see Robin Horton, 'Stateless Societies in the History of West Africa' in J. F. A. Ajayi and Michael Crowder, eds., *History of West Africa*, Vol. I, London, 1972, pp. 78–119.
68. NAK/BORGDIST/6 Borgu Provincial Record Book, 1905.
69. Lombard, *Structures de type 'féodal'*, pp. 62, 98, 102–3.
70. NAK/ILORPROF/5/2907 'Notes on the Customs of the Busa [sic.] at Illo' by Mr. Nicholson of the Education Department.
71. Hallett ed., *Niger Journal*, p. 106.

72. Clapperton, 1829, p. 111.
73. *ibid.*, p. 313.
74. *ibid.*, p. 98.
75. This is based on field-work by Haliru Idris Suleiman and the following reports by British Administrative Officers:
    NAK/ILORPROF/5/2907 'Notes on the Bussawa' by A. B. Mathews; 'Report on the Burial Place and Rites of the Kings of Bussa' by Walter Nash, 1926.
    NAK/SNP/13 × 14/K.C. Series K.6 'History of Bussa' by T. Hoskyns-Abrahall; 'Notes on Old Bussa' by D. F. Heath.
76. Clapperton, 1829, p. 74.
77. Lombard, *Structures de type 'féodal'*, pp. 330 ff.
78. *ibid.*, p. 345.

II · Early Foreign Administration in British Borgu

1. Sir E. Hertslet, *The Map of Africa by Treaty*, third edition. Reprinted London 1967, Vol. II, p. 481.
2. Anene, *The International Boundaries of Nigeria*, p. 208.
3. *ibid.*, p. 207.
4. Hertslet, *Map of Africa*, II, p. 122.
5. Cited in Anene, *The International Boundaries of Nigeria*, p. 221.
6. Cited in Lombard, *Structures de type féodal*, p. 387.
7. Hertslet, *The Map of Africa*, I, p. 122.
8. For the negotiations between France and Britain see J. E. Flint, *Sir George Goldie and the Making of Nigeria*, London, 1960, Chapter 12; Anene, *The International Boundaries of Nigeria*, Chapter 6; Margery Perham, *Lugard: The Years of Adventure* 1858–1898, London, 1956 (hereinafter referred to as *Lugard I*). For Lugard's account of the race to Nikki see Margery Perham and Mary Bull eds., *The Diaries of Lord Lugard*, Vol. IV, London, 1963.
9. Gabriel Hantoaux, the French Foreign Minister, told Sir Edmund Monson, the British Ambassador in Paris, that he was very worried that the officers in West Africa might lose their heads and precipitate a war 'for objects which in themselves cannot be worth so grave a calamity'. Quoted by Flint, *Sir George Goldie*, p. 290.
10. Cited by Perham in *Lugard*, I, p. 668.
11. Commandant G. J. Toutée, *Dahomé-Niger-Touareg*, Paris, 1897, p. 263.
12. Lombard, *Structures de type féodal*, p. 392.
13. T. Hoskyns-Abrahall, 'History of Bussa'.
14. Brigadier Sir James Willcocks, *From Kabul to Kumasi: Twenty-Four Years of Soldiering and Sport*, London, 1904, p. 225.
15. *ibid.*, p. 191.
16. *Colonial Annual Reports: Northern Nigeria*, No. 346, 1st January 1900–31st March 1901.
17. *ibid.*, no. 377, 1st January–31st December, 1901.
18. *ibid.*, no. 409 for 1902.
19. Lenfant, *Le Niger*, p. 127.
20. *ibid.*, p. 126.
21. NAK/ILORPROF/3353A/Kemble to Lugard 30.4.1902.
22. *ibid.* Kemble's Monthly Report for Borgu Province for September 1903. Kemble wrote that the Kings of both Kaiama and Bussa corroborated this version of events. See also NAK/BORGDIST/6 Borgu Provincial Record Book, Wawa, 1905.

23. Lenfant, *Le Niger*, pp. 122–5.
24. NAK/ILORPROF/3353A/Kemble to Lugard 30.4.1902.
25. *ibid*.
26. *ibid*. 31.5.1902.
27. *ibid*. Kemble's Monthly Report for February 1902.
28. *ibid*. Kemble's Monthly Report for May 1902.
29. *ibid*. Kemble's Monthly Report for July 1902.
30. *ibid*. Kemble's Monthly Report for April 1903.
31. *ibid*. Kemble's Monthly Report for May 1903.
32. *ibid*. Kemble's Monthly Report for July 1902.
33. *ibid*.
34. *ibid*. Kemble's Monthly Report for October 1902.
35. *ibid*. Kemble's Monthly Report for November 1902.
36. *ibid*. Kemble's Monthly Report for March 1903.
37. *ibid*. Kemble's Monthly Report for April 1903.
38. NAK/SNP/15/ACC.52/Anderson's Monthly Report for July 1903.
39. *ibid*.
40. *ibid*. Anderson's Monthly Report for August 1903.
41. *ibid*. Anderson's Monthly Report for September 1903. It is at this stage that reports use the title King interchangeably with Chief or its Hausa equivalent, Sarki/Seriki.
42. *ibid*. Anderson's Monthly Report for July 1903.
43. *ibid*. Steven's Monthly Report for December 1903. Unless otherwise indicated, all that follows from p. 58 to p. 61 is based on that report.
44. There seems to be quite a deal of confusion as to the date of Kitoro Gani's accession. The official records of later years frequently give his date of accession as 1902, e.g. NAK/ILORPROF/104/1925 Gazetteer of Borgu Division by Hoskyns-Abrahall, A.D.O. Borgu, December 1925. This is also the date given in S. J. Hogben and A. H. M. Kirk-Greene, *The Emirates of Northern Nigeria*, London, 1966, p. 584. We shall however consider 1903 as the actual year of his accession.
45. Information collected by Haliru Suleiman Idris, July–August 1971.
46. NAK/SNP/6/1/19/1904.
47. NAK/SNP/450 of 1905; NAK/SNP/1249 of 1905; and NAK/SNP/3782 of 1904.
48. NAK/ILORPROF/3352B. Kemble's Monthly Report for January 1904.
49. NAK/SNP/7/907/1912.
50. NAK/SNP/15/ACC.52/1903.
51. NAK/SNP/ACC.52/December 1903.
52. NAK/BORGDIST/6 Borgu Provincial Record Book—Yashikera.
53. NAK/SNP/15/ACC.2 Borgu Monthly Report—December 1903.

III · The End of Borgu Province
1. NAK/BORGDIST/5.
2. The following account is based on correspondence in NAK/SNP/ACC.76 'Captain Anderson, 1904'.
3. NAK/BORGIST/5.
4. NAK/BORGDIST/6.
5. NAK/SNP/15/ACC.76. Anderson to Lugard 20.7.1904.
6. *Colonial Annual Reports*—Northern Nigeria 1904, No. 476, p. 282.
7. *ibid*., p. 284.
8. NAK/BORGDIST/5.

9. *ibid.*
10. NAK/BORGDIST/6.
11. *ibid.* Minute of 8.12.1904.
12. NAK/ILORPROF/3352B.
13. NAK/BORGDIST/DOB/QHR/1.
14. *Colonial Annual Reports*—Northern Nigeria 1904 No. 476.
15. NAK/SNP/7/6/15/1151/1905.
16. Larymore, *A Resident's Wife in Nigeria.*
17. A. F. Fremantle ed. *Two African Journals and other Papers of the late John Morton Fremantle C.M.G., M.B.E.* Printed for private circulation, 1938.
18. NAK/BORGDIST/DOB/QHR/2 Borgu Quarterly Report for March 1906.
19. *ibid.*
20. Larymore, *A Resident's Wife,* p. 163.
21. *ibid.,* p. 161.
22. NAK/BORGDIST/QHR/2 Borgu Quarterly Report for March 1906.
23. NAK/SNP/7/7/1663/1906.
24. NAK/BORGDIST/QHR/2 Borgu Quarterly Report for March 1906.
25. Larymore, *A Resident's Wife,* p. 168.
26. *ibid.,* pp. 177–8.
27. *ibid.,* pp. 99ff., and also Robert Heussler, *The British in Northern Nigeria,* London, 1968.
28. NAK/BORGDIST/DOB/QHR/2 Borgu Quarterly Report for September 1906.
29. NAK/ILORPROF/3353A/Borgu Province Monthly Report for February 1902.
30. NAK/SNP/7/1539/1907 Borgu Quarterly Report for December 1906.
31. Fremantle, *Two African Journals,* p. 49.
32. *ibid.,* p. 93. Tribute to Fremantle by Lord Lugard.
33. *ibid.,* pp. 51–52.
34. NAK/SNP/7/1858/1907 Borgu Annual Report 1906.
35. Fremantle, *Two African Journals,* p. 53.
36. *Colonial Annual Reports*—Northern Nigeria, 1904, p. 251.
37. NAK/SNP/7/784/1908 Kontagora Report for 1907.
38. NAK/SNP7/1858/1907.
39. NAK/SNP/6/3/176/1907.
40. NAK/SNP/7/784/1908 Kontagora Report December Quarter 1907.
41. NAK/BORGDIST/DOB/QHR/3 Bussa and Kaiama Reports December Quarter 1909.
42. NAK/BORGDIST/DOB/QHR/4 Bussa and Kaiama Reports June Quarter 1910.
43. NAK/SNP/907/1912 Kontagora Province Annual Report, 1911.
44. NAK/BORGDIST/DOB/QHR/5 Bussa and Kaiama Reports for 1911. The police were actually away from 7th–28th March 1911.
45. NAK/SNP/403/1912.
46. NAK/BORGDIST/DOB/QHR/3 June Quarter Report 1907.
47. NAK/BORGDIST/DOB/QHR/3 Bussa and Kaiama Reports June Quarter 1909.
48. NAK/BORGDIST/DOB/QHR/4 Bussa and Kaiama Reports March Quarter 1910.
49. NAK/SNP/7/4097/1908 Kontagora Province Report June Quarter 1908.
50. NAK/BORGDIST/DOB/HIS/3.
51. NAK/BORGDIST/DOB/QHR/5 Bussa and Kaiama Reports for 1911.

52. NAK/BORGDIST/DOB/QHR/3 Bussa and Kaiama Reports for 1909.
53. NAK/SNP/7/2376/1911 Kontagora Province Report March Quarter 1911.
54. NAK/BORGDIST/DOB/QHR/5.
55. NAK/BORGDIST/DOB/HIS/3. Confidential Report on Kitoro Gani by T. C. Newton, Assistant Resident Bussa, 19/4/1911.
56. All the above is from NAK/BORGDIST/DOB/QHR/5 Bussa and Kaiama Reports 1911.
57. NAK/SNP/6/3/176/1907.
58. NAK/BORGDIST/DOB/QHR/4 Bussa and Kaiama Reports for 1910.
59. NAK/SNP/2371/1909 Kontagora Province Report March Quarter 1909.
60. NAK/BORGDIST/DOB/QHR/5.
61. NAK/BORGDIST/DOB/QHR/4.
62. NAK/BORGDIST/DOB/HIS/3.
63. NAK/SNP/7/3648/1911.

IV · The Deposition of Kitoro Gani

1. See Michael Crowder and Obaro Ikime, Introduction to *West African Chiefs: Their Changing Status under Colonial Rule and Independence*, Ife and New York, 1970.
2. NAK/BORGDIST/DOB/QHR/6.
3. NAK/BORGDIST/DOB/AR/3.
4. NAK/BORGDIST/DOB/QHR/5 and NAK/SNP/7/185/1912: Blakeney Res. Kon. to C.S. Northern Nigeria 10 June 1912. 'I had already infod. Mr. Clarke that the Jekada or Kofa must be done away with and that the D.H. together with the Village Head are alone responsible for the collection of tax.'
5. NAK/SNP/4037/1912.
6. NAK/BORGDIST/DOB/AR/3.
7. NAK/SNP/7538/1912.
8. Lord Lugard, *Political Memoranda*, London, 1919, No. 49.
9. NAK/BORGDIST/DOB/AR/3.
10. *ibid.*
11. NAK/BORGDIST/DOB/QHR/6.
12. NAK/SNP/4037/1912.
13. *ibid.*
14. NAK/BORGDIST/DOB/QHR/6.
15. NAK/SNP/7358/1912.
16. NAK/BORGDIST/DOB/QHR/6.
17. Bodleian Library, Oxford: Joyce Cary Papers. Cary to his wife 26.6.1917.
18. NAK/SNP/CR/108.
19. *ibid.*
20. *ibid.*
21. NAK/BORGDIST/DOB/QHR/7.
22. NAK/SNP/10/354p/1913.
23. NAK/BORGDIST/DOB/QHR/7.
24. P. G. Harris, *Sokoto Provincial Gazetteer*.
25. NAK/BORGDIST/DOB/HIS/3.
26. NAK/SNP/10/704p/1913.
27. NAK/BORGDIST/DOB/QHR/7.
28. *ibid.*
29. NAK/SNP/10/27p/1914.
30. NAK/SNP/10/155p/1914.

31. NAK/SNP/10/709p/1916.
   The problem of accurate dating for the events of this period is hampered by the records themselves. Successive district officers attribute different dates to major events in the history of Bussa. In NAK/SNP/0/5/54/1918 Sabukki's tax agitation is dated 1912. It is however clear that it took place in 1913, since Clarke mentions that he sent the ring leaders before Kitoro Gani for trial and he did not return until 30th December 1912. His own first mention of the affair is in his December quarterly report for 1913. NAK/BORGDIST/DOB/QHR/7.
32. Information collected by Haliru Suleiman Idris, July–August, 1971.
33. ibid.
34. NAK/BORGDIST/DOB/QHR/7 and NAK/DOB/AR/5 and NAK/SNP/5/54/1918.
35. NAK/BORGDIST/DOB/AR/5.
36. ibid.
37. NAK/SNP/10/423p/1914 File No. 1.
38. ibid.
39. NAK/BORGDIST/AR/5.
40. ibid.
41. NAK/SNP/10/584p/1914.
42. NAK/SNP/10/128p/1915.
43. There seems to be some confusion in the amounts here. The incidence was raised in 1913 from 2/6d to 2/9d, which was one of the causes of the anti-tax agitation led by Sabukki. In his Annual Report for 1914 (NAK/BORGDIST/DOB/AR/5) Clarke specifically states that Dwyer raised the incidence from 2/6d (not 2/9d) to 4/–.
44. NAK/BORGDIST/DOB/AR/5.
45. NAK/SNP/10/128p/1915.
46. ibid.
47. NAK/SNP/10/27p/1914 File No. 1.
48. NAK/SNP/10/251p/1915.
49. NAK/SNP/10/726p/1914. All that follows is, unless otherwise indicated, based on this file. The other file which deals with this patrol is NAK/SNP/10/14p/1915.
50. See Michael Crowder, 'West Africa and the 1914–18 War', *Bulletin de l'I.F.A.N.* T. XXX, ser. B, no. 1, 1968, pp. 227–247.
51. NAK/SNP/10/251p/1915.
52. NAK/SNP/10/67p/1913.
53. NAK/SNP/8/42/1915.
54. ibid.
55. ibid.
56. ibid.
57. The above is based on NAK/SNP/10/150p/1918 and NAK/SNP/8/42/1915.
58. NAK/SNP/8/42/1915.
59. ibid.
60. NAK/BORGDIST/DOB/BOU/3.
61. ibid.
62. NAK/SNP/8/42/1915.
63. ibid.
64. ibid.
65. NAK/SNP/9/10/3405/1923.
66. ibid.

NOTES

67. *ibid.*
68. *ibid.*
69. NAK/SNP/10/14p/1915.

V · Sabukki's Rebellion

1. NAK/SNP/10/387p/1915.
2. Unless otherwise indicated the sequence of events below is based on NAK/SNP/10/331p/1915.
3. NAK/SNP/10/31p/1915 and NAK/SNP/10/32p/1915. See also Akinjide Osuntokun, 'Disaffection and Revolts in Nigeria during the First World War 1914–18' (unpublished paper). Toronto, 1971.
4. NAK/SNP/10/331p/1915 16.6.1915.
5. NAK/BORGDIST/DOB/HIS/2.
6. Information collected by Haliru Suleiman Idris, July–August 1971.
7. By 1920 the population of Bussa was only 13,615, less of course Rofia which was not returned until 1927. NAK/BORGDIST/DOB/AR/12/1920.

	Population of Bussa in 1920				
	Male	Female	Children	Total	sq. Mile Area
BUSSA	1246	1256	1207	3709	2500
ALIYARA	985	938	996	2919	1150
WAWA	1574	1488	1200	4262	2500
AGWARRA	929	825	971	2725	144
	4734	4507	4374	13615	6294

i.e. 2·1 per square mile.

8. Emir of Borgu, *History of Bussa*.
9. NAK/SNP/10/387p/1915.
10. NAK/SNP/10/341p/1915.
11. Emir of Borgu, *History of Bussa*.
12. NAK/SNP/10/331p/1915 War Diary of Colour-Sergeant Kerry enclosed in letter from H.Q. W.A.F.F. to Secretary, Northern Provinces, Zungeru 23.10.1915.
13. NAK/SNP/10/331p/1915 21.6.1915.
14. *ibid.*, 24.6.1915.
15. *ibid.* Goldsmith, Lt-Governor Northern Provinces, to Hamilton-Browne, Resident Kontagora 24.6.1915.
16. This is reconstructed from NAK/SNP/8/2/183/1915 and NAK/BORGDIST/DOB/HIST/2.
17. NAK/SNP/10/331p/1915 War Diary of Colour-Sergeant Kerry.
18. NAK/SNP/10/331p/1915 Hamilton-Browne, Resident Kontagora, to Secretary, Northern Provinces, 12.7.1915, enclosing letter from Clarke, D.O. Yelwa, dated 5.7.1915.
19. *ibid.* Governor-General's Deputy, Lagos, to Lt-Governor Northern Provinces, Zungeru, 12.7.1915.
20. *ibid.* Quoted by Campbell-Irons, Ag. Resident of Kontagora, to Secretary, Northern Provinces, 5.8.1915.
21. *ibid.* War Diary of Colour-Sergeant Kerry.

REVOLT IN BUSSA

22. A[rchives] N[ationales] du S[enegal]/3F1 Noufflard, Lt-Governor of Dahomey to Commandant de Cercle, Parakou, 1.7.1915.
23. *ibid*. Commandant de Cercle, Borgou, to Lt-Governor of Dahomey 5.7.1915.
24. NAK/SNP/10/331p/Acting Resident Kontagora to Secretary, Northern Provinces, Zungeru, 19.8.1915.
25. A.N.S./3F1/Commandant de Cercle, Parakou, to Lt-Governor of Dahomey, 14.7.1915.
26. *ibid*. Commandant de Cercle, Kandi, to Lt-Governor of Dahomey, 6.7.1915.
27. *ibid*. Lt-Governor of Dahomey to Governor-General, Dakar, 3.9.1915.
28. *ibid*.
29. NAK/SNP/10/331p/1915.
30. NAK/SNP/10/364p/1916.
31. *ibid*.
32. NAK/SNP/10/331p/1915. Report by Hamilton-Browne, Resident Kontagora, to Secretary, Northern Provinces, 1–15. 7.1915.
33. Source mislaid.
34. NAK/SNP/37/1913.
35. NAK/SNP/8/25/1916.
36. Emir of Borgu, *History of Bussa*.
37. NAK/SNP/10/815p/1915. Dwyer, Acting Resident of Kontagora, to Secretary, Northern Provinces, Zungeru, 24.12.1915.
38. *ibid*. Hamilton-Browne, Resident of Kontagora, Minute of 8.3.1916.
39. NAK/SNP/10/747p/1915 Temple to Dwyer 19.11.1915.
40. *ibid*. 19.11.1915.
41. *ibid*. 19.11.1915.
42. *ibid*. 8.12.1915.
43. *ibid*. 6.12.1915.
44. *ibid*. 6.3.1916.
45. *ibid*. 18.12.1915.
46. NAK/SNP/17/7/K.C. Series/K.2227.

VI · Two Murders in Bussa

1. This chapter, except when otherwise indicated, is based on the three trials of Turaki before the Kontagora Provincial Court contained in NAK/SN/13/O/P.C./40/1916 and NAK/SNP/13/O/P.C/117/1916. I have only recorded as facts those, gleaned from the three trial records, on which all witnesses agreed, or which were not denied by the defendants or witnesses. Where a fact was in dispute, and the evidence for it was not accepted by the Court, I have indicated this in the text. I have also made it clear when 'facts' are supported only by evidence which was ruled to be hearsay.
2. Zakara was to deny this but both Mallam Isa and Turaki himself told the Court that he had given this order.
3. Turaki, trying to place the blame for the man's condition on Zakara, told the Court at his first trial that it was he who loosened Gani of Kagogi's bonds. But both Garuba and Gemmu stated that the man was released from his bonds before Turaki's arrival.
4. This is on the evidence of Mallam Isa as to what Badaburde later told him. Badaburde in his evidence said that Gani did not speak to him.
5. Mallam Matakure steadfastly denied to the Court that he had told Turaki that Aliu had ordered that Gani should be shot if he were caught. Aliu, too, denied ever giving such orders. But several witnesses testified that Matakure had in fact told Turaki that Aliu's orders were to shoot Gani.

6. NAK/SNP/8/2/183/1915.
7. *ibid.*
8. *ibid.*
9. NAK/SNP/O/P.C./40/1916.
10. *ibid.* L. S. Tew, Legal Adviser to the Lieutenant-Governor, Northern Provinces, 7.2.1916.
11. NAK/SNP/O/P.C./117/1916.
12. *ibid.*
13. *ibid.*
14. *ibid.*
15. NAK/SNP/10/386p/1916.
16. NAK/SNP/10/224p/1916.
17. *ibid.*
18. *ibid.*

VII · First Reforms and a Second Rising

1. NAK/SNP/8/25/1916.
2. *ibid.* Hamilton-Browne, Resident Kontagora, to Secretary, Northern Provinces, 10.3.1916.
3. *ibid.*, 17.3.1916.
4. *ibid.*, 4.4.1916.
5. *ibid.*, 25.5.1916.
6. *ibid.*, 6.6.1916.
7. *ibid.* and NAK/BORGDIST/DOB/3.
8. NAK/SNP/10/525p/1916.
9. Emir of Borgu, *History of Bussa*.
10. NAK/SNP/481p/1916 Hamilton-Browne to Secretary, Northern Provinces, 12.7.1916.
11. *ibid.*
12. *ibid.*
13. *ibid.*, 19.7.1916.
14. *ibid.* Hamilton-Browne to Secretary, Northern Provinces, 16.10.1916.
15. NAK/SNP/10/709p/1916.
16. *ibid.*
17. National Archives of France. Section Outre-Mer. Mission 1919. Rapport fait par M. Ch. Phérivong, Inspecteur-Général Ier Classe des Colonies, concernant affaires des cercles de Djougou et du Borgou a l'époque due 30 Janvier 1919 et explications fournies par le Lt-Gouverneur p.i. de la Colonie du Dahomey, referred to hereafter as Rapport Phérivong.
18. All the above is based on Rapport Phérivong 'Affaire de Bembereke'.
19. The above is based on Rapport Phérivong.
20. NAK/SNP/10/709p/1916.
21. *ibid.*
22. *ibid.*, 12.12.1916.
23. NAK/SNP/10/709p/1916. 9.2.1917.
24. *ibid.*, 26.2.1917.
25. *ibid.* Lugard to Lt-Governor, Northern Provinces, 14.12.1916.
26. *ibid.*, 31.12.1916.
27. *ibid.*, 17.4.1917.
28. NAK/SNP/10/735p/1916.
29. NAK/SNP/10/207p/1917 minute by Lugard of 13.2.1917.

REVOLT IN BUSSA

30. *ibid.* C. T. Laurence, Clerk of the Executive Council, to Lt-Governor, Northern Provinces, 5.7.1917.
31. *ibid.* Report on Trial by Hamilton-Browne, Resident Kontagora, 25.7.1917.
32. *ibid.* Duff, Acting Resident Kontagora, to Secretary, Northern Provinces, Kaduna, 7.5.1918.
33. *ibid.* Duff to Secretary, Northern Provinces, Kaduna, 6.7.1918.
34. *ibid.*, 9.9.1918.
35. *ibid.* Acting Secretary, Northern Provinces, to Resident Kontagora, 1.10.1918.
36. NAK/ILORPROF/104/1925. Gazetteer for Borgu Division by T. Hoskyns-Abrahall, A.D.O. Borgu, December 1925.
37. See Pierre Alexandre, 'Chiefs, *Commandants* and Clerks: Their Relationship from Conquest to Decolonization in French West Africa', in Michael Crowder and Obaro Ikime eds., *West African Chiefs: Their Changing Status under Colonial Rule and Independence*, Ife, 1970, pp. 2–13.
38. Emir of Borgu, *History of Bussa*.
39. NAK/SNP/10/734p/1916 E. J. Arnett, Resident Sokoto, to Hamilton-Browne, Resident Kontagora, 12th August 1916.
40. *ibid.* The files are not very clear as to the date Arnett first raised his complaint against Abba. There is some indication that he first mentioned his activities in relation to the quesion of 'prevention of migration to Kontagora Province' Minute Paper No. 398p/1915.
41. NAK/SNP/10/570p/1913.
42. *ibid.*
43. *ibid.* Hamilton-Browne, Resident Kontagora, to Chief Secretary, Government of Northern Nigeria, Zungeru, 30.9.1913.
44. *ibid.*
45. *ibid.* G. S. Browne, for Acting Chief Secretary, Government of Northern Nigeria, to Hamilton-Browne, 17.10.1913.
46. NAK/SNP/10/231p/1916.
47. NAK/SNP/10/734p/1916.
48. *ibid.* Hamilton-Browne, Resident Kontagora, to Secretary, Northern Provinces, Zungeru, 27.11.1916.
49. NAK/SNP/9/10/3405/1923 formerly SNP/751p/1916.
50. *ibid.*
51. *ibid.*
52. *ibid.*
53. NAK/SNP/8/2/183/1915. Hamilton-Browne to Secretary, Northern Provinces, 26.4.1916.
54. NAK/SNP/9/16/3405/1923.
55. *ibid.*
56. *ibid.*
57. *ibid.*
58. *ibid.*
59. *ibid.*, 3.3.1917.
60. *ibid.* Lugard to Goldsmith, Lt-Governor, Northern Provinces, 12.3.1917.
61. *ibid.*
62. NAK/SNP/18/CR/108 Hamilton-Browne, Resident Kontagora, 31.12.1914
63. *ibid.* Hamilton-Browne, Resident Kontagora, 4.4.1917.
64. *ibid.* H. S. Goldsmith, Lt-Governor, Northern Provinces, 19.4.1917.
65. *ibid.* J. C. O. Clarke to Secretary, Northern Provinces, 6.10.1917.
66. NAK/SNP/8/6/65/1919.

NOTES

67. NAK/SNP/18/CR/108. H. S. Goldsmith, Lt-Governor, 25.5.1920.
68. *ibid.* 'Application for Colonial Appointment' 13.4.1905.

VIII · The Reign of Kijibrim

1. NAK/SNP/10/417p/1917.
2. Joyce Cary Papers: Cary to his wife 4.5.1917.
3. Cited in Molly Mahood, *Joyce Cary's Africa*, London, 1964, p. 35.
4. Joyce Cary Papers: Cary to his wife 13.5.1917 and 14.5.1917.
5. *ibid.* Cary to his wife, 26.6.1917.
6. NAK/SNP/10/82p/1918.
7. NAK/SNP/10/417p/1917.
8. Joyce Cary Papers: Cary to his wife 12.10.1917.
9. Joyce Cary, *The Case for African Freedom*, London, 1941.
10. Joyce Cary Papers: Cary to his wife 22.9.1917.
11. NAK/BORGDIST/HIST/3 Diggle to Resident Kontagora 21.12.1917.
12. *ibid.* Resident Kontagora to Secretary Northern Provinces 26.4.1918.
13. *ibid.* H. S. Goldsmith to Resident Kontagora 31.5.1918.
14. *ibid.* Diggle to Resident Kontagora 28.6.1918.
15. NAK/SNP/10/502p/1918.
16. NAK/SNP/10/503p/1918.
17. *ibid.* H. S. Goldsmith to Hamilton-Browne 5.11.1918.
18. NAK/SNP/10/5p/1920. Kontagora Annual Report puts the restored area at 180 square miles but NAK/SOKPROF/2/11/84/1919 Yelwa Annual Report puts it at 144 square miles. See also NAK/SNP/10/401p/1918.
19. NAK/BORGDIST/DOB/BOU/8.
20. NAK/BORGDIST/DOB/BOU/17.
21. See Mahood, *Joyce Cary's Africa*.
22. *ibid.*, p. 47.
23. NAK/BORGDIST/DOB/ASR/9 Secretary Northern Provinces to Resident Kontagora 20.12.1919.
24. Joyce Cary Papers: letter to his wife 27.1.1919.
25. Mahood, *Joyce Cary's Africa*, p. 45.
26. NAK/BORGDIST/DOB/HIS/82 Handing-over Notes: Cowper to Campbell-Irons.
27. NAK/BORGDIST/AR/12/1920.
28. NAK/BORGDIST/DOB/HIS/82 Campbell-Irons to Izard 13.10.1920.
29. *ibid.*
30. *ibid.*
31. NAK/BORGDIST/DOB/AR/12/1920.
32. This is based on the Emir of Borgu's *History of Bussa* and information collected in Bussa by Haliru Suleiman Idris during July and August 1971.
33. NAK/BORGDIST/DOB/AR/12/1920.
34. NAK/BORGDIST/5 Political Officer's Diary: entry by Izard for 10.4.1921.
35. *ibid.:* entry for 10.10.1921.
36. NAK/BORGDIST/DOB/AR/13/1921.
37. Rhodes House Library, Oxford, *Diary of Sir Chandos Hoskyns-Abrahall*. I am very grateful to Sir Chandos Hoskyns-Abrahall for permission to quote from his diary.
38. *ibid.:* entry for 24.2.1921.
39. *ibid.:* entry for 8.7.1921.
40. *ibid.:* entry for 14.8.1921.
41. *ibid.:* entry for 9.1.1922.

42. Letter from Sir Chandos Hoskyns-Abrahall to the author dated 4.6.1972.
43. Hoskyns-Abrahall Diary: entry for 26.8.1921.
44. Information gathered by myself and Haliru Suleiman Idris on various visits to Bussa.
45. NAK/BORGDIST/DOB/AR/16/1922.
46. NAK/SNP/9/9/899/1922.
47. NAK/BORGDIST/DOB/AR/16/1922. The actual date of its return was 6.8.1922, when the staff and letter were received by Hoskyns-Abrahall. NAK/BORGDIST/5 Political Officer's Touring Diary: entry for 6.8.1922.
48. NAK/BORGDIST/5 Political Officer's Diary: entry for 21.10.1922.
49. NAK/BORGDIST/5 Political Officer's Diary: entry by T. Hoskyns-Abrahall for 27.2.1922.
50. Hastings, *Nigerian Days*, p. 211.
51. Unless otherwise stated this chapter is based on NAK/BORGDIST/5 Provincial Court Record Book. Evidence against Kissoin, 1923.
52. NAK/BORGDIST/5 Political Officer's Touring Diary, 1923: entry by T. Hoskyns-Abrahall for 20.4.1923. 'S.B. says that everybody roared with laughter when Kissoin was after S.B.'
53. *ibid.*: entries for 21.3.1923 and 28.2.1923.
54. *ibid.*: entry for 20.4.1923.
55. NAK/BORGDIST/DOB/AR/17/1923.
56. NAK/SNP/OP/C./279/1924 *Rex* v. *Kissoin of Bussa*.
57. Unfortunately the actual minutes of the trial of Kissoin are not in the file NAK/SNP/OP/C./279/1924 in the Kaduna archives, having been sent to the Chief Justice at Lagos. They are not in the Ibadan archives, though under NAI/CSO/26/1179/Vol. XI they appear in the list of Murder Case files where they should be No. XIII, but are not available. There is however a pencil note in the above file saying that the minutes are with *SNA* (Secretary, Native Affairs). Fortunately the transcripts of evidence made by Hoskyns-Abrahall are very full on both the murder and the assassination attempt, and the witnesses agree in all essential details. Given that Kissoin was sentenced to death and was given no recommendation to mercy, and given that by the time of the trial 21 months had elapsed since the murder, we may safely assume that the evidence given for his extradition and for charging him was essentially that on which he was convicted. It is a pity that we do not have his version of events, if indeed he gave it, for it will be recalled Turaki had said nothing in his own defence at his second murder trial.
58. NAK/BORGDIST/4/Court Minute Book *Rex* v. *Sabi Zakara*, D. H. Agwarra c. 40 years.
59. NAK/BORGDIST/5: entry for 3.1.1923.
60. P. G. Harris, *Sokoto Provincial Gazetteer*, p. 292.
61. NAK/SNP/10/150p/1918.
62. NAK/SOKPROF/3/1/C.4 and NAK/SNP/17/7/KC Series/C.193.
63. Harris, *Sokoto Provincial Gazetteer*, p. 292
64. NAK/BORGDIST/DOB/HIS/81 Handing-over Notes, 1923.
65. NAK/BORGDIST/5 Political Diary: entry for 9.12.1923.
66. NAK/BORGDIST/DOB/AR/17/1923.
67. NAI/CSO.26/12687/Vol. 2 Ilorin Province Annual Report 1924.
68. NAK/BORGDIST/5: entry for 21.8.1924.
69. NAI/CSO.26/2/13556 Restoration of Kitoro Gani.
70. NAK/BORGDIST/5: entry for 3.10.1924.

IX · The Restoration of Kitoro Gani

1. NAK/SNP/18/CR.47 Annual Report on Chiefs, Ilorin Province.
2. NAI/CSO/26/File No. 13556.
3. *ibid.*
4. *ibid.* S. M. Grier for Acting Chief Secretary to Clifford.
5. *ibid.* 20.10.1924.
6. *ibid.*
7. NAK/SNP/18/CR.47 Hoskyns-Abrahall on Kitoro Gani 1924/1925.
8. NAK/BORGDIST/DOB/AR/19/1924.
9. *ibid.*
10. *ibid.*
11. NAI/CSO/26/2/File No. 13556 G. S. Browne, Secretary, Northern Provinces, to Chief Secretary, Lagos, 29.4.1925.
12. NAK/BORGDIST/DOB/AR/20/1925.
13. NAK/BORGDIST/5 Political Officer's Diary: entry by Walter Nash 29.4.1925.
14. *ibid.*, 7.5.1925.
15. *ibid.:* entry by Hoskyns-Abrahall for 12.7.1925.
16. NAK/BORGDIST/DOB/BOU/17.
17. *ibid.*, 22.7.1926.
18. *ibid.*, 6.8.1925. Nash to Resident, Ilorin.
19. *ibid.*
20. *ibid.*
21. *ibid.*
22. *ibid.*
23. *ibid.*
24. NAK/SNP/17/7/KC. Series/KC. 2227 Resident Ilorin to Secretary, Northern Provinces, 10.8.1926.
25. *ibid.* Resident Sokoto to Secretary, Northern Provinces, 13.8.1926.
26. *ibid.*
27. *ibid.* Minute by Webster, Resident Sokoto, 5.9.1926.
28. NAK/BORGDIST/DOB/BOU/17 Diggle, D.O. Gwandu, to Resident Sokoto, 23.9.1926.
29. NAK/SNP/17/7/KC. Series/K. 2227 Diggle, D.O. Borgu, to Resident Kontagora, 13.4.1918.
30. NAK/BORGDIST/DOB/BOU/17 Resident Sokoto to Diggle, D.O. Gwandu, 1.10.1926.
31. *ibid.* Nash to Resident Ilorin, 26.10.1926.
32. *ibid.* Resident Ilorin to Nash, 13.10.1926.
33. *ibid.* Resident Sokoto to Diggle, 1.10.1926.
34. NAK/SNP/17/7/KC. Series/K. 2227. Joint Report of Messrs. Molyneux and Nash 23.10.1926.
35. *ibid.* Resident Ilorin to Senior Resident Sokoto, 10.11.1926.
36. *ibid.* Resident Sokoto to Resident Ilorin, 3.1.1927.
37. NAI/CSO.26/12687/IV Ilorin Province Annual Report. Secretary, Northern Provinces, 11.3.1927.
38. NAK/SNP/17/7/K.C. Series/K. 2227 Chief Secretary, Lagos, to Secretary, Northern Provinces, 10.3.1927.
39. *ibid.* Secretary, Northern Provinces, to Chief Secretary, Lagos, 31.3.1927.
40. NAI/CSO.26/13556.
41. NAI/CSO.26/12687/IV.

X · The Second Deposition of Kitoro Gani

1. NAI/CSO.26/12687/IV Ilorin Province Annual Report for 1926.
2. NAK/SNP/18 C.R. 47 Annual Report on Kitoro Gani for 1926.
3. NAK/BORGDIST/DOB/AR/21/1927.
4. NAK/BORGDIST/5 Diary: entry for 7.12.1926.
5. *ibid.*, 27.8.1927.
6. *ibid.*, 7.10.1927.
7. *ibid.*, 25.10.1927.
8. *ibid.*, 17.12.1927.
9. NAK/BORGDIST/DOB/AR/22/1927.
10. NAK/BORGDIST/DOB/AR/23/1928.
11. *ibid.*
12. *ibid.*
13. NAK/BORGDIST/5 Diary: entry for 14.11.1928.
14. *ibid.*, 14.4.1928.
15. *ibid.*, 25.6.1928.
16. NAK/BORGDIST/DOB/AR/24/1929.
17. NAI/CSO.26/12687/VIII/Ilorin Province Annual Report for 1929, minute of 27.2.1930.
18. NAK/BORGDIST/DOB/AR/25/1930.
19. NAK/BORGDIST/DOB/HIS/78 Handing-over Notes 1931: Capt. L. C. Schlotel to B. A. Roberts A.D.O. (in case of indisposition).
20. NAK/BORGDIST/32/Touring Bussa by B. A. Roberts A.D.O. 1932.
21. *ibid.*
22. *ibid.*
23. *ibid.*
24. NAI/CSO.26/12678/X/Annual Report for Ilorin Province 1932.
25. NAK/BORGDIST/32 Touring Bussa.
26. *ibid.* Heath to Roberts 4.1.1932.
27. *ibid.*
28. NAK/BORGDIST/5 Provincial Court Record Book, Trial of Jibrim, Ma'aji.
29. NAI/CSO.26/13556 H. A. James, Acting Secretary Northern Provinces, to Chief Secretary Lagos, 18.4.1933.
30. NAK/BORGDIST/32 Touring Bussa by B. A. Roberts A.D.O. 1932.
31. NAI/CSO.26/13556.
32. NAK/BORGDIST/32 Handing-over Notes: Roberts to E. R. Rowse 5.3.1933.
33. NAK/ILORPROF/5/1926 Heath to Nash 12.3.1933.
34. *ibid.* Heath to Nash 18.3.1933.
35. *ibid.* Nash to Heath 23.3.1933.
36. NAK/BORGDIST/32 Handing-over Notes: Roberts to Rowse 5.3.1933. 4.4.1933.
37. NAK/DOB/HIS/78 Handing-over Notes: Heath to Major B. Glasson 23.5.1933.
38. NAK/BORGDIST/DOB/AR/28/1933.
39. NAK/SNP/18/C.R./47 Annual Report on Kitoro Gani for 1933.
38. NAK/BORGDIST/DOB/AR/28/1933.
39. NAK/SNP/18/C.R./47 Annual Report on Kitoro Gani for 1933.
40. NAK/BORGDIST/5 Diary: entry by Major B. Glasson 31.3.1934.

NOTES

41. NAK/BORGDIST/DOB/HIS/78 Handing-over Notes: Glasson to Heath 13.11.1934.
42. NAK/BORGDIST/DOB/AR/29/1934.
43. NAK/SNP/18/C.R./47 Annual Report on Kitoro Gani for 1934.
44. NAI/CSO.26/16553/S.4. Unfortunately the D.O.'s Political Diary (NAK/BORGDIST/5), for this period i.e. from 6.12.1934 to 21.8.1935, is blank.
45. NAK/BORGDIST/DOB/AR/30/1935.
46. NAI/CSO.26/16553/S.4.
47. *ibid.* Glasson to Resident Ilorin 16.5.1935.
48. *ibid.* Secretary Northern Provinces to Chief Secretary Lagos, 13.6.1935.
49. NAI/CSO.26/13556 Secretary Northern Provinces to Chief Secretary Lagos, 14.6.1935.
50. *ibid.* Auditor to Chief Secretary Lagos, 19.6.1935.
51. *ibid.* Secretary Northern Provinces to Chief Secretary Lagos, 14.6.1935.
52. *ibid.*
53. *ibid.* Secretary Northern Provinces to Chief Secretary Lagos, 23.7.1935.
54. *ibid.* Chief Secretary Lagos to Governor, 30.7.1935.
55. *ibid.* Governor to Chief Secretary Lagos, 2.8.1935.
56. *ibid.* Resident, Ilorin, 3.8.1935.
57. *ibid.* Resident, Ilorin, 10.9.1935.
58. NAK/BORGDIST/5 District Officer's Political Diary, 1935: entry by R. E. Beevor for 21.8.1935. This account of Kitoro Gani's deposition and exile and the accession of Babaki as Emir of Bussa is based on the report of the Resident of Ilorin, F. de F. Daniel, to the Secretary Northern Provinces in NAI/CSO.26/13556 and the diary kept by R. E. Beevor, District Officer, Borgu, in NAK/BORGDIST/5.
59. NAI/CSO.26/13556 Resident Ilorin to Secretary Northern Provinces, 10.9.1935.
60. NAK/BORGDIST/5 District Officer's Political Diary 1935: entry by R. E. Beevor for 29.8.1935.
61. *ibid.*: entry for 6.9.1935.
62. *ibid.*: entry for 7.9.1935.

Epilogue

1. NAK/SNP/17/3/24024 Resident Ilorin to Secretary Northern Provinces, 11.4.1935.
2. NAI/CSO.26/2/12687/XI Ilorin Province Annual Report 1937.
3. NAI/CSO.26/12687/XII Ilorin Province Annual Report 1938.
4. NAK/SNP/17/3/24024.
5. NAI/CSO.26/2/12687/XII.
6. NAI/CSO.26/2/12687/XIII.
7. NAK/ILORPROF/5134/S.5.
8. NAK/ILORPROF/NAC/63.
   Borgu N.A. Council
   (a) Emir of Borgu as President.
   (b) 2 titled members of Bussa N.A.
       (Ubandoma Bussa and Galadima Bussa.)
   (c) 1 titled member of Kaiama N.A. (Madawaikin Borgu).
   (d) 1 person nominated as Adviser on Moslem Law.
   (e) 4 cattle-owning Fulani, nominated.
   (f) 15 elected members.

9. See the file NAK/BORGDIST/DOB/HIS/31. Retirement of Haliru Kiyaru, which contains a series of letters from people in Kaiama to the District Officer, the Resident, and the Premier of the Northern Region protesting against the reduction in status of Kaiama from an emirate to a district. One of the letters is from Ahmadu Yaru Mora Tasude, son of the late Emir Mora Tasude.

Index

Abba, political agent, 105, 118, 135, 142, 154–7, 181, 238–9, 241
Abdu, 212–14
Abdulai, 59
Abdullahi of Jabo, 107
Abershi, Abdullahi (Sarkin Yauri), 37, 97, 108, 110–12, 127–8, 196; made Emir of Kontagora, 128
Abershi of Yauri, Dangaladima, 38
Abson, Lionel, 36
Adamu, Madi, 37
Afwoingi, 133
Agba, Sabi, founder of Kaiama, 35
Agwarra, 37, 93, 97, 106–7, 111, 114, 133, 156, 165, 170–1, 174, 183, 190, 198, 202–3, 206, 213, 214, 219, 224, 226, 242
Ajia, *see* Umoru, Ajia
Alafin Oluewu of Oyo, 34, 119–20, 220
Alafirarou, 121
Alberke, 159
Alexander, C. H., 186
Aliu of Jabo (later Sarkin Yauri), 97, 105, 107–8, 110–12, 118–19, 125–9, 133–7, 139, 145, 150, 155–7, 159, 165, 174, 183–4, 191, 196, 198
Aliu, Umoru dan, 157
Aliyara Bisalla, 111, 113–16, 124–5, 140
Aliyara district, 99–101, 103, 109, 150, 174, 190, 192, 204, 206, 226
Anderson, Captain P. W., 45, 56–7, 65–7, 69–70
Anene, J. C., 34
Anglo-French Convention, 1890, 46, 49
Argungu, Emir of, 156
Argungu, Mainassara, 134, 138
Arki, Mai, 42, 69, 80

Ashanti, 20, 25; uprising in, 49
Atacora, 149: mountains, 20, 146; Somba of, 148
Auna, 221

Baba, 58, 60–1
Babaki, Wuru, 175, 190, 193, 202–4, 206, 213, 219–22, 224, 228: appointed Emir of Bussa, 221–2; becomes Emir of Borgu, 229
Babana, 48, 151, 181
Babanawara, 69, 72
Bachabi, Ali, 147–8
Badaburude, 39, 41, 132, 134, 174
Badagry, 20, 25
Baguène, 146–7
Bajibo, 47, 65, 128
Bakarabonde, 39, 41, 59, 174, 178, 219
Ballot, Victor, 47
Bamarubere, 27, 40, 41, 58
Bamode, 41
Banara, 23, 103, 105
Bariba, 120, 160, 162, 189; language, 21
Barjibelo, 196, 198
Barruwa, 46
Batafu, chief minister, 41, 42, 59, 93, 99
Batomba, freemen, 25
Bécou, 146, 148; 'affaire Bécou', 146
Beevor, R. E., 216, 220–1
Beit-el-Mal, Native Treasuries, 93
Bell, Sir Hesketh, 92
Bello, Barje, 38
Benue river, 45
Bera, 120
Bere Bere, royal bodyguard, 42
Beresondi, 29, 41
Beresuni, 41
Berlin Conference, 1884–5, 44

267

Béroubay, 149
Bimbereke, 146–9
Bindiga, Daudin, 92
Bindiga, Dowdu, 60, 114, 131, 134, 140
Binger, L. G., 46
Bio, 214–18
Birnin Kebbi, 123, 158, 190
Bissashe, 153
Biyo, 26
Black, Dr., 242
Blake, L., 108
Blakeney, Major J. E. C., 62, 92–5, 98–9, 101, 103, 105, 128
Bogo-Yaru, 122
Bokko of Puissa, 114
Boko language, 21
Borgawa (people of Borgu), 20, 49, 72, 86, 97, 106, 120–2, 129, 146, 160, 225
Borgu, 17, 18, 20–1, 23–37, 39, 43–50, 52, 55–7, 59–60, 62–7, 69–72, 74–84, 86–8, 91, 93, 95–6, 100–1, 103–6, 115, 120–1, 127–8, 130, 143, 146, 150, 154, 158–9, 161, 166, 170–1, 173, 176, 182, 186, 190, 194, 202, 204, 217, 220, 222, 224, 226, 228: rebellion in, 148–9; West, 229
Borgu Native Authority, 229
Bornu, 20, 30–1; Shehu of, 29, 64, 94
Boroboko, 35
Boyd, A. R., 81–2, 92, 94, 99, 107
Bretonnet, Lieutenant, 47–8
Browne, G. S., 163
Buai, 28
Bueru, 35
Bussa Native Administration, 212–13
Bussa, West, 93

Cameron, Sir Donald, 91
Campbell, M. J., 229
Campbell-Irons, A., 119, 142, 173–4
Cannotville, 47–8
Carter, F. E. L., 215–16
Cary, Joyce, 18, 24, 95–6, 165–9, 171–3; Works, *The Case for African Freedom*, 167q.
Chad, Lake, 46
Chado, 116
Chakanda, 121

Clapperton, Commander Hugh, 19–20, 21, 24–5, 30–1, 34, 35–7, 39–42
Clarke, J. C. O., 81, 84, 91, 96–101, 103–6, 108–10, 112–14, 116–21, 125–9, 131, 133–6, 138–42, 155–7, 163–4, 189, 242
Clifford, Sir Hugh, 18, 177, 182, 188–90
Colonial Annual Report, 78
Colonial Development Fund, 226
Corey, Mr., 96
Cotonou, 148
Cowper, H. W., 165–6, 171, 173–4

Dahomey, 20, 23, 45–8, 65, 70, 102, 113, 120, 148–50, 170, 181–2, 225; King of, 20
Dakar, 121
Dakara, 153
Dan Galadima, 110
Daniel, F. de F., 218, 220, 226
Darbai, Daudu, 134, 138
Decoeur, Captain, 30, 46
Delphic League, 34
Dendi (traders), 26
De Putron, P., 81–2, 87
Diggle, P. R., 81, 92, 94–5, 98, 129, 139, 143–5, 150–4, 166, 169–71, 184, 197–9
Djougou, 23
Dogo, Kisan, 34, 48, 50–1, 53–5, 57–9, 61
Duff, E. C., 155, 169–70, 183–4
Dukku, 125, 142
Dupigny, E. G. M., 85–6, 88, 93
Duthoit, 146
Dwyer, Fergus, 69, 71–2, 74, 78–80, 86, 99, 100, 107, 118–19, 124–9, 135–7, 140, 142, 163, 183; proposes deposition of Kitoro Gani, 79–80

Eaglesome, Mr., 65, 70
Edward-White, Lieutenant, 53

Farquhar, Lieutenant, 102
Ferlus, Commandant de Cercle of Borgou, 121, 146–8
Festing, Colonel, 52
Fort Goldie, 49–50, 57, 63, 65
Fourneau, Captain, 65–6

INDEX

France, expansionism of, 44-6
Fremantle, Major J. M., 75-7
Fulani, 24, 25-6, 34-5, 37, 50, 74, 77, 83, 98, 127, 150

Gaba, Layan, 114, 151, 191
Gaiye, 151
Gajere, 34-5, 58-9
Galadima, Nda, 34
Gallo of Yauri, King, 37, 197
Gambia, 45
Gamzo, Bisheru, 131, 137
Gando (state slaves), 21, 25-6
Gangan Kisra, 29
Gani, compound owner, 132
Gani, Kitoro (Sarkin Bussa), 17, 18, 26, 42, 53, 57, 59-61, 64, 65, 67, 69, 70, 72, 76-83, 85-8, 92-4, 97, 99, 100, 106, 110-11, 113-14, 124-5, 129-30, 134, 142-5, 155, 167, 170, 174, 178, 182, 186-93, 197, 201, 202-13, 215-23, 230, 237: proclaimed King of Bussa, 60-2; deposition of, 124-5; deportation of, 143; restoration of, 188—90
Gani of Bussa, 136
Gani of Kagogi, 131-5, 137-8
Gani of Wawa, 133-5, 137-9
Gani, state festival, 22, 42-3
Ganikassai, 113, 180-1
Garafini, 115, 118-19
Garuba of Wawa, King, 52-4, 56-7
Garube, mijindadi, 132
Gbakashe, Dodo Lilai, 114
Géay, Commandant de 121, 149, Cercle of Kandi
Gebbe, 198; wars of, 36-7, 196
Geli, 113
Gemmu, 131-2
Gendenne, 78
Gendi, Wuru, 158
George V, King, Coronation of, 88
George VI, King, Coronation of, 226
Gepp, N. M., 81
Gera, 58, 60-1
Geriayidadi, 59
Germany, administration in Africa, 45
Gheria, 120
Gidan Lalle, 145-6, 149, 151, 154
Gill, H. C., 204-5
Glasson, Major B., 215, 217-18

Godo, Garba, 114
Gold Coast (Ghana), 45
Goldie, Sir George, 45
Goldsmith, H. S., 110-12, 117-18, 122, 124, 140, 145, 152, 161-4, 169-71
Gonja, 20, 25
Grier, S. M., 188-9
Guèra, Bio, 146, 148-9
Guinea, 45
Gulbin dan Zaki, 111
Gumji, 153-4
Gungawa Islands, 97, 107, 128, 184, 196, 198
Gunu, son of Kitoro Gani, 206-7, 214
Gwanara, 203, 228-9
Gwandu, 37, 39, 45, 197-8, 224; Emir of, 38
Gwen, 160

Hadejia, Emir of, 75
Haliru, Emir of Kaiama, 28, 177, 202, 204, 226
Hamilton-Browne, Major W., 96-7, 102-8, 110-13, 117-26, 136-7, 139, 141, 143-5, 150-3, 155-9, 161-3, 165-7, 169-71, 197, 242
Harris, P. G., 183-4
Hastings, A. C. G., 178
Hausaland, 20
Headmen, names of, 58, 59
Heath, D. F., 205-7, 211-16, 224-5
Hermon-Hodge, Hon. H. B., 22, 130, 182, 186, 188, 191, 194, 197, 199-200, 202; Works, *The Gazetteer of Ilorin Province*, 22q.
Holli-Kétou, 146
Hollidjé, 148
Hoskyns-Abrahall, Theodore, *later* Sir Chandos, 22, 29, 175-7, 181-2, 184-91, 193, 197, 202; Works, *History of Bussa*, 194q.
Houlgate, Assistant Resident, Borgu, 81
Howard, Assistant Resident, Borgu, 107

Ibadan, 225
Ibrahim, Ma'aji of Bussa, 184
Idris, Musa Baba, 28n., 35
Idris, Suleiman Haliru, 28
Ife, 29-30

269

Igbetti, 220
Igboho, 120
Ilesha, 23, 36–7, 49–50, 70, 80–1, 103, 105, 120, 158–60, 167, 203, 228–9
Illo, 20, 23, 26–7, 29, 31, 34, 39–40, 50–1, 55, 65, 67, 77–8, 85, 100, 160, 194, 197–8, 201, 230
Ilorin province, 25, 34–6, 47, 71, 124–5, 130, 143–4, 155, 159, 182, 186, 193–4, 200, 205, 214, 220, 224–6
Imoru, 133–4
Indirect Rule system, 18, 22, 90–1, 172, 191, 203, 212–14, 224
Isa, 98, 115, 131–4, 138, 144
Islam religion, 23
Ivory Coast, 45–6

Jabo, 184
Jebba, 65, 84, 116, 220, 225
Jibrilu, son of Abdullahi Abershi, 97, 107–8; deposition of, 112–13
Jibrim, 207–12, 214, 217–18
Jimi, Emir of Kaiama, 95, 105, 110, 154
Jingima, 120
Jones, N. P. M., 204

Kabe, 145, 149, 151
Kaduna, 169–70, 172, 197, 225
Kagogi, 26, 113, 150, 178–80, 207
Kaiama, 19, 21, 22, 23–5, 27–31, 34–7, 44, 48–50, 57–8, 61–2, 65–7, 74, 77–8, 80–1, 84, 91–2, 95–6, 98, 101–6, 108, 110–11, 116, 119, 121, 123–4, 126, 129–30, 135, 144, 154–5, 157–62, 165, 167, 170–3, 178, 190–1, 193, 203–5, 208, 213, 218, 220, 225–6, 229
Kaiama, King of (Mora Tasude), 19, 36, 49, 51, 53, 61, 64, 70, 71–2, 74, 80, 82, 88, 92, 94–5, 106, 116; death of, 95
Kainji, 19, 115, 229
Kali, 36, 119–20
Kalkami, 38, 198
Kamberri, 36–7, 86, 106, 110, 193, 196–7, 205
Kamerun (Cameroon), 45, 100, 113
Kandi, 23, 122, 147–9, 152, 160
Kania, 117
Kankaye, 114

Kano (city), 25, 90, 94, 158, 239
Kano (Borgu village), 145–6, 149, 151
Kantama, King of Wawa, 52–4, 117, 173–4, 204, 206–7
Kaoje, 20, 56, 74, 78, 100, 194, 197, 201, 230
Kawara, 38, 198
Kebie, Woru, 69
Kemble, Harry, 27–8, 50–7, 62, 65–7, 70–1, 74–5, 107, 196–7
Kenubwe, 153–4
Kerry, Colour-Sergeant, 117, 119–21
Kibari, 52
Kibe, 38–40
Kigera, 111, Musa Mohammed, Emir of Borgu, 230
Kijera, 160
Kijibrim, Kiwotede of Bussa, 113–14, 116, 118, 124–5, 144–5, 150, 160, 162, 165, 167, 170–1, 174–8, 180–7, 190, 193: appointed Sarkin Bussa, 144–5; installed as Emir, 162; attempted assassination of, 180–2; deposition of, 183–7
Kika, 160
Kikwissoin, 173
Kingdon, Donald, 189
Kiotedi, 107
Kishi, 35, 120, 189, 225
Kisra, 38, 39, 64, 148; legend of, 26–9, 34
Kisra Nikki dynasty, 28
Kissanti, 185–6
Kissera (*see also* Kisra), 80
Kissoin, 134, 144–5, 173, 178–82
Kiwotede, 41–2, 111, 113, 115, 119; see also *Yerima*
Kofas, 42, 124, 203
Kolo, 143
Kongiri, 179–81
Kontagora province, 38, 55, 62, 70, 76, 78–82, 92, 96, 100–2, 113, 116, 118, 121–8, 135–6, 142–3, 145, 154, 165, 170–1, 173, 177–8, 183–4, 186, 188, 194, 201, 224, 238, 241–2: Report, 103, 140
Kouandé, 23 47
Kpera, Sero, King of Nikki, 34–6
Kunji, chief, 80, 83, 157
Kunji, town/district, 37, 85, 88, 93, 98, 100, 109, 111, 156–7, 170–1, 194, 196–201, 230

INDEX

Kura, Yerima, 158, 161–2, 167, 177
Kushi, Sabi, 114
Kuta, 114
Kwara (claimant of Bussa throne), 48, 52–3
Kwara State Government, 230
Kwarra, 174

Lafagu, 56, 85, 100
Lafiya, Mallam, 209–10, 214–15, 219
Lagos, 25, 45, 81, 89–90, 102, 110, 119–20, 122, 172, 186–7, 200–1, 220, 225
Lamu of Bode, historian, 30
Lander, Richard, 21, 25, 30–1, 34–5, 36–7, 39–40, 42
Langrishe, Mr., 51, 55
Larymore, Captain H. D., 71–2, 74–6, 105, 239
Larymore, Mrs., 19, 71–2, 74–5, 230; Works, *A Resident's Wife in Nigeria*, 71q.
Leaba, 54, 56, 93, 111, 116–17
Lefilliâtre, Monsieur, 148
Lenfant, Capitaine, 50–2
Lewis, Captain P. E., 203–4
Liman, 41
Lokoja, 61
Lombard, Jacques, 21, 39, 43, 48
Lonsdale, Captain, 186, 194
Lugard, Sir Frederick, *later* Lord, 17, 30, 35, 36, 46, 49, 50, 53–4, 57–8, 60–2, 64, 66–7, 69–70, 71–2, 89–90, 93, 101–2, 110, 117, 120, 126, 128, 152, 154–5, 161–2, 172, 224–5, 237; appointments, 89
Luma, 151

Madoko, 41
Magaji, 55
Maidanda, 146
Malali, 113, 116
Malendo river, 112
Mallams, 27, 41
Mama, 119
Mande, 26
Mashi (Sarkin Yashikera), Emir of Kaiama, 95, 105, 109, 116, 119, 121, 134, 154–5, 158
Matakure, 131, 134–5, 138–9
Mazandawa, 133
Mellis, Captain, 52

Mill, John, 63, 65
Mockler-Ferryman, Captain, 20
Mohamma, 131, 137
Mokwa, 221
Molyneux, District Officer of Yauri, 199
Momman, 208
Mori, 120
Moshi, 120
Moshi, river, 20
Munai, 115
Mura-Bane-De, 161
Murata-Sudi (*see also* Tasude, Mora), 161
Musina, 115
Muslims, 23, 70n.

Naganzi, 113, 121
Nagwamatse, Ibrahim (Emir of Kontagora), 37
Nash, Walter, 190, 193–4, 196–9, 202, 204, 214
Native Authorities, 90–1, 93, 104, 170–1, 176, 203, 211, 213, 224
Ndagi, Mai, 193
Newton, T. C., 81–8, 92
N'Gaski, 70, 97, 105, 106–7, 111, 157, 171, 184
Niganzi, 114
Niger Coast Protectorate, 45
Niger province, 186
Niger, river, 19–20, 23, 24, 26–7, 35, 37, 44–7, 50, 55, 65, 69, 78, 97, 116, 128, 174, 180, 196–7, 204, 215, 221, 225, 229; Rapids, 22
Nigeria, 17–18, 23, 113, 122, 173, 189, 222–5, 229–30: Northern, 17, 21, 46, 47, 64, 65, 69n., 70n., 78, 81, 83, 89–91, 98; Southern, 89, 91
Nigerian Borgu, 64; divisions of, 64
Nikki, 21–2, 25–31, 34, 35–7, 39, 43, 46–8, 57, 62–4, 102, 113, 121, 146–7, 158, 160–2, 181, 229; King of, 28, 36
Noma, Daudin, 157
Norton-Traill, Assistant Resident, Borgu, 81
Noufflard, Governor of Dahomey, 121–2, 148–9
Nupe, 20, 40, 47

271

Nyasa, Lake, 164

Odudawa, 29
Ojo (Woru Yoru), 36
Okuta, 23, 36–7, 49–50, 70, 80–1, 103, 105, 158–60, 203, 226, 229
Oli, river, 226
Oluewu of Oyo, Alafin, 34
Onitsha, 102
Ouidah, 36
Oyo, 20, 25, 29–30, 34, 35–7, 220

Palmer, H. R., 194, 200–1, 205
Parakou, 23, 48, 146, 148
Park, Mungo, 19, 21, 221; 'ring', 221
Patengi, 114
Phérivong, Charles, 146–7
Philip II, of Macedon, 34
Phillips, Lieutenant, 65–6
Porto Novo, 45–6, 122, 146–7
Potashi, 55, 126
Puissa, chief, 80
Puissa, town, 128

Renard, Commandant, 149
Roberts, B. A., 205–8, 212–15
Rofia, 37, 156, 194, 196–201
Rowse, E. R., 213
Royal Niger Company, 45–9, 208, 215

Sabbuki, 17, 99, 113–20, 122–3, 126, 128–31, 140, 142–6, 149–52, 169–70, 172–3, 181, 185–6, 191, 193
Sabi, founder of Nikki, 160
Sabi, scribe of Agwarra, 214
Sabi, son of Kisra, 26
Sabiboga, 175, 180–1
Sabikushi, 119
Salisbury, Lord, 47
Samba-Biu, 113
Sangwa, 26
Sankara, Hassan, 121
Sansani, 113
Sarakolle, 26
Savé, 147
Schlotel, Captain L. C., 205
Segu, 44
Shagunu, 26, 113, 115, 118, 133, 149–51, 174–5, 191, 207
Shaki, 225
Sharpe, Major, 78–9, 82, 87, 105, 107, 239

Shebenna, 115
Shekwana, 114
Sierra Leone, 45
Smith, Captain, 178, 181, 183–4
Sokoto caliphate, 20, 25, 34, 39, 45, 46, 54, 69n., 76, 78, 83, 85–6, 90, 107, 127, 145, 153, 156, 158, 160, 170, 186, 194, 197, 199–200, 224; Emir of, 64, 94
Somba, 20
Songhai empire, 20, 27
Stevens, Lieutenant, 57–63, 66, 237
Sudi, Murata (*see also* Tasude, Mora), 159
Sukki, 119
Suku Suku, Wuru, 116, 119
Sule, 179

Tasude, Mora (King of Kaiama), 19, 36, 49, 51, 53, 61, 64, 70, 71–2, 74, 80, 82, 88, 92, 94–5, 116, 158; death of, 95
Telu, 240
Temple, C. L., 99, 102, 126, 143
Tew, L. S., 137, 143
Thumbu, 114
Thumbu Baba, 114
Toga, founder of Wawa, 27
Togo, 45, 100
Toro, Dan, of Bussa, King, 34, 37–8, 45, 58–9, 61, 185, 197
Toutée, Commandant G. J., 47
Trenchard, Lord, 226
Tribute Collection, 128
Tukolor caliphate, 44
Tukura, 127
Turaki, 92–3, 99, 110–11, 113–16, 124–5, 128, 130–42, 144, 155, 178–9, 237

Umaru, Mallam, 207
Umoru, Ajie, 111, 114, 115–18, 124, 133–4
United Africa Company, 226

Vera, 114
Vermeersch, 52
Vignon, Félix, 146

Wallace, William, 69
Warra, 118, 150, 204, 208, 215
Wassangari, 22, 25–6, 42, 48

INDEX

Waters, Captain, 102–3, 112
Wawa, chief, 80
Wawa, town, 19, 23–7, 30–1, 34, 37, 39, 40–1, 48–9, 52, 54, 56, 93, 111, 116–17, 119–20, 126, 160, 173, 190, 226; King of, 41, 80
Webster, G. W., 197–9
Western Borgu Sub-Native Authority, 229
Wete Futani Gerede, 42, 114
Whitworth, Lieutenant, 150–2
Willcocks, Colonel, 49
Williams, Dr., 74
Woodhouse, C. M., 200
Woru, son of headman of Bissashe, 153–4
Woru, son of Kisra, 26–8
Woru, spectator, 179
Woro Yaru, King of Yashikera, 56, 62–4

Yakubu, 131–2
Yambushidi, 113
Yangbasso, 100
Yaru, King of Yashikera, 63
Yashikera, 23, 36–7, 49–50, 56, 57, 62–3, 80–1, 103, 111, 154, 158–60, 167, 172, 228–9
Yaurawa, 37
Yauri, 20, 23, 35, 37, 54–6, 81, 87–8, 96–8, 100–1, 105, 107–8, 110–11,

Yauri (*contd.*)—
124–9, 141, 159–60, 162, 165, 171, 173, 183–4, 193–4, 106–9, 224: Emir of, 87; Greater, 108
Yelwa, 50, 55–6, 84, 91–2, 97, 100–1, 104, 105, 107–8, 110, 112–13, 116, 120, 123, 128, 133–5, 139, 142–3, 152, 158, 162–3, 166, 173, 194, 196, 199, 238; Judicial Council, 157
Yerima (or *Kiwotede*), 41
Yola, 96
Yon Magara, 40–2
Yoru, 179
Yoruba, 29–30, 35, 45, 72
Yorubaland, 20, 25, 29

Zakara, Sabi, 114, 131, 133–4, 136–8, 140, 174, 183
Zali, 114–15
Zambara, 115
Zhinkina, 41
Zinder, 149
Zugu, 160
Zugu(r)ma, 55, 125–6
Zuma, 42
Zungeru, 66, 86, 96–7, 101–2, 105, 116–19, 121, 129, 131, 136, 145, 150, 241
Zuru, 113, 117–120, 150

THE LIBRARY
ST. MARY'S COLLEGE OF MARYLAND
ST. MARY'S CITY, MARYLAND 20686

JS
7656.9 Crowder, Michael.
.B88   Revolt in Bussa.
1902